Don Eberly's well-documented book is one of the best surveys of today's wide-ranging reassessment of how countries develop, what works and what does not work in foreign aid, and cutting-edge innovations in aid delivery. The book could make Alexis de Tocqueville smile.

ANDREW NATSIOS
Presidential Envoy to Sudan; former administrator of USAID

Drawing on a wealth of experience, Don Eberly offers a bold vision for combating global poverty in an evolving world. This is a timely argument for civil society as a flexible means to engage and empower the world's poor.

DR. WALTER MEAD
Council on Foreign Relations

Don Eberly addresses the positive social and economic aspects of globalization. *The Rise of Global Civil Society* is a clarion call to leaders in government as well as those in the private sector to reach out to the poor as producers, consumers, and partners in enterprise as an alternative to handouts.

JACK KEMP
former Secretary of Housing and Urban Development

If you have ever doubted that the United States has an important role to play in world development, read this book. Eberly argues, clearly and persuasively, that the world's biggest constituency for the "American values" of the market, the rule of law, and democracy are the poor of the developing world.

HERNANDO DE SOTO
author of The Mystery of Capital

Don Eberly is a leading theorist and practitioner of civil society—he helped give birth to today's civil society movement in the United States. This book takes the idea global, showing how an energized civil society not only can change the world, but is already doing so.

DAVID BLANKENHORN
president of the Institute for American Values

Eberly's analysis is required reading for international philanthropies and development agencies who need to understand the current realities of development assistance.

CAROL ADELMAN
director of the Center for Global Prosperity at the Hudson Institute

The Rise of Global Civil Society is a work of extraordinary breadth and depth. Eberly's experience in key assignments at the highest levels of government give him a unique vantage point, and his expertise infuses every chapter of the book.

GEORGE WARD
former U.S. Ambassador and Coordinator for
Humanitarian Assistance in the U.S. mission in Iraq

Anyone in international business should read this book. Eberly describes the dynamic force-multiplying interaction of technology, communications, compassion, and civic norms and practices in Third World (and Second World) countries. He reveals both the surprising scale and important nuances of a new and hope-filled force in our age.

WILLIAM W. ADAMS
former chairman and president of Armstrong World Industries

Don Eberly has been at the forefront of the struggle to preserve and strengthen civil society. His work in the White House and internationally has led him to invaluable insights about the delicate relationship between government and civic entrepreneurs.

STEVE GOLDSMITH
chairman of the Corporation for National and Community Service

This book clearly shows how community associations, entrepreneurship, property ownership, and integration into the world economy improve the lives of the disadvantaged and strengthen democratic practices. It is essential reading for those seeking more effective ways to advance liberty and prosperity in developing countries.

JOHN SANBRAILO
executive director of the Pan American Development Foundation

Few tasks are more urgent for American foreign policy than building the "infrastructure of democracy," as President Ronald Reagan said nearly 25 years ago. Don Eberly offers a timely set of strategies and insights on how to do exactly this, based on years of experience around the world.

JOHN SULLIVAN
executive director of the Center for International Private Enterprise

The profusion of nongovernmental organizations dedicated to doing good around the world seems like an unalloyed blessing—a fast-off-the-mark alternative to the ponderous and impersonal institutions of government. But as Don Eberly argues cogently in this timely new book, it also raises a host of difficult questions. We are lucky to have a guide so knowledgeable and perceptive to help us parse the complexities.

WILL MARSHALL
president of the Progressive Policy Institute

Companies, philanthropy, governments, multilateral agencies, religious groups, civil society, diasporas, and others are working in a variety of new alliances because we have collectively concluded that we can solve the world's pressing problems by working together. Don Eberly's book is about development's future.

DAN RUNDE
former director of the Global Development Alliance, USAID

At a time of enormous and often confusing global change, Don Eberly provides a hopeful vision of how the four revolutions—economic, political, cultural, and technological—can result in global commitment to civil society. This book is a blueprint for how America can help lead the world toward decisions that base policy on the best aspirations of humankind.

ROBERT S. WALKER
*former U.S. Congressman; chairman of Wexler & Walker
Public Policy Associates*

The Rise of Global Civil Society offers insight about the brave new multipolar, multisector world that we are moving into, and the vital role that civil society organizations will play in its development. This is an important book to have in your library if you want a well-rounded perspective on the forces shaping modern events.

Stephen Jordan
senior vice president and executive director of the Business Civic Leadership Center, U.S. Chamber of Commerce

Eberly carefully documents the emergence and evolution of important new trends in the way society—especially in America—is now tackling some of the really big ills it faces. For those of us engaged on this front daily, he provides a heartening reminder that great progress is being made.

Kurt Hoffman
director of the Shell Foundation

With a discerning eye, Don Eberly surveys the global landscape, tracing out the feature missing from most analyses: the untapped power of a global civil society rooted in mutual respect and the rule of law. He reveals the exciting roles that social capital can play at the grassroots level, while reminding Americans of the compassion that has made their country great.

Chris Seiple
president of the Institute for Global Engagement

Don Eberly has experienced how some of the hardest problems of our age can be uniquely addressed by civil society precepts that are less purely American than they are essentially human. *The Rise of Global Civil Society* is very good news for those who care about the world their children will inherit.

David Legg
managing director of Gobal Business Development at Gerson Lehrman Group

THE RISE OF GLOBAL CIVIL SOCIETY

DON EBERLY

THE RISE OF GLOBAL CIVIL SOCIETY

*Building Communities and Nations
from the Bottom Up*

Encounter Books · New York · London

First edition published in 2008 by Encounter Books,
an activity of Encounter for Culture and Education, Inc.,
a nonprofit, tax exempt corporation.
Encounter Books website address: www.encounterbooks.com

Manufactured in the United States and printed on
acid-free paper. The paper used in this publication meets
the minimum requirements of ANSI/NISO Z39.48–1992
(R 1997) (Permanence of Paper).

FIRST EDITION

LIBRARY OF CONGRESS CATALOGING-IN-PUBLICATION DATA

Eberly, Don E.
The rise of global civil society : building communities and nations
from the bottom up / Don Eberly.
p.   cm.
Includes bibliographical references and index.
ISBN-13: 978-1-59403-214-1 (hardcover : alk. paper)
ISBN-10: 1-59403-214-9 (hardcover : alk. paper)
1. Civil society. 2. Voluntarism. 3. Public welfare. I. Title.
JC337.E24 2008
300—dc22
2007050698

10 9 8 7 6 5 4 3 2 1

CONTENTS

Poverty Reduction in the Age of Globalization

IF YOU HAVE picked up this book, you are probably among the millions of Americans who are concerned about global developments and about America's place in the world. Leaders and citizens alike want to know whether attempts by American citizens and their government to promote democracy and free enterprise are having any positive effect.

The Rise of Global Civil Society is designed to reach a broad general audience that is interested in global trends affecting the future of freedom and our way of life. It draws from my experience in senior positions at the White House, at USAID (United States Agency for International Development), the nation's primary agency for relief and development, and at the State Department, including a term as a senior advisor in Baghdad—as well as conversations with many of the nation's top policy leaders, scholars, and advocates—to provide a first-hand view of economic development and democratic nation building around the world today. This book also attempts to answer some basic questions: Are the forces of progress and democratic values winning? If so, where and how?

The news is dominated by terrorism and extremism, as well as a bungled and seemingly open-ended conflict in Iraq. Is there any good news anywhere? America's reputation abroad, we are reminded again and again by ubiquitous polling, is at an all-time low, and many citizens are embarrassed and frustrated by the fact that a country so closely identified with the highest democratic ideals could be so unpopular in so many places. Why, they ask, are we so broadly despised?

Given the tumultuous conditions in many regions of the world, many have come to doubt that efforts to improve the lot of humanity in the Third World can succeed in the face of sectarian conflict, Islamic radicalism, and anti-Americanism. Perhaps we should just return home and concentrate on building secure borders.

Many others, however, sense that behind the more troubling news there may be a promising new global era emerging, although they are uncertain what form it is taking and how it will affect them as Americans. Globalization, for good or bad, is shifting the tectonic plates. It is also bringing innovative approaches to advancing democracy and confronting poverty.

Conventional efforts by elite policy experts and bureaucracies to bring about prosperity in the twentieth century have mostly failed. As a result, confidence in "top-down," bureaucratic solutions is declining, while confidence in "bottom-up" innovation by business and non-profits is growing. The twenty-first century will see more social entrepreneurship, private philanthropy, public-private partnerships, and grass-roots linkages involving the religious and civic communities. There will be less of the traditional approaches to "helping," and more partnering with and empowering of indigenous institutions. The key to meeting development challenges in the future will be to harness the best of both the public and the private sector so as to foster experimentation with approaches that rely on markets and on civil society, and that engage the poor as partners.

The work of building and maintaining the democratic state must involve citizens operating in their own communities. This book examines recent efforts by policy leaders in Washington to transfer more responsibility for social welfare to local and nongovernmental institutions. Private voluntary organizations, faith-based partnerships, and a proliferating array of NGOs—aided by communications technology and unprecedented mobility—are spreading real capacity as well as the norms of civic community and private enterprise around the globe.

In the new era, business too has an expanding role in generating technical innovations that are directly and powerfully beneficial to the poor. American business ingenuity will help the poor in the most remote Third World villages.

In the midst of these promising trends, there is also much to be sobered by, especially the problems that arise from ethnic and sectarian division. In the Arab Middle East and other traditional Muslim societies, there is a resurgence of tribalism and identification with religious factions. Dozens of nations are at or near civil war conditions. This book addresses the deeper questions of religion in relation to civil society, particularly in the Islamic world.

In this context, the rush to democratize strikes many as misguided. Democracy cannot be instituted simply by forcing elections on nations that remain in a state of underdevelopment. Moving hastily to achieve the symbolically satisfying results of an election can even produce "illiberal" outcomes. Genuine democracy is not possible without democratic citizens. Moreover, the experience of recent years suggests that the U.S government is ill positioned to push democracy on a reluctant world. The institutions and values of democracy are most likely to advance through the continued outflow of assets from the American private sector, including business, civic, philanthropic, academic, and faith-based organizations.

Chapter One details the first global "associational revolution," involving an explosive growth of nonprofits, NGOs, and thousands of civic, professional, and advocacy-oriented groups, many of them tied together by technology and promoting democratic values worldwide. This movement, I argue, is America's most consequential export, and it presents the greatest hope for economic and political progress. The tendency to join or create voluntary associations, which Alexis de

Tocqueville identified as distinctive to America and a key to its democratic success, is now also a trend on every continent, thanks to the increasing connectedness of the world. This global web of civil society is providing the world's destitute in remote locations with information and knowledge relevant to improving their condition.

Chapter Two surveys the strategies that are now being used successfully to reduce poverty and build healthy communities at home and abroad. The problems of community are similar in every location. Strategies to bring about "comprehensive community transformation" domestically are the same strategies that are being adopted to transform conditions in Third World countries. The approach is to replace top-down, state-dominated programs with broad partnerships involving flexible organizations working within the communities. The essential ingredients are local ownership and innovation.

Chapter Three reviews the great foreign aid debate. America is in the process of reassessing what works and what doesn't work in the area of government aid programs to the developing world. Many have accused the United States of being stingy, but without taking into account the massive outflow of private assistance in the form of philanthropy, university partnerships, NGOs, and even remittances. What really matters, this book argues, is whether a particular intervention —private or governmental—is producing results in poverty reduction and effective institution building.

Chapter Four describes the shift that is under way in how the U.S. government delivers assistance to the world. Neither traditional aid nor aid agencies have a monopoly any longer. Instead, there is a growing role for public-private partnerships and private aid alliances, as well as a movement of private businesses into such areas as emergency assistance and relief. Numerous partnerships with local poor communities involving private sector players are yielding results that traditional aid programs cannot replicate.

Few trends are more promising for the future of global prosperity and democracy than the emergence of international movements promoting corporate citizenship and social responsibility. Chapter Five discusses the corporate citizenship practices of volunteerism, community partnerships, and targeted philanthropy. Many corporations see the call to citizenship as inseparable from their pursuit of a stronger bottom line and have made it a part of their branding and marketing. Philanthropy is also being transformed by the "social entrepreneur" —a socially concerned business person who offers his expertise and business acumen for solving a particular social problem.

The capital that already exists in poor countries far exceeds the combined value of foreign aid, investment by the private sector, and philanthropy. Trillions of dollars are currently held by the poor, but this wealth is trapped in the underground economies of poorly managed Third World nations. Chapter Six describes how such innovations as microenterprise and microfranchising are tapping native capability at "the bottom of the pyramid."

The Third World is in the midst of a bottom-up revolution in entrepreneurial capitalism that is bringing economic opportunity and hope to millions of poor families. Fueling this movement are hundreds of NGOs that are establishing microlending and business development programs, including rural co-ops and credit unions. Local and regional economies in places like India are growing from the seed-planting success of microenterprise initiatives. Numerous private organizations are promoting legal and institutional reforms to strengthen property rights and establish sound business regulation. The poor will no longer be ignored when they are finally seen as producers and consumers.

Drawing from my experience as the director of private assistance for tsunami reconstruction at the State Department, I describe in Chapter Seven the phenomenal growth of private emergency relief and reconstruction assistance being offered to communities in crisis. While U.S. government assistance after the Asian tsunami disaster of 2004 totaled $657 million, private donations from individuals and corporations approached $2 billion. A new global e-philanthropy contributed greatly, with funds for victims raised almost instantly via the Web. Faith-based programs got worldwide support for their relief efforts, and American business stepped up to provide hands-on assistance of the kind once offered exclusively by government emergency relief programs.

Of all the major trends in world affairs, perhaps the most consequential has been the prominent role of religion and culture in national and regional affairs, particularly in Asia and the Middle East. Chapter Eight analyzes religion as a factor in generating the best and the worst of civil society. What emerges is a hopeful view that while extremist movements may gain short-term advantages, most citizens desire more freedom and prosperity, and they will push for more open societies. Attention is given to the complex currents within the Islamic faith affecting such values as tolerance, diversity, and openness to innovation.

Chapter Nine aims to make sense of the stunning rise of anti-Americanism. While America stands at the apex of influence, and while American products and ideas are known everywhere, animosity toward America has reached unprecedented levels. This chapter examines how America's private sector and civil society may be far more effective than its government officials and policies in spreading American values throughout the world. In many ways, direct government efforts are the least effective means of advancing America's interests.

Even where hostilities toward official America are high, local attitudes toward the American people remain largely positive. On the other hand, America's cultural exports often have a negative influence on international opinion, especially in traditional Islamic communities. Chapter Nine suggests that more efforts be made at promoting people-to-people, institution-to-institution ties, in order to expose the world to the real America.

Chapter Ten explains how civil society is the foundation stone of democratic nation building. There are no shortcuts to building democratic nations. It is not possible to build viable democracies from the top down or from the outside in. Instead, democratic habits, skills, and aspirations must be cultivated inside societies to support the formal institutions of democracy. Traditionally, it has been the voluntary associations of civil society that afford individuals the opportunity to

practice in their daily lives the values and habits of trust, collaboration, and mutual respect. A rush to formal democracy can actually
create space for undemocratic elements to move in and dominate the
process.

Chapter Eleven visits the vexing problems of conflict and reconciliation in the context of nation building. The horrifying experience
of the Rwandan genocide in 1994, and the subsequent attempt to
build a viable democratic state there in the heart of Africa, illustrate a
range of internal transformations that are required for democracy to
take root, along with political institutions and rule of law. This chapter describes the work of reconciliation and building trust in Rwanda,
and the broad effort to replace an ideology of ethnic hatred with a
moral vision of citizenship wherein ethnic categories are eliminated.

Chapter Twelve makes the case that the only path to free and
prosperous nations is by way of cultivating democratic citizens.
Democracy as it is understood in Western political theory is not
merely about politics and the state; it is about civil society and local
community habits. Too many attempts at building formal democracy
sidestep the difficult issues of culture, religion, race, ethnicity, and a
variety of attitudinal factors that often militate against liberal democracy. Building the seedbed for democracy requires promoting a
global civic culture to incubate the attitudes and habits that produce
healthy democratic societies.

The concluding chapter offers a guide for a variety of actors
across all sectors—government, business, philanthropy, NGOs, and
private individuals—on how to apply the observations and recom-
mendations that flow from the previous chapters. It is presented as a
roadmap to encourage more effective efforts at promoting freedom,
democracy, and prosperity around the world by individual Americans
and their civic, educational, business, and philanthropic organizations.

CHAPTER ONE

Compassion:
America's Most Consequential Export

THE WORLD HAS entered a promising new era that is certain to yield advances in democracy and new opportunities for the world's poor. If the twentieth century was about top-down, rule-driven bureaucracy, the twenty-first century will be about social entrepreneurs, private philanthropy, public-private partnerships, and global grass-roots linkages involving the faith and civic communities. We are entering an era of "bottom-up" innovation and discovery. In our lifetimes, major advances will be made in reducing global poverty and in eradicating disease and illiteracy.

The world is in the midst of tectonic shifts in how the poor are viewed and how poverty is confronted. Just as America has learned much from its domestic experiment with state-dominated antipoverty programs, we have learned important lessons from over four decades of experimentation in international development. Attempts by development policy experts to bring prosperity through command-and-control bureaucracies have mostly failed. The government dominated the past. Nongovernmental entities and forces will dominate the future. The key will be to find new ways to harness the best of both the public and the private sector to create a new era of experimentation, one that relies on markets and civil society, with the poor everywhere serving as partners in their own development.

I

Any discussion of world poverty must start with the recognition that news from the Third World is often staggeringly bad. Three billion of the planet's inhabitants—fully half the world's population—live on two dollars a day or less. According to the United Nations, 842 million are chronically hungry.[1]

Many believe we are paying a heavy price for continued economic globalization. The natural resources upon which we all depend are being depleted. The destruction of forests and streams, the disappearance of species, and worsening pollution stand as reason to question the wisdom of growth-based strategies if they will result in more of the same.

Other forces impeding progress are rampant anti-Americanism, tribalism, and Islamic extremism. Perhaps the most worrisome is the seemingly intractable ethnic and sectarian conflict that is oblivious to the boundaries of nation-states, and which in some cases is exacerbated by rapid democratization. Some observers describe a retreat of nation-states altogether in the poorest regions, yielding to private "statelets" run by criminal gangs and militia.

Somewhere between forty and fifty of the world's poorest countries appear to be hopelessly dysfunctional, with rising populations and declining GDPs leading to Hobbesian conditions of joblessness and violence. Thirty countries are on the brink of civil war, according to Georg Kell of the United Nations. Sixty countries are crippled by systemic corruption. Although many will profit from globalization, others will languish in conditions of extreme poverty, disease, and illiteracy. For these "basket case" countries, solutions may not be found soon enough, if they can be found at all. Direct foreign investment and other positive trends of development may likely pass them by, and the global community may have to consider new approaches to confronting the grave humanitarian conditions that will result.

These are daunting challenges, and conditions in some regions may continue to worsen. Scholars are divided on whether the dominant trends in the world are toward democratic openness and market-led prosperity, toward fragmentation, or toward some incoherent combination of the two for the foreseeable future. Even so, there is a growing sense that the conditions exist for general improvements in Third World economies and for strengthening social and economic institutions. We know far more today about how to build communities and nations. Top-down approaches to social justice and empowerment are losing their value and appeal. Civil society, combined with small-scale enterprise and trade, is poised to contribute much to the reduction of persistent and extreme poverty in the twenty-first century.

This is an era in which American business ingenuity will aid the poor in the most remote Third World villages. American private firms will routinely partner with small businesses in the developing world to supply badly needed components for business success, from IT to improved storage, processing, marketing, and distribution. Globalization brings its own problems but also expands and accelerates the delivery of solutions.

This is the era in which America's research and knowledge products will bring unimagined benefits to the world's poor. Technical solutions to problems plaguing the Third World are proliferating at a dizzying pace. For almost every major development problem—killer diseases, water and sanitation problems, agricultural productivity issues, environmental depletion—there is a known remedy and successful models of application. Accompanying bleak environmental forecasts is a growing hopefulness that we can feed the planet while conserving the world's resources through sustainable agriculture and forestry practices. Today, the means exist to advance economic growth in ways that are ecologically sound.

The poor "do not need much to meet their basic nutrition," says Stephen C. Smith, a development professor. In most cases, "an extremely small amount of money would be enough for people to escape under-nutrition traps."[2] Referring to the modest interventions by Bill Gates and others to control ancient calamities such as river blindness and leprosy, the columnist Nicholas Kristof remarked, "It is exhilarating to see how little it takes to make a difference."[3]

Few Americans realize the scale of problem solving that American

3

universities, firms, and philanthropies are engaged in. For instance, if the disease scourges of the Third World are reversed, it will be American science that is credited with the success. The rapid development of vaccines by U.S. medical science has already pretty much eliminated polio, measles, and the guinea-worm disease. The Bill & Melinda Gates Foundation is investing $200 million in clinical trials of six new TB vaccines, and research continues to advance on vaccines for HIV/AIDS and malaria. A major drive is being made to adapt available treatments to African circumstances, such as applying iodized salt to prevent stunted growth, and oral rehydration technologies to fight diarrhea.[4]

This is the era of unprecedented opportunity for creative public-private partnerships in which the traditional boundaries that separate government and the private sector begin to blur. It is an age in which government will increasingly use its own resources to leverage private sector assistance and development know-how. State aid agencies will frequently settle for being the minor partner in development enterprises.

This is an era in which exploding outflows of private assistance make the debate over official foreign aid less and less reality-based. The United States is constantly taking heat from the international community and foreign aid advocates for being stingy in its foreign assistance. Yet the public commitment of taxpayers' dollars, now exceeding $20 billion annually, doesn't begin to compare to the increasing contributions being made every year by American firms, universities, congregations, and NGOs.

Not long ago, the work of economic development was monopolized by a handful of U.S. and international institutions. Today, that monopoly is gone and state agencies are wrestling with their own declining importance. The World Bank has been "since World War II the world's largest poverty-fighting institution," writes Bob Davis, but now it "competes with what it estimates are as many as 230 other agencies focusing on poverty and health care, which are run by billionaires, celebrities and individual nations." Institutions like the World Bank slowly lose relevance when developing nations have access to capital in global capital markets and numerous private sector collaborators.[5]

This is the age in which the trillions of dollars currently held by the poor, but trapped in the underground economies of poorly managed Third World nations, will be harnessed for productive enterprise. The capital that already exists in poor countries far exceeds the combined value of foreign aid, investment by the private sector, and philanthropy.

This is the era of a global corporate citizenship movement in which CEOs aspire to be social entrepreneurs and companies look for ways to combine profit with social responsibility. Growing numbers of corporations are embracing a creed that promotes volunteerism and combines business investment with strategic philanthropy and even hands-on emergency assistance. For example, after the tsunami that devastated the Indian Ocean region in December 2004, dozens of large corporations immediately activated their prearranged emergency response systems, with databases of staff experts who had signed up in advance to volunteer, donate products, provide supply chain expertise, and build IT and communications systems. Entire operating units were deployed to sponsor the construction of clinics, schools, and homes.

This is the era of technology in which barriers are blasted and people are empowered. It is an age in which something so basic and accessible as the cell phone is driving innovation in the poorest nations and protecting the newfound sovereignty of free citizens.

It is a new day altogether for closed societies and for states that not long ago could get away with repressive crackdowns and not face significant consequences. When hundreds of thousands of people gathered in the streets of Kiev to preserve Ukrainian democracy, and in Brazil to protest corruption, and even in Egypt to challenge the political dominance of President Mubarak, citizens were empowered by a range of new technologies. Citizen uprisings throughout 2007 in such places as Burma, Pakistan, and the Republic of Georgia all had one thing in common: the reality of new technology and its capacity to defeat the most determined and creative efforts to impose political controls.

When Buddhist monks in Burma took to the streets, the Burmese junta responded by closing borders, cutting phone lines, and blocking streets. But no police state tactic was capable of preventing "citizen correspondents" from transmitting messages by cell phone to fellow citizens and beaming photos and news accounts to a global audience that quickly came to their defense. In one of the most heavily censored countries in the world, the monks and their sympathizers were able to post messages on Facebook, send text messages and e-mails, transmit news accounts to blogs, and slip tiny messages out on e-cards. They used Internet versions of "pigeons" to courier news and images to embassies and nongovernmental organizations.[6]

Governments are now facing entirely new kinds of choices. The only way they can destroy the inherently liberalizing effects of modernization is to remain part of the shrinking community of extreme police states such as North Korea. The first and smallest step forward to modernization results in an irreversible spread of communication technology, and with it the exposure of more and more citizens to new ideas.

This is the era of global civil society, in which voluntary associations are proliferating and creating the first global electorate. As one observer put it, the world is in the midst of an "associational revolution," which is producing a "power shift" of potentially historic dimensions.[7] Another observer predicted that "the role of the nongovernmental organization in the twenty-first century will be as significant as the role of the nation state in the twentieth century."[8]

We are in an age in which the power of the World Wide Web is still in its early stages of development. Human beings from the remotest villages will no longer be isolated from the global community. National and international NGOs will link up with indigenous civil society, carrying Web connections and mobile phone service into the farthest reaches of the planet, giving a voice and visibility to the marginal and the forgotten.

The growing dominance of the Web in organizing human activity worldwide is beginning to transform development aid itself. Today, IT platforms designed by private firms offer a clearinghouse on thirty thousand development projects, allowing a private firm or nonprofit to connect with projects, find partners and workers with the specialties they need, and quickly team up with government agencies to get the job done. One website offers a development workers' "MySpace," which enables a health worker in Nairobi to compare notes with a colleague in Kenya on how to improve the managing of vaccine supply chains.[9]

Globalization and technology are driving deep change in how development bureaucracies work. Like it or not, development agencies long accustomed to managing monopolies through vertical structures are now forced to succeed in a flattened environment where rapid information exchange pretty much ensures that they have less information than the thousands of firms, nonprofits, and civil society organizations they have to partner with. Good and effective agencies are those that have mastered the process of "sector blending," whereby effective partners in private business or the growing number of development firms are quickly identified and mobilized.

The same Web systems are organizing information for private investors like never before, ensuring that firms in poor countries that might have long languished in obscurity now show up on someone's electronic watch system and become eligible for capital investments. A growing number of developing countries are establishing their own stock markets, allowing worthy firms to draw capital out of private hands and giving poor citizens an opportunity to own a piece of local firms.

This is the "century of the nonprofit," in which nonprofits, fueled by a growing private philanthropy, form at a faster pace than businesses, creating careers for college graduates with degrees from a growing number of universities that offer majors in nonprofit management. In the recent past, nonprofit social enterprises were largely dismissed as inferior to those of the government, run by well-intentioned but bumbling nonprofessionals. This condescension is coming to an end as the nonprofit sector now routinely scores higher public approval ratings than the government in its response to disasters such as the Asian tsunami and Hurricane Katrina.

This is the era, in short, of "bottom-up" participatory civil society and market-based private enterprise. The tendency of Americans to join or form voluntary associations "of a thousand kinds," as Alexis de Tocqueville observed, is becoming a global phenomenon in the twenty-first century. Philanthropy, volunteerism, and civic association are no longer uniquely American.

This is the era, most importantly, in which the lessons learned from decades of trial and error are yielding bold new innovations. Much has been learned about the limits of foreign aid and remote top-heavy bureaucracies laden with development policy planners. Writing in the *Financial Times*, John Kay reports the demise of the idea that "central coordination and direction, and the uniform implementation of best practice, are bound to improve performance." Central planning, he says, is giving way to a rapidly changing world environment in which "success comes not from the inspired visions of exceptional leaders, or prescience achieved through sophisticated analysis, but through small-scale experimentation that rapidly imitates success and acknowledges failure." [10]

The new era starts with an appreciation of the limitless potential at the bottom of the pyramid, the power of participatory democracy, and the importance of local institution building. The language of this new era is social capital, capacity building, philanthropy, and global democratic civil society.

THE FALSE FEARS OF GLOBALIZATION

The opposite of poverty is prosperity. Much of the debate over poverty for the past several decades has focused on charity and foreign aid as remedies. Yet while the world was haggling over which countries might be able to donate a billion or two more annually, China and India created $700 billion in new economic development. Their bold departure from stagnation and poverty happened in large part because they figured out how to participate in globalization. The problem with much of Africa, the Middle East, and Latin America is *too little* globalization.

Most people have heard only half the story of globalization. The arguments against globalization normally focus on the alleged movement of more power and wealth upward into the hands of the already powerful few. The antiglobalization movement creates a picture of rapacious American or multinational corporations scouring the earth for quick profits and displaying little regard for the poor, their cultures, or even the sovereignty of their nations. Little attention has been paid to how globalization is moving resources and poverty-reducing technologies downward and outward to the poor.

Global integration has been proceeding for centuries; the only difference today is that the pace of change is accelerating through technology. Naturally, the first actors to exploit global opportunities are those who already have resources and access. But it is a fallacy to assert that globalization can only expand the wealth and power of the privileged, especially the multinational corporations, while leaving everyone else behind.

The global status quo has been bad for the poor. When they are seen as irrelevant to wealth creation, they are dismissed as merely indigents to be taken care of by a government program or private charity. When the Third World poor are reached by technology and discovered by a spreading global capitalism, they become potential producers, customers, and citizens.

A closer look at global trends will suggest that the ultimate result of globalization may be the opposite of what critics have argued. Giant institutions, be they governments or corporations, may eventually lose clout, while the forces of globalization will drive capital, information, and connection to markets in the most remote reaches of the developing world.

The Third World is now its own frontier for investment, partnerships, and social experimentation, and not merely the recipient of charity. The hottest development ideas have little to do with charity;

instead, they are innovative entrepreneurial concepts like micro-finance, microfranchising, and private investment. Private equity initiatives for Africa and Latin American are proliferating. What the developing world needs is enterprise and capital, according to the *New York Times* columnist Thomas Friedman.

Africa in particular "needs many things, but most of all it needs capitalists who can start and run legal companies, and more Bill Gates, fewer foundations," says Friedman. He elaborates: "What Africa needs most is more 'patient capital' to spur its would-be capitalists. Patient capital has all the discipline of venture capital—demanding a return, and therefore rigor in how it is deployed—but expecting a return that is more in the 5 to 10 percent range, rather than the 35, and a longer payback period." Friedman remarks that "people grow out of poverty when they create small businesses that employ their neighbors. Nothing else lasts."[11]

Others have even argued that the poor will launch the next wave of entrepreneurship and innovation, driving a new round of global trade and growth. C. K. Prahalad, in his influential book *The Fortune at the Bottom of the Pyramid*, describes how globalization can open up new vistas of investment and wealth creation for the poor.[12] Long ignored by First World corporations is the enormous wealth that could potentially be created by what Prahalad has termed "the bottom of the pyramid" (BOP), which includes the three billion people who live on less than two dollars a day. "What if we mobilized the resources, scale, and scope of large firms to co-create solutions to the problems at the bottom of the pyramid?" he asks. "Why can't we mobilize the invest-ment capacity of large firms with the knowledge and commitment of NGOs and the communities that need help?"[13]

The answer to these questions is: we can and we will. Doing so requires moving beyond simplistic and polarizing views of globaliza-tion. "Like all other major social movements," Prahalad says, global-ization "brings some good and some bad." We need to set aside pointless debates that pit global versus local, or small versus large firms, or NGOs versus business.[14] These divisions and distinctions are increasingly passé as the world becomes flatter—a trend that benefits the powerless, as Friedman argues in *The World Is Flat*.[15]

How then can we harness the global changes that are inevitable so as to build capacities among the poor? What is a strategy for poverty alleviation that embraces the best of globalization in the twenty-first century?

The shrinking of the globe and the integration of economic production is unfortunately applying downward pressure on wages for some low-skilled workers in America. But it is delivering an equal measure of benefit to low-skilled workers in the developing world. The supply chain for major firms is flattening to include people never before esteemed as contributors to the production process.

New resources and communications technology in the hands of the poor will lead to rising expectations, manifested in social and political movements. The poor will discover the means to speak directly for themselves, which will alter the message that is heard from advocates who claim to speak for them. Global advocacy groups with an ideological agenda have often been more committed to opposing American business or foreign policy than to genuinely helping the poor. Their remedy for poverty is almost always more foreign aid, without conditions. But when the poor speak for themselves, a different message often emerges. They are usually not against the market and are more critical of their own government's failures than they are of America.

In India, for example, the training and employment of 245,000 workers to process international phone calls is generating demands for additional reforms of the Indian government. India has graduated from the status of poor nation into an emerging economic giant in Asia, potentially rivaling China, with a new favored status vis-à-vis the United States. While there has been an explosion of major businesses in and around the urban areas, however, many rural workers have been blocked from economic opportunity by flawed government policies. The poor of India are expecting more from their government and are making their voices heard.

On these developments, Friedman cites Pratap Bhanu Mehta of the Center for Policy Research in Delhi:

> This is not a revolt against the market, it is a protest against the state; this is not resentment against the gains of liberalization, but a call for the state to put its house in order through even more reform. . . . The revolt against holders of power is not a revolt of the poor against the rich; ordinary people are far less prone to resent other people's success than intellectuals suppose. It is rather an expression of the fact that the reform of the state has not gone far enough.[16]

He is referring to the rights of the poor to receive minimal justice from the legal system, to register land, to start a business, and to win some protections against corruption.

Friedman concludes that the most important forces against poverty in India and elsewhere are "not those handing out money," but rather the indigenous NGOs that are "fighting for better governance, using the Internet and other modern tools of the flat world to put a spotlight on corruption, mismanagement and tax avoidance."[17] These new populists are not targeting the wealth of the developed world; rather, they are determined to break down obstacles in the way of empowerment and development at home.

The real poverty fighters are not drifting around the halls of the United Nations, the International Monetary Fund, or the World Bank. They are working at the village level. As Friedman remarks, "You don't help the world's poor by dressing up in a turtle outfit and throwing stones through a McDonald's window. You help them by getting them the tools and institutions to help themselves."[18]

EXPORTING CIVIL SOCIETY

If asked to identify one of America's major exports, most people would probably not think of nonprofits or NGOs. But one of the most positive aspects of globalization is the expansion of the voluntary sector worldwide. America's heritage of strong voluntary associations and civil society is spreading around the world. Globalization is providing opportunities for America to export the civic norms and practices that form the building blocks of democracy and small-scale entrepreneurial capitalism everywhere.

Nongovernmental organizations have had a celebrated place in America's social history. In his survey of American social life in the nineteenth century, Tocqueville spoke of a powerful "tendency" he observed:

> Americans of all ages, all conditions, and all dispositions constantly form associations. They have not only commercial and manufacturing companies, in which all take part, but associations of a thousand kinds, religious, moral, serious, futile, general or restricted, enormous or diminutive. The Americans make associations to give entertainments, to found seminaries, to build inns. To construct churches, to diffuse books, to send missionaries to the antipodes; in this manner they found hospitals, prisons and schools. If it is proposed to inculcate some truth or foster some feeling by the encouragement of a great example, they form a society.[19]

Central to America's founding vision was the idea that the state would not be dominant; it would not undermine the vital operation of private voluntary organizations, which filled numerous roles that were as publicly beneficial as the functions of government. This tendency to leave much of public business to private voluntary organizations has been called "decentralist republicanism," and traditionally it has distinguished America from the political systems of Europe and Asia. Much of the Third World has had a long history of tribal and caste systems and has suffered under various forms of autocratic rule that resist sharing power with private nongovernmental institutions.

Civil society emerged with such dynamism in America because so much space was kept open for private associations and because those associations were buttressed by America's principles of religious freedom and pluralism. But the impulse to form associations is universal, a part of our social nature. It seems to emerge the moment freedom of association and expression is granted, and then it becomes a force multiplier for more political liberalization and empowerment. As more and more nations are discovering, any society that seeks to preserve freedom and maximize the conditions for human flourishing will take care to create or preserve a vibrant nongovernmental sector.

Thanks to easier travel and accessible communications technologies, even the smallest local association now has global connectedness. The number of private organizations with international operations in Tocqueville's era in the nineteenth century was thirty-two. Today, although precise figures are not available, estimates of the number of international NGOs range up to forty thousand.[20] Some of these are devoted to advocacy, while others focus strictly on the delivery of humanitarian aid. According to a 2004 survey of private voluntary organizations (PVOs) by USAID—the United States' lead relief and development agency—the largest 503 humanitarian organizations gave $7.1 billion in private assistance to the developing world in both cash and in-kind benefits.[21]

Taken together, private voluntary associations operating in the international arena are the newest and most influential actors in global politics. The former White House assistant Stuart Eizenstat has dubbed this new global force "the Fifth Estate."[22]

Through the latter half of the twentieth century, many people thought the giant professional institution of the central government held the greatest hope for mankind. Some even predicted a steady waning of voluntary organizations in the face of an omnicompetent state. Today, private voluntary organizations that engage and mobilize citizens are emerging as the greatest social and political phenomena of the twenty-first century.

Building "new communities" will be the top priority in all countries in this century, according to Peter Drucker, an eminent business consultant and scholar. Accomplishing this will be the task of "the non-government, non-business, non-profit organization."[23] The twentieth century saw an explosive growth in the business and government sectors. The idea that government could and should supply the community needs of an urban society through "social programs" dates back to World War II. That idea has failed, says Drucker; the social programs of the last fifty years have, "by and large, not been successes."[24] It is equally clear that "the private sector—that is, business—cannot fill that need either." Only the social sector can create communities for citizens. What the twenty-first century needs above all, Drucker maintains, "is equally explosive growth of the nonprofit sector organizations."[25]

Drucker describes voluntary group action at the community level is "that peculiarly American form of behavior." In his view, "nothing sets this country as much apart from the rest of the western world as its almost instinctive reliance on voluntary, and often spontaneous, group action for the most important social purposes."[26]

A powerful display of the American inclination toward voluntary action was the spontaneous surge of private engagement in the immediate aftermath of Hurricane Katrina, which devastated the Gulf Coast region of the United States. While 60 percent of the $3.6 billion in private donations went to the American Red Cross, individual Americans on their own initiative created four hundred new nonprofits to channel donations and volunteer assistance to victims. The friendliness of American policy toward nonprofit innovation was also put on display when the IRS instituted a fast-track approval system that processed some applications in as little as eight days.[27]

THE CENTURY OF THE NONPROFIT: THE GOLDEN AGE OF PHILANTHROPY

There are a variety of ways to measure the health of the nonprofit sector, including the number of nonprofits currently operating, employment by nonprofits, and the quantity of philanthropic dollars

flowing into the nonprofit sector. All indicators register dynamic
growth for the nonprofit sector both domestically and internationally.

It is a sector with proven momentum and resilience. Even during
the business boom of the 1990s, nonprofits grew more briskly than
the rest of the economy. The number of Americans employed by nonprofits has doubled over the past twenty-five years. Over a million
nonprofit organizations now operate in America, employing 12.5
million people and forming at a rate that exceeds business startups.
The nonprofit sector constitutes 7.5 percent of the U.S. gross domestic product (not including health care and public education). Worldwide, the nonprofit sector constitutes almost 5 percent of GDP.[28]

Fueling growth in the nonprofit sector is a burgeoning private
philanthropy, arising from unprecedented new wealth in America and
from tax code incentives to channel portions of that wealth toward
the social good. The number of private foundations has tripled since
the early 1990s. According to the most recent survey, Americans give
over $250 billion annually to private charity.

On the global stage too, growing wealth will likely feed more private philanthropic endeavors in the twenty-first century. The number
of families with assets over $30 million has risen to 77,700, accord-
ing to the latest survey by Cap Gemini and Merrill Lynch. The number of billionaires worldwide is growing fast. Forbes reports that 350
of the world's 691 billionaires live in countries other than the United
States.[29]

Many observers of private philanthropy are predicting a new
golden age of giving as tens of trillions of dollars are passed from one
generation to another. The scale of this capacity to give is staggering.
Paul Schervish of Boston College predicts that by the middle of the
century, somewhere between $31 and $41 trillion of inherited wealth
will be available for philanthropy, in addition to what the parent generation will simply give away on their own. "More and more people
have more money than they want to leave to their children," says
Schervish.[30]

The American view of wealth and the relative importance of the state versus the private market differs substantially from European attitudes. In America, the restless pursuit of wealth has long been viewed as contributing to social health The public sees the pursuit of private wealth as beneficial to the common interest in that it supplies government coffers with revenues and provides enormous reserves of capital that generates consumer credit and jobs. Moreover, the spirit of commerce and enterprise is seen as promoting social harmony, since those who seek happiness and satisfaction through competition in the marketplace are less likely to foment social strife.

While Americans have always regarded the pursuit of earthly riches as an aspect of freedom, they also believe the rich bear a special social responsibility. Hording wealth or using it for purely private ends has always been discouraged. As Andrew Carnegie famously said, "The man who dies rich, dies disgraced."

The private sector is viewed differently in Europe, where the private provision of services is more likely to be seen as an indication of government failure. But this attitude is changing. Many Europeans have come to recognize the limits of the state in solving social problems. More recent trends suggest that much of Europe is coming to regard civil society as complementary to state action. Countries across the European Union, and even China, have recently been working to foster a philanthropic spirit, partly through greater tax code friendliness.

The British government, for example, has organized a private giving campaign to boost charitable activity and has offered more generous tax treatment of private donations. Charles Handy, a British management guru who has written about the rise of philanthropy in England, says "there is a mood now in Britain that there are niches that the government doesn't fill, and that if you have talent, money and time you should get into these gaps." Thirty years ago, by contrast, "a businessman would have said 'I pay my taxes, the government should do it.'"[31]

For a long period, Americans dramatically outpaced others in their tendency to volunteer and support private organizations. In

1990, for example, while only 18 percent of Americans said they belonged to no private association, 61 percent of the French and 64 percent of the Japanese reported having no such commitment. But newly collected data suggest that the principle of civic responsibility is becoming more of a global phenomenon.[32] For example, Lester Salamon of Johns Hopkins University and Helmut Anheier from the University of California, Los Angeles, have found that civil society has become a major force in many countries over the past decade, its presence "far more widespread than typically thought." In one recent year, 60,000 nonprofits were created. In Germany, the number of associations tripled over ten years. Sweden, known for its extensive welfare state, showed some of the highest participation rates in civil society. Salamon and Anheier document the emergence of a "global associational revolution of extraordinary scope and dimensions."[33]

What is perhaps most promising is the proliferation of NGOs in developing countries. Michael Edwards of the Ford Foundation has assembled data indicating that in numerous Third World countries, the rise of indigenous civil society is a key factor in the ascent of the development ladder. One of the largest surveys of the nonprofit sector ever conducted, covering twenty-two countries, found over one million such organizations operating in India, 210,000 in Brazil, 17,500 in Egypt, and 15,000 in Thailand. One in twelve jobs in the countries surveyed were supplied by nonprofits. In places like Ghana, Zimbabwe, and Kenya, the nonprofit sector now provides 40 percent or more of education and health care services.[34]

Another distinctive feature of the American civic landscape is the dynamic role of religious congregations and faith-based philanthropy. The *Economist* describes religion in America as "a powerful force for generosity." There are more than 250,000 religious organizations in the United States, adding up to almost a quarter of all American non-profits.[35] Religious giving accounts for a staggering 62 percent of all donations in the United States, according to the Center on Philanthropy at Indiana University. Every income group in America, from rich to poor, is more inclined to give to religious than to secular non-profits.[36]

A review of data on American civic life shows clear differences between secular and religious people in all key indicators of civic engagement, including charitable giving and volunteering. Professor Arthur Brooks of Syracuse University reports that "religious people are 25 percentage points more likely than secularists to give money (91 percent to 66 percent), and 23 points more likely to volunteer time (67 percent to 44 percent)." He also found that the more serious the religious engagement—regular worship attendance, for example—the higher the level of charitable commitment.[37]

In this respect too, it appears that American patterns of philanthropy are migrating across continents. For instance, aid authorities in Britain report that 10 percent of the donations going to the nation's five hundred largest private organizations are now directed to faith-based organizations. Populations with little prior record of donating to religious NGOs are discovering the effectiveness of faith-based organizations, including American religious charities. During the historic outpouring of private donations that followed the tsunami disaster in the Indian Ocean, several faith-based humanitarian organizations in the United States were surprised to find hundreds of millions of dollars in donations flowing into their coffers from Australia, Europe, and Japan.

The best illustration of this trend is World Vision, a prominent Christian humanitarian organization whose annual budget now approaches $2 billion. According to World Vision's most recent annual report, $92 million came from Germany, $74 million from Hong Kong, $273 million from Australia, $247 million from Canada, $34 million from New Zealand, and $25 million from Japan.

At the same time, new philanthropic institutions are flowering around the world. Helmut Anheier, an expert on foundations, has reported that foundations are booming in Italy. A study by the Bertelsmann Foundation reveals that the startup rate for new foundations in

Germany is now 800 to 900 annually, up from 200 per year in the early 1990s. As in the United States, the creators of this wealth tend to take an active role in the operation of the private foundations they set up, applying their business skills and vision to their new role as social entrepreneur.[38] The Comparative Nonprofit Sector Project at Johns Hopkins University recently studied thirty-seven nations and found that when hospitals, charity schools, voluntary aid societies, and professional associations are all tallied up, total operating expenditures for nonprofits worldwide now reaches $1.6 trillion.[39]

In the face of public perceptions that state bureaucracy is not the most effective means to confront problems, government institutions are turning to partnerships with nonprofits to accomplish their mission. Public surveys reveal that private voluntary organizations are regarded as honest, capable, and transparent, in spite of occasional scandals involving large NGOs. The trend toward more public-private partnerships is promising more efficient aid.

Government functions increasingly are being transferred to the nonprofit sector, which is viewed as less entangled in red tape and more focused on results. Total government aid to domestic and international nonprofits reached a record $78.6 billion in 2004.[40] USAID has had a lot of success in moving programming in this direction through the Global Development Alliance, which leverages private dollars and incorporates private sector practices in its programming.

NGOs can often move faster and more effectively than government agencies burdened by heavy bureaucracy. More importantly, they are going beyond the notion of "development as delivery," the idea that what matters is the volume of assets that flow into a poor community, and instead are focusing on the assets that are already in place, waiting to be harnessed for economic growth. Most NGOs specialize in delivering a particular service such as education or health care, and most now resemble corporations in their management systems and talent. As Nicholas Stockton, former executive director of Oxfam, puts it, "There's a market for good works, and it's big business."[41] NGOs and nonprofits are capitalizing on partnerships with major institutions. According to Johns Hopkins, fees paid to nonprofits by major institutions such as schools and hospitals account for about half of the global nonprofit revenue base, or $880 billion a year.

TECHNOLOGY AND KNOWLEDGE PRODUCTS

Americans often envision charity as donations of private cash from businesses and individuals to humanitarian groups, which then go forth to deliver services. But this view doesn't begin to capture the variety of services that are routinely contributed by American individuals, firms, universities, and civic organizations. Just as powerful is the flow of knowledge products and the development benefits of our science and technology.

For example, scientists have completed the genetic mapping of the rice plant, making it possible to develop seeds that are more drought-resistant and can grow in colder climates. Irrigation technologies are evolving rapidly. Systems for delivering clean water efficiently can make an enormous difference in defeating poverty, as women are freed up from hours of walking each day to purchase water and can instead spend the time cultivating microenterprises. American entrepreneurs are figuring out how to install solar energy systems to power clinics, schools, and cybercafés.

One of the three major deficits that the UN's Arab Human Development Report identifies as crippling the Arab world is a simple lack of knowledge. But that will inevitably change as the barriers to acquiring technical knowledge are broken down in an increasingly open global community.

I was part of the first group of American civilians to enter Iraq following the military invasion. Iraq's knowledge class had been forcibly cut off from the civilized world for three decades under Saddam, and all of the nation's science and engineering information was badly dated. We visited a lab at a technical school and found bottles of chemical compounds used for basic research that were dated 1985, which was about the time when progress in Iraq slowed to a complete halt.

Some of us rushed to help stand up IT platforms so that knowledge products could immediately be transferred to eager scholars and technocrats, who immediately went to work applying them to building a new nation. With IT, it is possible for Third World countries to overcome barriers such as the high cost of books by building ties to U.S. publishing houses, technical schools, medical and law schools— ties that are formed by the transmission of technical knowledge through phone lines. Many schools and businesses volunteered to partner via long-distance Web connections with civic and educational institutions on the ground.

Whenever an NGO enters a country to provide humanitarian aid, it brings along technologies that are made available to the communities it serves. The most important example is the cell phone. In the *New York Times*, Sharon LaFraniere reported on the boom in mobile phone use in rural Africa, by far the poorest continent on earth. According to LaFraniere, "Africans had never been big phone users because nobody gave them a chance." Today, 76 million, or roughly 9 percent of Africans, are mobile subscribers. This new electronic connectivity is allowing the poor to overcome one of the great obstacles to economic advancement: isolation. Cell phone technology, says LaFraniere, "is a social and economic godsend." [42]

The greatest advantage of the cell phone is that it allows for productive use of time. Now, when a rural woman takes her four-hour daily trek for water, she pulls out her cell phone, checks in with her husband who is working in a steel factory 250 miles away, takes care of her banking, monitors her ailing mother who is bedridden in a clinic several towns away, and orders supplies for her microenterprise.

One study found higher rates of economic growth in those developing countries where the percentage of households with cell phones grew significantly in recent years. The rural poor can open bank accounts and do banking from a distance with otherwise inaccessible branch networks. "I used to keep my money in an envelope stuffed under my mattress," said Mpanza, a community worker in Soweto. "With banks, you need lots of papers, but with this one, all you need is a cell phone." Using text messages, account holders pay for goods, transfer money to friends, and have their salaries paid into cellular accounts.[43]

Mobile phone subscriptions in Africa grew by 104 percent between 2001 and 2003, from 25 million to 51 million. Now, 60 percent of Africans are within reach of a signal. Along with affordable wireless service comes the potential for increased e-mail and Internet access as well. This form of electronic empowerment will dramatically expand the connection of the poor to information and global markets.

Spreading the Norms of Democratic Society

Outflows from America are generally measured in terms of the large contribution that citizens and businesses make in the form of money and material goods, such as medicine and food. These are substantial contributions to the world, but this emphasis misses the real impact of American institutions, volunteers, and NGOs.

Wherever American nonprofits, religious congregations, and civic organizations are present in the developing world, they are helping to establish new legal and social norms and an ethic of citizenship—the foundations of nation building. Where American firms are at work, acting on the principles of corporate social responsibility, they are helping to modernize business practices, improve corporate ethics, reduce state corruption, and promote sound property law. Their community investment strategies are creating an entire new class of local nonprofits that are nurturing habits of philanthropy where they have never before existed.

The proliferation of global civil society also presents real challenges. Many NGOs are not advocating democratic capitalism. A significant minority see world progress as dependent upon checking American power and restraining multinational corporations. These NGOs can be counted on to supply the armies of protestors at World Bank and IMF meetings.

Many critics of NGOs are raising questions about the agenda for global civil society, asking, "Whose democracy is it anyway?" Gary Johns of the Institute for Public Affairs in Australia sees a danger that big advocacy-based NGOs will crowd out the voices of "the unorganized." There is "a new breed of civil society regulators—advocacy NGOs," says Johns, "and their activities have implications for representative democracy." Whereas civil society organizations such as churches, trade unions, and NGOs are normally viewed as vehicles for promoting private initiative, many international advocacy groups want, in effect, to regulate civil society.[44]

Most NGOs, however, are part of a worldwide pro-democracy network, functioning as the conveyor belt for badly needed reforms. Along with American corporations, they are at the forefront in advancing human rights, economic empowerment for women, rule of law, transparency and sound governance. For instance, in Banda Aceh, Indonesia—one of the most corrupt and conflict-prone regions in Asia—several hundred U.S. and international NGOs are partnering with local civil society to promote reform, modernization, and conflict resolution.

One of the things that policymakers have learned with certainty about effective international development is that state reforms are an indispensable element of the process. The poor cannot be well served without healthy institutions, both private and governmental.

NGO ACCOUNTABILITY AND THE PROBLEM OF BIGNESS

The image most people have in mind for civil society is small, simple organizations fueled by idealism and enlisting nonprofessional volunteers. But today, humanitarian and relief organizations are taking a remarkable new sophistication into the field, owing largely to standards of professionalism that have been forced upon them by private donors and their government partners. The so-called fifth estate unquestionably contributes much to international development, but in some ways it may undermine the basic spirit of civil society.

Today, large nonprofits can regularly be heard selling themselves to donors on the basis of their success at simulating business models. They advertise their advanced management systems and sophisticated methods for measuring outcomes. Often, they are pushed to organize in this fashion by the grant-making foundations that fund them, who have become infatuated with outcome measurements. Believing that professionalization is always best, these donors are imposing management objectives on nonprofits.

While large nonprofit institutions are important partners with government and bring vital resources of their own into international development, it was not the modern management systems that so fascinated Tocqueville. Intrinsic to the notion of civil society is the idea of space where ordinary citizens gather, deliberate, and carry out programs and plans for their own improvement. The power of civil society has always been its capacity to enlist the charitable commitment of individual citizens. America's rich history of private organizations is a narrative filled with stories of heroic citizens, often acting inefficiently and sometimes clumsily in pursuit of social ideals and aims.

A question that often arises is whether NGOs today are becoming like other megastructures run by a credentialed elite, and are not really empowering individuals at the grass roots, whether at home or in the countries they serve. As Lester Salamon put it, "America's charities have moved well beyond the quaint Norman Rockwell stereotype of selfless volunteers ministering to the needy and supported largely by charitable gifts," even though their success continues to be linked to this older image.[45] Fundraising still runs on images of simple acts of caring by presumably unpedigreed volunteer workers.

Can bigness coexist with the idealism and moral purpose of volunteerism? Are giant nonprofits a part of civil society at all?

There are certain ironies attached to the emergence of giant NGOs. Typically, NGOs are skeptical, if not hostile, toward large corporations and their political attitudes. Yet in their size and operations, they have come to resemble those for-profit corporate giants. Many NGOs have annual budgets in the hundreds of millions, with several now over a billion dollars. "These groups are huge and diversified, just like multinational businesses," says Professor Jagdish Bhagwati of Columbia University.[46]

Professor Bhagwati is among those who don't necessarily see the growth of NGOs in size and savvy as a straightforward plus. He says that big NGOs, like large for-profit firms, are driving to maximize their place in the market, always seeking new markets and too frequently "expanding beyond their expertise."[47]

Lester Salamon says that the pursuit of new markets and money leads to a tension between the nonprofit sector's "distinctiveness imperative," the things that distinguish it from business, and its "survival imperative." At what point, he wonders, does the nonprofit become so indistinguishable from the business firm that it altogether loses whatever advantages it might bring (not to mention its tax-exempt status)?

According to John Barkdull and Lisa Dicke, "global civil society organizations operating at all levels have adopted the bureaucratic form to some extent. As the major NGOs have grown, they have become more hierarchical, bureaucratic and professionalized." This trend, they say, raises serious concerns about "their democratic integrity."[48] How much do they actually model out democratic, as opposed to bureaucratic or corporate, ideals and practices?

The problem isn't just bigness. A growing chorus of critics can be heard questioning the practices of many NGOs. For example, they may inadvertently cause dependency by giving out food while doing nothing to encourage local agricultural production. Programs may be launched without sufficient funding to complete them, or a disease may be addressed in ways that almost guarantee it will continue. NGOs may display a very limited understanding of the local culture. But the concern raised most often is the question of "to whom" NGOs report and give account.

Some advocacy-based NGOs, especially human rights groups, enjoy political platforms that are available to no other entity and carry almost unquestioned moral authority. Human rights organizations are the eyes and ears of humanity in developing countries and make an invaluable contribution to the advance of justice. Their pronouncements are taken as authoritative, even if they lack an in-depth comprehension of local circumstances.

In Rwanda, for instance, President Paul Kagame is attempting to build a new nation following a genocide in which nearly one million Tutsis were slaughtered. This requires keeping over fifty thousand perpetrators in crowded prisons, cracking down with militia where necessary, and monitoring press outlets that were partly culpable during the genocide. Yet human rights groups, showing little understanding of the political-military context, regularly make pronouncements on practices that are nearly unavoidable for a nation seeking to recover from calamity.

According to Stuart Eizenstat, some civil society groups have been criticized for urging other institutions to make themselves more accountable, while demonstrating "a notable reluctance to evaluate how accountable they themselves are to the constituencies they purport to represent."[49] In all too many cases, NGOs fail to practice the transparency and accountability they routinely recommend for governments and corporations. The fifth estate, says Eizenstat, is "unelected, often unaccountable, and has been criticized (not always unfairly) as a self-appointed spokesperson for groups that may or may not endorse the actions taken on their behalf."[50]

On whose behalf do NGOs speak? How exactly have they been authorized? Should these large organizations be considered a part of civil society at all, or are they mostly auxiliary systems of, and operationally indistinguishable from, the governments that provide the greater part of their funds?

SOUND GOVERNANCE

As the power and capacity of nongovernmental organizations grow, so will the need for oversight and accountability. The answer to the problems associated with size and bureaucratization in major NGOs is to establish standards of democratic practice that are universally applied within the organizations themselves. Just as corporations are regularly admonished to be accountable to their stakeholders, NGOs must be accountable to theirs: funders, clients, and the constituencies whose views they claim to represent when they engage in advocacy. NGOs must demonstrate comprehensive accountability, because they are a principle means by which checks and balances are maintained on government.

As the World Bank advisor Alfredo Sfeir-Younis explains, civil society not only empowers the voiceless poor, it also provides exposure to the practice of governance. Civil society follows "a traditional set of norms and governance structures similar to those of 'quantitative' democracies, e.g., majority voting."[51] It is needed to address the many "normative issues" in development that can't be resolved through top-down bureaucratic structures.[52]

Even NGOs that announce humanitarian objectives as their primary mission are doing far more than delivering money or services. Their very presence in a country can be transformative—by empowering women, fostering participatory democracy, and introducing modern practices through technology. In embodying democratic values, they unavoidably contribute to the building of local democratic institutions and practices.

Wherever civil society organizations form, and whatever their size, mission, or characteristics, they must model out democratic practice and offer citizens opportunities to learn the habits of democratic decision making. The more capacity that is created among community-based groups to do the work of healing and caring, the less pressure there will be on top-down bureaucratic systems. Public officials and private NGO managers alike should think seriously about how to protect and nurture the varied groups and associations that are the building blocks of society, as Robert Nisbet put it. If the twentieth century brought destruction to the little platoons of civil society, the twenty-first century can be a time of restoration.

CHAPTER TWO

The Core Elements of Community and Nation Building: The American Debate

COMMUNITY BUILDING and nation building are treated together in this book, because in many ways they are intimately connected and interdependent. It is impossible to have a strong nation grounded in democratic values without vibrant nongovernmental institutions. National health and strength grow from the vitality of basic institutions such as family, neighborhood, congregation, and civic association.

Free nations are designed for free people. The institutions of free nations are shaped with self-governing citizens in mind. Much of the work of building and maintaining the democratic state is done by citizens operating within communities. Nations are not artificial constructions; they rise up out of cultural and social conditions. Similarly, the renewal of nations and the transformation of communities are not mostly orchestrated from above; they come from the bottom up and the inside out.

America's experiment in self-government cannot be fully understood apart from the role played by nongovernmental institutions. Ben Franklin alluded to this function when he said, "We've got ourselves a republic, if we can keep it." By republic, he meant a system in which many powers and responsibilities would be left to private voluntary associations of free people. Franklin raised doubts about the durability of this republican order for the simple reason that the natural tendency is to atrophy. The health of a republic is dependent on the vitality of civil society and the voluntary actions of the people.

Perhaps no other system of government on earth has made a greater effort to balance the powers of the state with those of the market economy and of civil society. This balance of interests and sectors can be represented as a three-legged stool: one leg represents the market, another the state, and the third is the social sector, consisting of families, neighborhoods, places of worship, professional guilds, and civic associations. Each leg of this stool must be firmly in place in order for a stable, well-ordered society to function.

Efforts to export American-style democracy sometimes emphasize one leg to the exclusion of the other two. Some will argue that economic growth is the panacea, only to discover that a flourishing business sector requires rule of law and sound governance. Others will focus on civil society without recognizing a need for political society —parties, elections, and sound rule. Some put an exaggerated confidence in a constitution, overlooking the organic way in which legitimate constitutional order takes root.

In the American political order, the social sector provides goods that neither the state nor the market can supply. The government can do a lot of things; it can maintain public order, manage the economy, establish justice, transfer resources, and provide a wide range of services. The government is constitutionally incapable, however, of performing the tasks of religious congregations, voluntary associations, or families.

The government can provide care in the form of social services, but it cannot create a society of caring people. The government can aim to strengthen community, but it cannot build community in the truest sense, an endeavor that requires people working together in a spirit of mutual obligation, trust, and cooperation. When "community" is mentioned, people often think of geographic location, architectural features, and perhaps demographic characteristics. But the real essence of community is organic and intangible, built on bonds of trust, shared values, and mutual obligation.

The Core Elements of Community and Nation Building

Few things have been more important to America's social order and capacity for self-renewal than the dynamic role played by voluntary associations and private charities throughout our history. Many of our enduring civic institutions arose through the initiative of citizen leaders. Many of our great social movements—for moral uplift, justice for women or children, reducing substance abuse, increasing literacy, or eradicating poverty and suffering—were led by social entrepreneurs and community organizers, not politicians. The reformist ideals and energies of civic America historically have not originated in government, but in the heartland, from the grass roots.

Civil society has made immeasurable contributions to ordering people's lives, transforming social conditions, and reforming laws where necessary. But the most important function of America's civil society may lie deeper, in the way it cultivates democratic values and habits. The great civic renewal movements of the past rose out of participatory democracy and also contributed to its vitality.

As Alexis de Tocqueville remarked, civil society is the incubator of citizenship. Love of nation and love of mankind start with the affective bonds that are cultivated in the little platoons of family and neighborhood. The voluntary associations that citizens join are the true building blocks of society, the place where "feelings and opinions are recruited, the heart is enlarged, the human mind is developed by the reciprocal influence of one person on another." [1]

Although the institutions of civil society cannot be created by legislative edict, the state of civic health is a matter of public consequence, making it a subject of public debate. Warnings of civic decline have been issued by social scientists such as Robert Putnam of Harvard University, who observes signs of American withdrawal into a private world of "bowling alone." [2] Putnam cites the influence of television, suburbia, and two-income families as factors contributing to the depletion of social capital—a term used by social scientists to mean the personal skills and social habits that are essential for democratic participation, such as trust, tolerance, and collaboration.

National policy debate through much of the twentieth century focused either on the powers of the state or on the capability of the free market to solve social problems and generate social health. The growth of the administrative state and the principle of central planning depended on devaluing all that was local, voluntary, or nongovernmental. We were told again and again that the social sector, or private charity, had little to offer in comparison with modern systems dominated by credentialed experts, with a monopoly on public resources.

But central planning has been largely discredited as a means to build prosperous democratic societies. The state has proven its shortcomings in solving social problems. Similarly, while free markets are crucial to encouraging prosperity, the market is not the sole basis of the good society either. Consequently, there is renewed interest in the community-building role of nongovernmental institutions, both at home and abroad. In recent years, governmental bodies have aimed to spark civic revitalization through leadership as well as legislation.

While some data seem to support a pessimistic outlook for civic health in America, several leading forecasters point to signs that the social sector may be poised for a great rebound. For example, there are indications of renewed interest in volunteerism across the entire age spectrum. Some are predicting a significant increase in volunteering among America's retired population—which is physically healthier than ever—in such activities as mentoring and organizing local charities. There are also signs of increased civic activism on college campuses and among America's youth, who are less inclined toward political action than toward local social enterprise. All told, almost ninety million Americans now volunteer, averaging more than four hours per week.

Perhaps the greatest opportunity for social and civic rejuvenation lies in the huge transfer of wealth that is about to occur—the largest in history. While baby boomers are inheriting their parents' wealth, they have also created enormous amounts of new wealth, which they will be handing over to their own children in the next decade. This new and inherited wealth, cumulatively measured in the tens of trillions of dollars, will make unprecedented resources available for charitable investment.

The new golden age of philanthropy is bringing fresh approaches to social problem solving. The current generation of civic capitalists give money away in much the same way as they made it—through small, flexible institutions that are highly focused and results-oriented.

Revitalizing civic institutions is not a partisan enterprise; in recent decades, it has received strong encouragement from senior figures of both major parties. In fact, a commitment to volunteerism and service may be one of the few things that bind Americans together as a nation. While there are deep social divisions along cultural and ideological lines, particularly over questions about the size and scope of government, civil society may help bridge the divide. There is more agreement over moral and cultural values than there is over the government's role in protecting them, so common ground may be found in strategies that scale down government programs while building up alternative private institutions and strengthening communities and families.

When people confront their differences through direct contact in civil society, a variety of things occur. They believe they are personally better off for having participated; they are more appreciative of those with whom they have clear differences; and they come to believe more strongly that civic connections make for a stronger nation.

Through a decade of involvement in the nonprofit sector as a social entrepreneur and another decade in the government promoting economic empowerment and civic renewal, I had the opportunity to advise key officials on a bipartisan basis—including a major Presidents' Summit on Volunteerism in 1996, occasional advice to the Clinton administration, and service in the administration of President George W. Bush for almost five years. I met thousands of volunteers, social entrepreneurs, and concerned business leaders who were promoting ideas for social improvement and for building stronger communities at the center. When I was in the White House working on the president's domestic compassion agenda, I encountered hundreds of leaders in the armies of compassion who were bringing hope to "the least, the last, and the lost" in the toughest neighborhoods in America.

When I moved into the international development field, I was frequently impressed by the level of engagement I found in American nonprofits working in the developing world. When I went to Iraq, one of the first things I did was organize a campaign to donate eighty thousand soccer balls from American children to Iraqi youth in an effort to win hearts and minds. Working through youth organizations and American soccer players, hundreds of local communities answered the call to promote good will. It occurred to me that no other society on earth would respond so rapidly or spontaneously to an invitation to participate in making the world a better place.

Later, working out of the State Department, I coordinated social programs and private donations for Iraq amounting to hundreds of millions of dollars. I also served as the director of private sector outreach and coordination for tsunami reconstruction at the State Department, where I watched the American private sector spontaneously come alive. Individuals and business firms gave $1.6 billion in private donations to the affected area—the most generous outpouring of private assistance in American history.

Private civic and charitable endeavors may be the key to greatness at home, and they are also the most potent force for good abroad. The tendency of individual Americans to act generously in response to need is universally appreciated, even where opinion runs strongly against American politics and government. It will take more than compassion and good public relations to win the war on terror, but the generosity of citizens does help significantly in winning hearts and minds abroad.

In all these ventures, I knew when I was around individuals who have a large view of their role as citizens, who don't wait for others to act, who see public problems as their own responsibility and not merely as issues to be addressed through the political process. These qualities represent citizenship at work, and it is hard to imagine a healthy nation without people who embody them.

President Bush began his administration hoping to make compassion his legacy. His signature initiative, as he often called it early in his administration, was the Office of Faith-Based and Community Initiatives. It was designed to bring a new approach to social problem solving and poverty reduction in the United States. one that was community-based and drew from all the civic assets of America's communities, including congregations and religious charities. It was my privilege to guide the planning process that established the initiative, to staff it, and then to serve as a deputy assistant to the president in that office during its first phase.

The president's campaign in 2000 promoted a new agenda that focused on effective, results-based compassion. "We will make a determined attack on need, by promoting the compassionate acts of others," he said. While he acknowledged that private charity was not a substitute for government action, he stressed that social services must "go first to the neighborhood healers," those groups that "are working *in* the neighborhoods, fighting homelessness, addiction and domestic violence." This approach, would "attempt to replace the failed compassion of towering, distant bureaucracies."

The new model of public policy would:

- Seek to reverse poverty and social pathology, not merely treat its symptoms.

- Evaluate the success of public programs in light of their impact on communities.

- To the greatest degree practical, rely on civic institutions and effective charities to achieve public purposes.

- Prize performance over process.

This was to be predominantly the work of civil society. In setting up the Office of Faith-Based and Community Initiatives, we announced our goal to: "energize civil society and rebuild social capital, particularly by uplifting small non-profit organizations, congregations and other faith-based institutions that are lonely outposts of energy, service and vision in poor and declining neighborhoods and rural enclaves."

Take note of the preferences expressed: small, local, faith-based, serving the poorest of the poor. There were many great things we could try to accomplish, but bringing support to the most deserving community organizations would be the greatest of all.

Implicit in the initiative was the idea that problems are rarely solved from remote locations, least of all by distant bureaucracies. Therefore, resources should be channeled not just to lower levels of government, but to charities and local caregivers who needed them the most. It was believed that these groups—which had been ignored or crowded out by larger institutions—were achieving results in their own neighborhoods.

Religious congregations and affiliated nonprofits have entered the spotlight as never before with their contributions to community health. Today, 18 percent of nonprofits in the United States claim a foundation in faith. Professor Robert Ruthnow of Princeton, author of *Saving America: Faith-Based Services and the Future of Civil Society*, has made the case that religious congregations and their affiliated social service organizations represent a unique form of social capital, based on their actual presence in neighborhoods and their provision of broadly supportive relationships. Ruthnow argues that faith-based organizations build "bonding social capital" within the communities they serve and "bridging social capital" by linking the poor and the nonpoor. In urban America, he reports, two-thirds of all congregations are involved in providing social services. The combined contribution of these congregations and faith-based nonprofits to the nation's social safety net is upwards of $12 billion annually.[3]

A relatively new phenomenon in urban America is the so-called "megachurches," which are known not just for their size, but for the range of community institutions and services they are creating. In many cases, they are organized around a comprehensive vision for community revitalization.

Windsor Village United Methodist Church in Houston, Texas, combines spiritual leadership with a broad vision for economic empowerment in the surrounding area. Founded by the Reverend Kirby John Caldwell, an investment banker turned ordained clergyman, the church has established numerous programs, all drawing from Caldwell's extensive experience in the private sector. It has created a health clinic, a bank, a private school, and a community college. One of its affiliated nonprofit agencies has sponsored a $173 million development program to offer affordable housing to low-income families. Other plans include a $68 million community center, a YMCA, a sports facility, a safe haven for abused children, and a shopping mall.[4]

As Windsor Village illustrates, the megachurch movement aims to do more than provide services to the poor. These congregations are building healthy institutions and transforming dysfunctional communities into vibrant living places, where people overcome their disadvantages to achieve independence and self-reliance.

Many of these emerging urban institutions are unafraid to partner with government agencies. The president's agenda included regulatory and legislative change as well as fresh support for civic enterprise and private philanthropy. Federal contracts and grants were to be made on a competitive basis to all organizations, including religious ones. Faith-based organizations were invited to come to the table in such a way as not to compromise their spiritual character or mission.

Another part of the initiative would be tax incentives to encourage charity. Due to a peculiar feature of the American tax system, three-quarters of all American taxpayers, or eighty million, did not itemize their deductions and thus would not benefit from charitable donations. A variety of tax code reforms were proposed to encourage more giving.

The unveiling of the president's community renewal agenda

prompted a vigorous debate about the basic responsibilities of the state and about the possibilities and limits of private voluntary action, a debate that continues today. One of the more remarkable responses came from the international community, which was a sure sign to me that what we were searching for in the poor communities was what many others around the world were searching for as well. We received inquiries from governments that had virtually no previous tradition of volunteer-based, nonprofit, civic, or faith-based programming, but wanted to learn how to plant the seeds of civil society within their countries, especially in poor communities.

Interest in the society-strengthening capacities of nongovernmental organizations is growing internationally, as reflected in academic studies, in the popular press, among public officials, and at policy conferences. New ideas to revitalize the institutions of civil society are being implemented everywhere—from poverty-ridden Third World nations and newly independent states of the former East Bloc to moribund welfare states in the West. All are coping with roughly the same phenomenon: weakened social institutions and civic enervation.

I will never forget the racially diverse delegation I received from South Africa who told a story of how, through the civil society sector and especially via an interfaith alliance, they were achieving progress in racial reconciliation, restoring social trust, and revitalizing neighborhoods. I asked them what was the key to this transformation. They said racial reconciliation was possible when individuals themselves, not politicians or the state, were sponsoring the work. No government programs could have produced the renewed sense of solidarity that this diverse group discovered in the course of working on civic projects together.

Neither will I forget the team of senior policy advisors from a leading European government who indicated they were searching beyond the traditional welfare state for remedies to urban decay. The visiting officials acknowledged that nothing was working to reverse the worsening conditions of the underclass. The only programs that seemed to be making a difference in people's lives were the urban religious congregations and locally operated faith-based social agencies—the only remaining islands of civic health in many underclass communities.

One delegation was from Prime Minister Tony Blair's administration in England. The British debate illustrates the shortcomings of both conservatives and liberals in their struggle to confront worsening urban social problems. The Labor Party, which historically could respond to the disintegration of urban neighborhoods only by calling for more social services, admitted that government was not fully up to the job. Conservatives, by contrast, had to deal with the legacy of Margaret Thatcher, whose free-market ideology purported that "there is no such thing as society."

Each party has to cope with the consequences of its own pattern of focusing on one leg of the stool at the expense of the other two. The Labor Party delegation informed me of their desire to strengthen the nonprofit sector. The Conservatives have announced a revised strategy for realizing their longstanding ideal of smaller government, saying that "the problem of fat government can be cracked by first thinking of ways of reducing the demand for government. . . . [R]educe demand and the supply problem will take care of itself."[5] In other words, focus on a cure for the problems that cause poverty and dependence—such as crime, addiction, and family collapse—and the need for government will decline.

When liberals acknowledge the limits of the state and conservatives admit that a society needs more than a market, we are hearing nuggets of socially consequential truth. First, democratic systems consist of more than individuals operating autonomously, either in a market economy or under the protective care of a massive central government. True social empowerment requires mediating institutions that act on behalf of the individual before the megastructures of the state and the market economy. Second, although modern states are dependent on civil society for social capital, they are in a weak position to regenerate it. They can devolve power to states and localities; they can foster more creative partnerships with civic organizations; and they can encourage donations to nongovernmental organizations. Civil society in the truest sense, however, must arise from a sense of mutual obligation and civic vision among citizens themselves.

President Bush's domestic initiatives accomplished more than is widely known. Although weaknesses in execution were repeatedly revealed, the objective of creating a level playing field for religious and secular poverty-fighting organizations alike was unassailably sound and is likely to remain a permanent part of the social policy landscape. Perhaps most important but least appreciated was the extent to which the same social policy doctrine guided a variety of other initiatives, including new directions in international development policy. In the end, the initiative that best embodied the principles of compassionate conservatism was the Millennium Challenge Corporation (discussed in Chapter Three), which targets funds to a limited number of developing nations that have agreed to embrace the internal reforms widely recognized as bringing economic progress. Other initiatives that featured innovative partnering were the Global Development Alliance at USAID, Volunteers for Prosperity, the President's Malaria Initiative, and the HIV/AIDS initiative. When combined, the international initiatives placed the administration in the category of having contributed more to international humanitarian and development priorities than any other since the Kennedy administration.

If the president's domestic compassion initiatives fell short of their promise, it was because the challenges of homeland security and confronting terrorism eclipsed everything else. Without a focused commitment to redesigning institutions, domestic programs continued to gravitate—as they usually do—toward the familiar scramble for federal dollars with a narrow focus on service delivery. And without a strategic framework of reform, the faith-based initiative came to be defined by religion, not results. Americans are faith-friendly but don't want the state promoting religion as such.

Nevertheless, these initiatives set the stage for a more comprehensive examination of how institutions work in poor communities,

both domestically and internationally. Research has presented overwhelming evidence that the two things that are actually proven to
deliver people out of poverty domestically are jobs and family; the
difficulty comes in figuring out how to produce jobs and two-parent
families in the poorest neighborhoods in America. By comparison,
government agencies do a poor job of reducing poverty. Social service programs are often fragmented, displaying neither interest nor
competence in transforming communities. A typical poor community has dozens of agencies, each offering its own narrowly focused
interventions, all of which prove insufficient because they don't lead
to a "tipping point" at which neighborhood antibodies can over-
whelm the viruses and push the entire community toward health.

What are community viruses? Joblessness, criminality, drug dependence, and the absence of fathers—social maladies that are mutually
reinforcing. Every poor neighborhood has its success stories of heroic
individuals who somehow overcome the odds. But these stories
rarely become the norm because social momentum is driving toward
dysfunction.

Both conservatives and liberals would improve their effectiveness
in reversing this momentum if they overcame certain tendencies
toward individualism—economic in the case of conservatives, cultural and behavioral in the case of liberals. Conservatives embrace the
individual operating in the market, but also call for strengthening the
family. Liberals suspect that this emphasis on family means returning
to the social agenda of the 1950s, with curtailed rights and opportunities for women. Liberals embrace the individual within the state.
When they say "it takes a village," conservatives suspect with good
reason that "village" is just a metaphor for the social service state.

Liberals would do well to embrace the social benefits of the sturdy
little platoons of family. Conservatives would strengthen their approach
by taking a new interest in building communities through the voluntary associations of civil society. And forward-thinking policymakers
would do well to capitalize on a potential convergence in social policy
thinking. A majority of liberal and conservative theorists have come

to believe it takes both a village and a family to achieve a lasting reduction of poverty. Liberals are realizing that healthy families are necessary to improve the lives of children. Conservatives are realizing that healthy communities reinforce their social objectives and minimize the need for government.

Conservatives favor work requirements for welfare recipients and a less intrusive government; liberals want a real social safety net, involving more government action if necessary. A compromise strategy is to focus on "building down" dependence on the state by building up alternative institutions that can restore social and economic health to poor communities. The debate must shift from social service reforms to resuscitating urban civil society. Liberals and conservatives should join together to evaluate every policy in terms of whether it encourages or discourages family formation and whether it multiplies or destroys community antibodies.

Religious congregations are the principal antibodies in America's poorest communities—the gathering place for entrepreneurs, civic leaders, and maintainers of neighborhood order. While they do not have the capacity to rescue all or even most of the poor where the government has failed, urban congregations are the most powerful islands of civic health and hope, providing the poor with role models and exposure to the social norms that generate self-sufficiency.

Civil society cannot be understood without an appreciation of the role that private voluntary organizations play in sustaining and transmitting values that are essential to human success. Peter Berger and Richard John Neuhaus, authors of the influential book *To Empower People*, have stated that "mediating structures are the value-generating, value-maintaining institutions in society. Without them, values become another function of the megastructures, most notably the state."[6] Publicly funded social strategies should involve working with the value-transmitting organizations that exist in every neighborhood to replace poverty-perpetuating habits with poverty-beating habits.

Although society's problems cannot just be dumped on the doorsteps of churches or charities, government should energize private action in every way it can. A new focus on empowering the social sector means a shift in resources and responsibilities:

> From the giant to the small.
> From the remote to the local.
> From the bureaucratic to the nonbureaucratic.
> From the impersonal to the personal.
> From the compartmentalized to the holistic.

These changes correspond to important trends in public attitudes. Americans have lost faith in the megastructures of the modern state that overpromise and underperform. People want to see policies that push back against the encroachment of pedigreed "social service professionals," which has suffocated citizenship and discouraged local action by nonprofessionals. More than anything else, taxpayers want to see results for dollars spent.

The American people are coming to believe that philanthropy should embody values of work and responsibility. The Pew Charitable Trusts released a national poll showing that large majorities of Americans believe that "local churches and places of worship together with local organizations such as Salvation Army, Goodwill Industries and Habitat for Humanity" are the most important problem-solving organizations in their communities.[7]

The findings were confirmed more recently in the aftermath of Hurricane Katrina, which struck America's Gulf Coast in 2005. Victims of the hurricane gave dramatically higher marks to private religious and charitable organizations such as the Salvation Army than to their government. In a survey, residents gave churches the most favorable rating for their contribution to emergency relief, followed by nonprofits in general. At the bottom was government at all levels.[8]

No one has suggested that private charity can solve the entire scope of complex urban problems. Clearly, government carries a major obligation to manage the big and expensive tasks. But large systems of government are not good at providing for the more personal care that families and neighbors frequently need. Grandiose notions of national community are being replaced with real, functioning local communities where people support each other as neighbors. Small nonprofits and faith-based organizations have the capacity to transform lives and mend broken communities.

These principles for building stronger communities have direct application to international development as well. The United States is now overhauling its programs to advance economic development in poor countries. For too long, our policies abroad were delivering the same dependency-producing results that domestic policies were yielding.

Civil society, whether in America's poorest cities or in the slums of sub-Saharan Africa, does not evolve in isolation from public policy. Laws and regulations set the rules of the game for the social and economic sectors. Thus, the centerpiece of the Bush administration's development policy has been promoting the reform of those laws and regulations, particularly as regards how communities and nations treat entrepreneurship and the assets of the poor. Even in their powerless state, the poor have talent and energy, they have assets, and they have capital that is often poorly managed and rarely organized to leverage economic empowerment. As the widely respected work of the Peruvian economist Hernando De Soto has shown, the way capital is treated has a huge bearing on how successful a community or a nation may be, whether it is a neighborhood in an American city or one of the poorest developing countries. The most effective strategies for human development in the twenty-first century will emphasize ideas, knowledge, and expertise, to assist the poor in better using their existing capital for productive investment.

Direct governmental assistance cannot compare to the power of civic or economic enterprise to fight poverty. America needs a new experiment in community-based poverty reduction, which begins with those who are "working in the neighborhoods, fighting homelessness, addiction and domestic violence," as the president said. One approach would be to conduct several pilot projects with multiple cities of various sizes. Each experiment, involving government at all levels, would concentrate public and private resources on achieving dramatic improvements over five years in rates of job creation, family formation and preservation, incarceration, and completion of high school.

Nonbureaucratic, market-oriented approaches to fighting poverty should be encouraged with more vouchering of services to the poor. Federal policymakers should inaugurate a new private sector war on poverty, all privately funded. Too much of today's charitable giving benefits middle-class and even elite institutions such as universities, hospitals, and museums, while too little reaches the poorest of the poor. The tax code should be revised to reward nonprofits and organizations that target their creative ideas on the poorest communities of America.

The ultimate objective in all this, whether domestically or internationally, is to elevate, empower, and bring hope to people. We must treat people as partners in their own development, with the right, the responsibility, and the capacity to govern their own lives and communities.

CHAPTER THREE

The Great Foreign Aid Debate:
Stingy or Generous?

> History tells us that the most successful cures for poverty
> come from within. Foreign aid can help, but like windfall
> wealth, can also hurt. It can discourage effort and plant a crip-
> pling sense of incapacity. . . . [A]t bottom, no empowerment is
> so effective as self-empowerment.
>
> DAVID LANDES
> *The Wealth and Poverty of Nations*[1]

JEFFREY SACHS DESERVES a lot of credit. As a leading development
economist who has traversed the Third World for several decades, he
has shown unmatched persistence in his advocacy for the poor. Team-
ing up with celebrities like Bono, he has been at the forefront of putting the cause of global poverty on the public agenda and keeping it
there when the temptation arises to ignore it. He is especially effective at conveying to Western audiences both the traps that ensnare the
poorest of the poor in their daily struggle for survival and the possibilities for elevating the poor above their precarious existence.

For example, Sachs tells of a meeting with two hundred members
of a Kenyan village, many of whom were hungry and ill yet also
resourceful and determined. In this village, few of the children
advance beyond the eighth grade because they lack the money for
tuition, supplies, and uniforms. Most families are home to at least one
child orphaned by the AIDS pandemic. Three-quarters of the families

reported having someone in their household suffering from malaria, and although everyone in the audience knew that the best available protection against the mosquito-born illness was simple bed nets, only two had them and were using them. Sachs found families living off tiny plots of land with severely depleted soil. The farmers were aware of methods to enhance production and all of them had used fertilizers in the past, but fertilizer was no longer affordable.

Stories like this one stir the conscience, and the mind races to dozens of simple and economical remedies that rich nations could offer.[2]

Sachs' principle nemesis, Bill Easterly, deserves a lot of credit too. Easterly believes that Sachs is a man of noble ambition who is mostly wrong, and that the consequences of following his costly schemes are terrible for the poor and the taxpayer alike. Reviewing Sachs' optimistically titled book *Ending Poverty*, Easterly describes the ideas presented there as "enthralling and maddening at the same time— enthralling, because his eloquence and compassion make you care about some very desperate people; maddening, because he offers solutions that range all the way from practical to absurd."[3] In fact, Easterly thinks that as long as the world is fixated on the Sachs solution, the poor in much of the developing world will likely remain poor in spite of what we do for them. That, he says, is the lesson to be learned from decades of trying to solve problems through development programs designed and delivered by elite policy professionals operating from remote places inside Western aid agencies.

Jeffrey Sachs and Bill Easterly are probably the most forceful and persuasive voices on opposing sides of the current debate on international development. Each represents a sizeable body of thought. As development economists who take academic research seriously, both marshal authoritative evidence for their position. Both are passionate about the poor and believe in their inherent worth and dignity. Neither dismisses the poor as lazy, stupid, or incompetent. Both believe that the developed world must do more for poverty reduction. And each believes the other is seriously misguided.

47

Sachs and Easterly both believe that sustained economic growth is the answer to poverty. Where they disagree is over what works to achieve it. Jeffrey Sachs believes that the path to Third World development is paved with lots more foreign aid, and that America is being stingy in its official foreign assistance budget. Serving as a special advisor to the UN secretary general, Sachs aims to get developed nations to accept and implement the UN's Millennium Development Goals, the principle objective of which is to raise annual foreign aid spending of donor nations to 0.7 percent of their GNP, adding an extra $70 billion annually to the fight against poverty.

Bill Easterly believes that America's helping hand is actually hurting, and that how much we spend matters less than how we spend it. In Easterly's view, Sachs' agenda for the poor appears to ignore the evidence of four decades of attempts to confront Third World poverty. Sachs maintains that "success in ending the poverty trap will be much easier than it appears," and that what is needed is simply more motivation and money.[4] Easterly sees this as "dangerous utopianism" and believes that today's utopian dreamers, like those of the past, know too little about the problem and disregard too many hard facts.[5]

Easterly predicts that Sachs' approach will fail, and that it will make the public even less inclined to support costly foreign aid ventures. Easterly is a scholar, but he casts aside the academic subtleties and polite policy jargon of the classroom to thunder irreverently about the failings of the Sachs school. In his book *The White Man's Burden: Why the West's Efforts to Aid the Rest Have Done So Much Ill and So Little Good*, he describes what he sees as a costly misadventure born of the hubris, gullibility, and guilt of the wealthy.[6]

For Easterly, the idea that more motivation plus money will solve the complex problem of world poverty is itself a problem, because it prevents a reassessment of the failed methodologies of the past. He charges that "spending $2.3 trillion (measured in today's dollars) in aid over the past five decades has left the most aid-intensive regions, like Africa, wallowing in continuous stagnation."[7] By promising what they cannot deliver, he says, "rich-world activists prolong the true nightmare of poverty."

Easterly defines much of the conflict over approaches to providing aid as "the West" versus "the Rest," and ties the grand designs of today's Western antipoverty warriors to the attitudes and strategies of colonialism in the past. The Enlightenment encouraged Europeans and Americans to imagine themselves as having a uniquely "meaningful history" and institutions that produced superior ideals. Meanwhile, the developing world was seen as having no real history or experience to draw upon. The "white man" thus got to play the starring role in a great drama of his own creation, living out a "self-pleasing fantasy" in which he had the power to save "the Rest." The colonialists of today, Easterly argues, are the bureaucratic "Planners" who have simply traded in the old coinage of "uncivilized" for the foreign aid industry's currency of "underdeveloped."[8]

To those like the musician-activist Bono who say "it's up to us," Easterly unapologetically retorts, "No it's not." He cites a lawyer-advocate from Cameroon who responded to the Live 8 benefit concerts of July 2005 by saying, "They still believe us to be like children that they must save by their willingness to propose solutions on our behalf."[9]

THE SCOPE AND NATURE OF POVERTY

The news regarding poverty is generally considered bad, especially for the poorest of the poor. There have been modest improvements in life expectancy, nutrition, and literacy. Though income levels for the poor are dreadfully low, they have risen somewhat over the past two decades. A number of countries once considered nearly hopeless are graduating into the family of developing nations through pro-growth strategies. It is possible to conclude, as USAID did in a recent report, that "development in the past half century has been extraordinary."[10]

But while there are some bright spots on the global poverty front, the statistics nevertheless tell an unsettling story of dehumanizing conditions. According to the United Nations Development Programme (UNDP):

- More than one billion people still do not have access to safe water; 2.6 billion lack access to sanitation.

- There are ten million preventable child deaths each year.

- 900 million people live in slum-like conditions without clean water or sanitation.

- 115 million children do not attend school.

- Almost three billion people—half the world's population—still live on less than two dollars a day.

Perhaps the saddest picture emerges in Africa. Many African countries have seen per capita income decline as populations have grown. Martin Meredith, author of *The Fate of Africa*, notes that of fifty countries on the African continent today, only South Africa and Botswana are better off than when they were freed from colonialism four decades ago, despite hundreds of billions in foreign aid being spent.[11]

One of the lessons about domestic poverty that has taken us a long time to learn is that not all poverty is the same. To truly understand poverty, one must disaggregate it. Even when looking at global averages, one must appreciate that some are getting poorer while some are becoming better off.

Among Jeffrey Sachs' many accomplishments is that he has educated a generation on the difference between the upwardly mobile poor and the extremely poor who are stuck at the very bottom. "Extreme poverty" describes the condition of the lowest one-sixth of income earners, those who live on one dollar a day or less. It is "the poverty that kills." The lowest one-sixth is "chronically hungry" and faces the "ravages of AIDS, drought, isolation and civil wars." Many in this category lack health care, safe drinking water, education for their children, and in many cases even rudimentary shelter. They are, according to Sachs, "trapped in a vicious cycle of deprivation and death."[12]

The picture is not all bleak. There have been successes, even within the category of extreme poverty. Around 1.2 billion people have gained access to clean water. Infant mortality has declined by 10 percent, and mortality among children under five has declined by 20 percent. Life expectancy has made modest gains in the developing world, and economic growth rates have increased slightly.[13]

The total number of people living on less then a dollar a day, according to the World Bank, dropped by 390 million (from 1.5 to 1.1 billion) between 1981 and 2005. Most of the good news, however, came predominantly from Asia. An economic boom in East Asia has resulted in a reduction of the extremely poor from 58 percent of the population in 1981 to 15 percent twenty years later. In South Asia, extreme poverty dropped from 52 percent to 31 percent during the same period.[14] But while conditions in Asia have been improving, the standard of living in sub-Saharan Africa has been plummeting.

These statistics factor into a great debate over America's role in global poverty reduction. Two major questions are: Is America stingy? And, is traditional foreign aid effective?

How Stingy Is America?

Jeffrey Sachs is best known for arguing that the United States is doing far too little to confront global poverty. Americans are often startled to hear that their country, the richest on earth, ranks "dead last" among advanced nations in its aid to the developing world.

What interests Sachs is "official development assistance" (ODA). Those who, like Sachs, insist that a country's "donor performance" be measured by percentage of GDP dedicated to official foreign aid take their direction from world development bodies like the Organization for Economic Cooperation and Development (OECD). The international aid community recently organized a campaign to get all countries to donate 0.7 percent of their annual earnings to the global fight against poverty. Given the enormous size of America's domestic economy, its aid-to-GDP ratio is bound to rank low among nations. Leading in the percentage category are Denmark, Norway, the Netherlands, Luxembourg, and Sweden, even though their annual dollar contributions are miniscule when compared with the United States.

But as critics of Sachs will quickly point out, this is not a fair or comprehensive measure of a country's generosity. There are multiple ways of looking at what a country does. And even under the system used by the foreign assistance establishment, the U.S. government has done far more in recent years than it is generally given credit for. Between 2000 and 2005, the Bush administration increased ODA at the fastest rate since the Marshall Plan, doubling official development assistance, from $10 billion to over $20 billion. U.S. donations represent the largest dollar value in aid by far, with Japan coming in a distant second at $8.8 billion. Bunched together on the second tier are Germany, England, France, and the Netherlands, followed by all other nations, who give miniscule sums of money.[15]

The American people and their government do far more for the poor than is measured in official development assistance, and they deserve more recognition for it internationally. In recent years, the United States has spent twice as much on global HIV/AIDS programming than all other nations combined. U.S. bilateral aid to Africa is now at over $3 billion annually, up from $1.1 billion in the last year of the Clinton administration, and accounting for one-quarter of every development dollar in sub-Saharan Africa.[16] The United States is the single largest contributor to multilateral development organizations, like the United Nations, the World Bank, and the International Committee of the Red Cross. The United States is the top importer of goods from developing countries, purchasing over $600 billion worth per year—eight times the amount that developing countries receive in aid from all sources.

If public aid growth is impressive, it can't begin to compare to the difference made each year by a wide range of activities involving the private sector. America's commitment of private sector resources far exceeds that of other nations and is growing every year, with private contributions to developing countries representing 62 percent of all worldwide charitable contributions. The Sachs approach to measuring generosity omits the many forms of engagement sponsored by the American private sector, including philanthropies, universities, businesses, and hundreds of religious and humanitarian enterprises that are producing results, often more effectively than government assistance programs.

Relying on a tracking system that measures official aid to the exclusion of all other forms of assistance wrongly implies that state aid is the most legitimate form of caring and that Americans are indifferent to Third World poverty. Under this system of counting, the $1.6 billion in private donations for tsunami reconstruction would not even register as part of America's contribution to international relief and development. Neither would remittances, which are now over $60 billion per year.

Also excluded from this official counting system are a wide range of exports that are highly valuable but especially difficult to quantify because they involve technical knowledge and ingenuity. What Third World communities often need more than money is our technical knowledge to boost agricultural productivity, enhance forestry techniques, improve health through better management of water and sanitation, and enable a host of other measures that directly affect poverty.

Perhaps most severely undercounted is giving by religious organizations. Because comprehensive records on religious giving do not exist, the figure of $7.5 billion commonly cited as the total amount given annually by religious organizations in all likelihood understates the actual amount substantially. The systems that do exist for tracking religious donations tend to count only large institutional giving, such as the amount spent by denominations on overseas activity and the money raised and spent by large faith-based NGOs. Many of the contributions made directly by congregations go unnoticed and untracked.

According to Carol Adelman of the Hudson Institute, who studies private philanthropy, the existing method of recordkeeping simply does not capture "the individual donations and projects of thousands of local churches, synagogues and mosques throughout America that give on a continual basis to overseas people and projects."[17] Adelman has assembled her own tracking system for private contributions in their multiple forms, in an attempt to challenge the lobby that says "America is stingy." Private assistance includes individual and corporate philanthropy, foundation grants, private religious and humanitarian organizations' activity, and remittances. Adelman claims that America's actual generosity is both undercounted and underappreciated.

America has always followed a different path in our approach to poverty, relying more on private charity and economic growth than on large volumes of government aid. Says Adelman, "Americans help people abroad the same way they help people at home—through private donations."[18] According to Adelman's index of private giving, Americans donated at least $95 billion to poor people abroad in 2005. When combined with official aid and U.S. private capital flows, this amount approaches $200 billion.[19]

Moreover, the more than $20 billion in official aid that the U.S. government provides the developing world annually does not include a variety of other forms of governmental assistance. In fact, only 52 percent of official aid is managed by USAID. In addition, Congress appropriates substantial monies for governmentally chartered organizations like the National Endowment for Democracy, which supports training in democracy programs in the developing world. Also, numerous programs to promote human development, such as cultural and educational exchange programs, are funded through the State Department. Aid in various forms also flows through multilateral institutions like the Overseas Private Investment Corporation (OPIC), the Inter-American Foundation, and the African Development Foundation.

Also missing from all official tracking systems is the rapidly growing portion of the military budget spent on emergency relief, rehabilitation, and conflict stabilization. For example, much of the $6.2 billion in aid delivered to East Timor, Bosnia, and Herzegovina went through military spending channels and was used for building roads, clinics, and schools. Few Americans are aware of the extent to which their armed forces engage in missions with humanitarian dimensions throughout much of the Third World.

REMITTANCES

A remittance is simply the payment of a portion of an immigrant or migrant worker's paycheck to relatives back home in the country of origin. Remittances have recently emerged as one of the most effective ways that America's amazing wealth-generating economy is lifting the poor, particularly in Latin America. Money sent home by immigrants is rapidly becoming a significant factor in regional and global economics, boosting democratic civil society and changing the way migration and immigration are viewed. It is also humanizing the process of globalization, which normally is presented as a matter of big business shifting its operations around the world in search of cheap labor, rather than workers moving to find new opportunities.

The growth in person-to-person assistance has been dramatic. According to one study, the global total of private remittances increased from $20 billion to nearly $160 billion between 1983 and 2006. Remittance payments to Latin America in particular have been skyrocketing. The Inter-American Development Bank (IDB) reports that migrant workers sent $45 billion to Latin America and the Caribbean in 2004, exceeding the combined value of both foreign investment and development assistance for the third year. The IDB also reports that immigrants who send money back to Latin America share approximately 10 percent of their paychecks, and these sums constitute between 50 and 80 percent of household income for those receiving the transfers. Remittances now account for at least 10 percent of GDP in six Latin American countries, running as high as 30 percent in Nicaragua. Annual payments to Latin America from the migrant and immigrant communities in six U.S. states now exceed $1 billion each, with twenty-four more states sending over $100 million each.[20]

Not all are comfortable including this category of private donations from the earnings of America's immigrant communities within the outflow of American generosity. But these are very substantial charitable donations made possible by America's dynamic private sector.

Mexico has been the biggest beneficiary of America's job and wealth-creating machine. In 2005, Mexican families received $17 billion from Mexican workers in the United States, almost twice the amount of four years earlier. According to Mexico's National Population Council, more than one out of ten families depend on remittances as their primary source of income. One state in Mexico, Zacatecas, reports receiving $1 million per day from its former residents.

The New York Times recently profiled a single town in Mexico— Valparaiso. Residents who left the city for jobs in the United States send home an estimated $100,000 a day, providing as much money to local residents in one month as the municipality will spend in one year. The mayor of Valparaiso, Alberto Ruiz, considers himself the representative of his city's residents on both sides of the U.S.-Mexican border. Shortly after being elected, Mayor Ruiz traveled to southern California, where he presented a list of public works projects he was hoping to get funded over backyard barbecues.[21]

Remittances are contributing to the creation of new political and social forces across Latin America, and are believed to be playing a role in strengthening democratic institutions. For one, the payments are spawning hundreds of "mom and pop" organizations to assist in their processing. These private associations, says one observer, "are filling in where more than a decade of free trade and foreign investment has failed to narrow the gap between the rich and poor."[22] Some migrants have formed political action committees to support candidates back home, and growing numbers are returning home to run for office. Having been exposed to how government is run in U.S. communities, these Latinos are making new demands for accountability on governments that have long been ineffectual and rife with corruption.

The United States may be the preferred destination because of its higher-paying jobs, but the movement of workers in search of jobs has accelerated in every region of the world. In 2001, the *Wall Street Journal* published a case study of how remittances had transformed the town of Pozorrubio, Philippines, population sixty thousand. One in ten of these people worked overseas, from Hong Kong to Los Angeles to New York, and thanks to their remittances the town was bustling with new stores and other businesses.[23]

In a mobile world, it is more and more common for workers to migrate to wherever opportunities exist, often within the region and sometimes to a new location within their own country. Bolivian workers migrate to Argentina, Nicaraguans to Costa Rica, and Haitians to the Dominican Republic, for example. Vietnamese who have moved to various new locations abroad are sending $2.6 billion home to their relatives. Remittances to the Muslim countries of the Middle East and North Africa are estimated to be in the neighborhood of $14 billion annually, four times the total foreign direct investment capital to the same countries.[24]

The story of remittances is not without its complications and controversies. The most obvious problem is that remittances are a product of what many in the United States believe to be an out-of-control immigration system. And if immigrants, legal or illegal, create challenges for America, their absence from their native communities has consequences as well. In some towns where the brightest and most energetic members are enticed away, the result is a serious drain on social capital. Jaripo is a town in Mexico that basically relocated to Stockton, California, leaving behind the poorest, oldest, and infirm. The remittance cycle is doing little to help revive the ghost town left behind. Local residents say that almost no new economic development is occurring.

Remittances are reported to have had distorting effects on the economies of Latin American towns. Although the inflow of wealth has a positive effect in spending for consumer goods, studies show that little is poured into wealth-creating activities such as saving and investment to expand the local economy. Some workers in Mexican towns refuse to work low-wage jobs in local factories, preferring to wait for more generous remittance payments to arrive.

The economic research on remittances is still in its early stages, so any attempt to draw major conclusions is probably premature. But the phenomenon may intensify the debate over why some communities and states are hospitable to enterprise and wealth creation while others are not. Why is it that migrants cannot generate wealth in their native communities and must travel elsewhere for opportunity?

Whatever their limitations, remittances are a powerful form of income distribution, transferring large sums of wealth from the United States to the Third World. Money that would otherwise not exist is flowing directly into the hands of the poor, becoming a vital form of private social welfare that strengthens family bonds and prevents many from sinking further into poverty.

AID: HOW EFFECTIVE?

Much as with domestic poverty programs, the criticism of foreign aid centers on its top-down, government-dominated nature. Both foreign aid and domestic poverty-fighting aid systems were products of the twentieth century, when confidence in large government solutions was running high. The Foreign Assistance Act, which started the process of foreign aid and the Great Society programs, was initiated under President John F. Kennedy.

Also surfacing in the great aid debate is the issue of scale—whether grand and comprehensive strategies or piecemeal approaches are best. Bill Easterly mocks the "Big Plan" approach of Jeffrey Sachs, with its promise to "end world poverty once and for all." The Sachs plan, he says, "covers just about everything, in mind-numbing technical jargon, from planting nitrogen-fixing leguminous trees to replenishing soil fertility, to antiretroviral therapy for AIDS, to specially programmed cell phones to provide real-time data to health planners, to rainwater harvesting, to battery-charging stations, and so on."

As Easterly sees it, thinking too big is the problem. "Big push" schemes are costly and wasteful; they mostly reward elite programmers; and they are rarely subjected to honest evaluation. According to its critics, aid programming that focuses on spending substantially more money probably means that more money will be spent on the wrong people. Much of the money passed through the foreign aid bureaucracy goes into programs designed by elite planners without local participation or input at the forefront. Whenever top-down programming designed by elites is favored, says Easterly, it results in grand "utopian" ideas that promise to "fix all problems simultaneously and quickly," but these programs rarely deliver what they advertise.

Easterly offers an alternative strategy: to select a few projects, do them well, and allow plenty of room for the poor to participate. Piecemeal reform "motivates specific actors to take small steps, one at a time, and then tests whether that small step made poor people better off." The piecemeal approach acknowledges that nobody "can fully grasp the complexity of the political, social, technological, ecological and economic systems that underlie poverty." Easterly says this approach eschews the arrogant idea that "we" know exactly how to fix "them."[25]

Easterly believes that with piecemeal approaches, agencies can be held responsible for their actions. Before taking an additional step, agencies must prove results from those already taken. Results follow from discrete management actions, such as vaccination campaigns, oral rehydration therapy to prevent diarrhea, clean water and sanitation programs that have delivered multiple benefits to villages, and other health programs that have reduced infant mortality.

If one believes that poverty is a function of too little money being invested in the poor, the solution becomes simply to transfer more money to the poor. If one believes, on the other hand, that effective aid should "teach a man how to fish" rather than simply give him a fish, the focus becomes the need to expand market-based growth.

Allowing money to dominate the focus is tempting. Outflows of money are concrete and easy to measure. Watching expenditures grow is certainly one indication of political will and seriousness. Money is often given for the simple reason that it satisfies the need to do something—which is always preferable to doing nothing when lives are at stake. The money solution may persist because it seems the moral thing to do, while allowing one's giving to be complicated by questions of effectiveness can seem immoral.

Effectiveness is less measurable than expenditures. While Americans are not against spending money, they have shown again and again that their patience runs thin when doubts arise about the effectiveness of how their money is being applied. In fact, a consistent American belief from the New Deal and Great Society to the present is that the key to human development is *not* mostly money. The preferred approach is promoting opportunities for self-improvement through economic growth produced by markets.

Giving priority to money has been the preferred approach of foreign assistance programming. It is the predominant approach of major international institutions such as the various agencies of the United Nations as well as Europe. The European foreign aid establishment goes to great lengths in encouraging financial aid. Finance ministers throughout the 25-nation bloc promoted a special tax on their people—an airline ticket tax—that would help finance development aid to Africa.[26] Generating major headlines prior to the G8 meeting in the summer of 2005 was a concerted effort by Europeans to generate a global agreement to reduce or cancel the debt of some thirty-eight countries that fall into the category of "highly indebted poor countries" (HIPCs).

The reason given for the appeal was compelling: So long as these countries spent much of their GDP on servicing their debt rather than investing in health, education, and infrastructure, they would not get themselves out of the poverty trap.[27] Not mentioned, however, was that the generous lending policies of the West may have helped create the trap in the first place. Despite $144 billion in loans, the

HIPCs saw their average per capita incomes decrease more than 25 percent over the course of the twenty-five years that the lending was occurring.

Whether the issue is debt relief or increased government expenditures, money is presented as the answer whenever development officials gather. When money is key, the fate of many rests in the hands of a few, namely a handful of leaders from rich industrialized nations. A *New York Times* editorial captured this in the lead-up to the G8 meeting in 2005: "Eight men are about to decide the future of hundreds of millions of people in sub-Saharan Africa." These eight men, according to the editorial, would determine whether "40 million young people will still be able to go to school and whether 300 million Africans will continue to lack access to clean water."[28]

Those who espouse the market school of economic development reply, "No, they won't. If it were up to Western leaders and Western aid budgets, these problems would have been solved a long time ago. The citizens of these nations will get clean water and education programs when their leaders decide these things are important." When Western leaders conclude that they have the solutions, it is inevitable that too little attention is given to corruption, theft, waste, civil strife, and state failure.

Jeffrey Sachs, who has spent his life advocating more aid money, is not against the market solution. He admits that sustainable local growth through job-creating enterprise is a big part of the answer. But he and others of his school maintain that the poorest of the poor will never achieve productive lives in the marketplace without the most basic investments in health and education. And such investment takes money that most poor countries do not have.

For the poor who live in disease-ridden, drought-prone, infrastructure-starved, and often landlocked countries, the market approach can smack of "boot-strappism" or "market Darwinism," as some have termed it. Markets are important, says Sachs, "but in my view, clean water, productive soils and a functioning health care system are just as relevant to development as foreign exchange rates." Sachs argues that just as the sources of poverty are multidimensional, "so are the solutions."[29]

The great aid debate has been heavily influenced by experience in Africa over the past two decades. Even those friendly to traditional aid admit the need for a change in direction. Those who advocate spending more money have a hard time explaining how it will make the difference. Per capita, Africa is the most generously aided continent on earth. Over the past twenty-five years, Africa has received $520 billion in official development assistance—a figure that does not include private investment or philanthropy. Neither does it include the continent's own oil revenue, which has tripled in the past five years.

Few would contest the evidence that the African continent is mostly worse off today than when foreign aid began pouring in, with some isolated exceptions. Raghuram Rajan, chief economist of the International Monetary Fund, says that the failure of this aid to advance economic growth in Africa is partly a function of the distortions that monetary aid creates in countries with weak institutions and underdeveloped economies. Aid tends to shift skilled labor from the private sector to the public sector and drastically reduce incentives to produce goods for export. According to the economist Walter Williams, as money has flooded into Africa, capital and talent have fled. "One unappreciated tragedy that attests to the wasted talents of its peoples is that Africans tend to do well all around the world except in Africa," writes Williams. "This is seen by the large number of prosperous, professional and skilled African families throughout Europe and the United States. Back home, these same people would be hamstrung by their corrupt governments."[30]

The general verdict on the impact of foreign aid is not very positive. While there has been a slight drop in the number of persons who are very poor, mostly in Asia and notably in China, this trend has little to do with aid. Where progress is occurring, it appears to be a function mostly of economic growth linked to the rule of law, as we will discuss later.

Thomas Dichter, who spent forty years of his life serving in a variety of positions involving international development, came to the reluctant conclusion late in his career that "aid has not worked, is not likely to work in the future, and *cannot* work." He added that he doesn't know a single colleague "with long field experience who believes wholeheartedly that aid has been effective." Dichter is not suggesting that we stop caring about the poor, but rather that foreign aid is not lifting them out of poverty. The bleak results, he maintains, stem from "the complex nature of poverty and the flawed nature of institutions and governments in poor countries."[31] Lasting poverty reduction takes time because economic growth takes time to generate.

The "aid industry" in the developed world has experimented with a new priority focus roughly every decade. In the 1950s, the focus was on import substitution and industrial development, in the belief that we could help poor countries leapfrog over stages of growth. Then came agriculture in the 1960s and 1970s, with an emphasis on cooperatives, agricultural marketing boards, and training of agricultural extension workers to pass along new techniques. At various times in the 1970s and 1980s there was also a big push to deal directly with the poor and to encourage grass-roots participation. Women emerged as a key factor in Third World development, as did urban slum reform.[32]

All these new ideas and paradigms, along with dozens of international proclamations and gatherings, "were motivated by a sincere commitment to do better," says Dichter, even as one failure led to another and hopes were pinned on one or another new idea. "Deep down, the aid industry has not changed much," he concludes, and "we must entertain the possibility that we have been fooling ourselves."

Mirroring the debate about domestic antipoverty strategies, Dichter says that "the aid industry is not prepared to deal with the fact that poverty is not just a material condition—something that is complicated enough—but it is also a matter of the social, cultural and political position many poor people occupy in their societies." For many people in developing countries, "it is about which caste, class, language, group, tribe, gender, or shade of color you were born into."[33]

What has perhaps stymied progress more than anything else is our failure to appreciate that neither foreign aid nor economic growth can be successful apart from rule of law and effective governing institutions. Many less-developed countries "have governments that are either autocratic or unstable or both, and more often than not they are also corrupt or repressive or both," Dichter points out, and these conditions limit the effectiveness of foreign aid.[34]

A Third Way: Conditionality

If history is any guide, foreign aid will continue to flow, and at more generous levels. No one—not even the most ardent aid foes—expects Western governments to do less. Everyone recognizes that major infrastructure projects such as roads, highways, schools, and hospitals are vitally important. The large private and public system that critics call the "aid industry" will continue to be supported. NGOs, through private aid as well as government contracts, will continue trying to ameliorate conditions.

The debate between giving money and promoting markets will continue. But another alternative, a third way, has been emerging.

If there is one big lesson in foreign aid over the past twenty years on which large majorities of experts and practitioners agree, it is this: For aid to be effective, it must be linked to broad reforms aimed at building strong institutions, rule of law, and sound government free of corruption.

Paul Collier of the World Bank presents the case for smarter aid, given with strict conditions. He suggests that aid be given only to countries where "policies, institutions and other circumstances make it atypically effective . . . avoiding countries where it is likely to be ineffective or even counterproductive." Like many others, Collier sees a place for official aid but believes that greater effectiveness depends on using it more sparingly.[35] That means using aid where it can leverage reforms within a country while bypassing some countries altogether if they show no interest in internal reform. If aid is going to confront poverty seriously, it must be used in a way that promotes behavioral change. Otherwise, chances are it is doing little good and may even be doing harm.

This conditional approach to aid has gained favor in the Bush administration, even as the amounts spent on aid have increased. Speaking at Harvard University, USAID administrator Andrew Natsios stated, "The central reason why some countries remain poor and other countries develop, and develop in terms of rapid rates of economic growth, centers around the issue of governance, of democratic governance." The failure of democratic governance, he continued, "is a central reason why some countries are stuck without growth, deeply mired in poverty and in chronic instability, corruption, and mismanagement." [36]

THE CORRUPTION CALAMITY

Among the most urgent and difficult problems that many Third World countries must confront in order to progress is corruption. According to Transparency International, a group committed to dealing aggressively with bribery and corruption, it is "one of the world's greatest challenges" and "a major hindrance to sustainable development." Studies indicate that corruption adds upwards of 10 percent to the cost of doing business for the private sector and as much as 25 percent to the cost of public procurement. It has "a disproportionate impact on poor communities and is corrosive on the very fabric of society." [37]

A country steeped in corruption is likely to divert large portions of whatever aid or direct foreign investment it is able to attract from abroad. One result is that aid from Western governments is cut or eliminated, and direct foreign investment dries up.

When corruption is rampant and rule of law almost nonexistent, life for the poor often becomes a state of bondage at the hands of warlords, drug bosses, and human traffickers. Many forms of corruption are so subtle that they evade detection even when the government is committed to fighting them. For ordinary citizens, bribing officials just to get a government service—like having your trash picked up or getting a vaccination for your child—can be a routine necessity, one that is woven into the local culture. Corruption can affect the most ordinary activities, from getting government checks to dealing with traffic violations to renewing passports or identity cards.

For businesses, just about any commercial transaction or any sort of permission to conduct business is susceptible to some form of corruption, such as having to pay off officials to import or export products. In many developing countries, the majority of work is done through projects that are never subjected to competitive bidding and are rarely if ever audited. A common practice by corrupt officials is to ask a contractor who is providing the government $15,000 in services to sign a receipt for the full amount while receiving only half the amount as payment.

In many countries, corruption runs so deep that it requires heroic and often life-threatening efforts to uproot. Advances are often reversed. This is especially true in much of Africa, which has received $300 billion in aid from Western nations since 1980, much of which is widely acknowledged to have dissipated into waste and fraud.

Nigeria is an example of a nation thoroughly crippled by corruption, where Western aid was mostly wasted or stolen. Repeated efforts have been made to fight corruption, with mixed results. Nigeria received $3.5 billion in aid from 1980 until 2000, not including World Bank loans or the $300 billion in earnings from lucrative oil and gas operations.

That $3.5 billion in aid is only slightly less than the sum that the Nigerian dictator Sani Abacha reported as having been looted during his five-year rule, according to Sharon LaFraniere of the *New York Times*. Audits disclosed that $836 million was poured into projects that were abandoned midway and never completed. Many more projects were completed but never made operational. The World Bank concluded that half of the projects initiated had little impact or were unsustainable.[38]

Rulers who come along promising corrective action have to confront habits of corruption among their own constituency, where corruption is longstanding and thoroughly entrenched in the culture. This is something few are willing to do. In Nigeria, Abacha's replacement in 1999 was Olusegun Obasanjo, who in an earlier career had helped found Transparency International. Only halfway through his second term was he able to fire or arrest three officials for misdeeds and open up government contracts for competitive bidding.

While there is a sense that progress is possible in Africa, there are still many roadblocks, corruption among them. A World Bank study showed that governance deteriorated in as many African countries as it improved between 1996 and 2004. Some went through cycles of improvement followed by major setbacks. For example, in Kenya, after two years of progress, a widely respected anticorruption czar quit in frustration, resulting in major cuts in aid by the United States and Germany.[39]

The Kenyan episode illustrates how the problem of corruption is inseparably connected to poverty. The country can barely feed its hungry citizens because, according to Emily Wax of the *Washington Post*, "past and previous administrations have looted the country's treasury in one corruption scandal after another."[40] In March of 2006, dramatic details were released of two major scandals in which high-level Kenyan officials stole $1.3 billion in public funds that had been allocated to irrigation and road projects. The money would have improved agricultural production and helped farmers reduce the devastating effects of recurring drought. According to Wax, "many Kenyans are blaming government corruption, not Mother Nature, for their dire situation." The crisis "highlights how government fraud and mismanagement can worsen, and in some cases create, food shortages."[41]

In another recent scandal, $300 million in contract money awarded to improve security and create tamper-proof passports disappeared into the pockets of senior officials. Kenyan political leaders "drive luxury cars, enjoy personal helicopters and live in sprawling villas," remarks Wax, while one-third of the children under five are malnourished.

The problem of corruption is acute in a country "where subsistence farming is a way of life for the population and where just one season without rain can mean widespread hunger."[42]

Prosperous Westerners who desire to alleviate these conditions of hunger and malnourishment have little choice but to question what can be done without a full-scale assault on government malfeasance, corruption, and incompetence. Clearly, humanitarian endeavors alone cannot supply long-term solutions to systemic abuse.

Similar patterns are playing out across Central and South America, where the democratic gains of twenty years have faced multiple setbacks. Fledgling democracies are imperiled by disillusioned publics who see democracy as powerless to end corruption as promised. Surveys of the region reveal that Latin Americans themselves see corruption as the most serious problem in their countries, and believe it is directly linked to the region's economic crisis; 80 percent believe that corruption has increased and that it is hurting business and economic growth. Jose Ugaz, a Peruvian anticorruption investigator for the World Bank, says, "The impact of corruption on our economies is huge, just huge."[43]

All across Central America, demonstrating that corruption is pervasive and also that law enforcement is committed to confronting it, "prosecutors are pursuing cases against current and former leaders who have lined their pockets," according to *New York Times* reporters Larry Rohter and Juan Forero.[44] The former Nicaraguan president Arnoldo Aleman is serving a twenty-year sentence for diverting funds. In Costa Rica, two presidents have been accused of taking kickbacks on lucrative government contracts. In Peru, public officials have been lynched by angry mobs demonstrating in the streets and eight leaders have been forced out of office in five years.

In all too many cases, the person who achieves power with anti-corruption promises goes on to govern through a small power base consisting mostly of friends and business cronies. When he ran for the presidency of Brazil in 2002, Luiz Ignácio Lula da Silva promised he would boldly confront the sordid practices of his country and guarantee the people a government freer of corruption. Shortly into Lula da Silva's term, numerous officials surrounding him were charged with embezzlement and fraud and were forced to resign. In the fall of 2005, fifteen thousand people marched through the major cities demanding "zero corruption" and insisting that nineteen legislators from six political parties linked to corruption be jailed. The demonstrators condemned the president who had won their support as an anticorruption crusader, saying, "a thief is a thief, friend or not."[45]

Progress in fighting corruption is often linked to broader efforts to improve a country's business climate. For example, Indonesia, long regarded as one of the most corrupt countries, is believed to have made considerable headway in reducing corruption in recent years. During the period when I worked on tsunami reconstruction at the State Department and traveled to the region to review progress, every single meeting with Indonesians brought forth a strong pledge to prove to the world that the billions in aid flowing into the affected area could be spent without corruption. At all levels of Indonesian government, from the president on down, a commitment was made to pursue corrupt elements. In Banda Aceh, the province of Indonesia hit hardest by the tsunami, a major crackdown in corruption resulted in a ten-year prison sentence for the provincial governor.

All reconstruction in Indonesia was consolidated under a highly respected Western-trained public manager, Dr. Kuntoro Mangkusubroto, who had staked his own credibility as well as the future of that region on the ability of his agency to handle the money with minimal corruption. Kuntoro saw an opportunity to use the tsunami disaster to make permanent improvements in the governance of his country based on Western standards of transparency and accountability. He and his president knew full well that any significant improvements they made in how that region is perceived could yield major breakthroughs for trade and investment.

Proof of progress is best displayed in how the people themselves judge a government's performance. In a mid-2005 worldwide survey of public perceptions on corruption conducted by Transparency

International, the Indonesians were found to be the most optimistic people on earth in their expectation that their country would continue to rein in corruption.[46]

Advocates of traditional foreign aid are often uncomfortable with a heavy emphasis on corruption. Accusing Third World governments of failing to confront poverty because of their own misdeeds sounds condescending and can easily lead to abrupt aid cut-offs, hurting the poor even more. And Western campaigns against corruption may be too quick to condemn cultural practices that can be explained by family and tribal traditions.

For Jeffrey Sachs, the assertion that African corruption "is the basic source of the problem does not withstand practical experience or serious scrutiny."[47] Sachs maintains that at least twenty-four African nations are run well enough that they could handle a major infusion of foreign aid, and that corruption or mismanagement is not a sufficient excuse to delay further action.

Others point out that uprooting corruption will take patience and generations to achieve, and even countries that are relatively well governed often can't seem to make it beyond the first rung on the ladder. Sound governance is important, Sachs remarks, but the more important ingredients are such things as "good harbors, close contacts with the rich world, favorable climates, adequate energy sources and freedom from epidemic disease." Countries with these advantages can escape poverty, and have.[48]

The preponderance of opinion today, however, is that preventing corruption is close to the highest priority in Third World development. Writing in *Foreign Affairs*, Ben Heineman and Fritz Heimann state that "the true impact of corruption is now widely acknowledged: corruption distorts markets and competition, breeds cynicism among citizens, undermines the rule of law, damages government legitimacy, and corrodes the integrity of the private sector." They conclude that corruption is a major barrier to development and deeply hurtful to the poor, a "systematic misappropriation by kleptocratic governments."[49]

Corruption robs the poor by chasing away everything that could help them—business investment, talent, and the aid that was intended for them, as the Nigerian and Kenyan examples point out. Research by the World Bank shows that levels of economic investment in a country are inversely correlated to rates of corruption, which is why promoting good governance now appears in the agendas of business, NGOs, and governments alike.

GOING WITH SOUND GOVERNANCE

In a 2000 study of aid effectiveness by a group of World Bank economists, the authors concluded that "development assistance can contribute to poverty reduction in countries pursuing sound policies." The study prompted the World Bank president to declare that confronting corruption is a foundational goal in Third World development. "We have learned that corruption, bad policies, and weak governance will make aid ineffective," he said.[50]

Clearly there are links between transparency, the rule of law, democracy, and free markets, and these linkages are being acknowledged in U.S. policy and law. In 2002, President Bush announced a new initiative called the Millennium Challenge Corporation, designed to produce better returns on investment for American foreign aid spending. The thesis behind the initiative is that economic development and sound governance are inextricably tied together. When pro-growth economic policies are in place and when government reforms are adopted, foreign aid can make a difference. In announcing the Millennium Challenge Corporation, the White House claimed that in sound policy environments, "every dollar of aid attracts two dollars of private capital." Conversely, where poor governance exists, "aid can harm the very citizens it is meant to help—crowding out private investment and perpetuating failed policies."[51]

Both experience and research confirm that American compassion can make a difference for the Third World poor if their governments care about their own development. Conversely, where the rulers of the poor are indifferent or even resistant to modernizing reforms, little good can be done from the outside. According to President Bush, "When nations respect their people, open markets, and invest in better health and education, every dollar of aid and every dollar of trade revenue and domestic capital, is used more effectively."[52]

To qualify for support under the Millennium Challenge Corporation, governments must demonstrate a commitment to three things: to governing justly (through rule of law, rooting out corruption, supporting human rights and political freedoms); to investing in their people (via education and health care); and to promoting economic freedom (through open markets, sound fiscal policies, and support for private enterprise).

The most important change that Third World countries can pursue to achieve rapid economic development is to create what development professionals call an "enabling environment" for entrepreneurship. This means passing a range of legal reforms to certify and protect land and property, to protect credit, and to reduce registration requirements for starting a business.

Many obstacles to business and trade are located within the developing countries and can only be addressed by them. However, developed nations must acknowledge their own role in excluding the poor from the world trading system through barriers and subsidies. Few policies subject America to more charges of hypocrisy than its generous and unjustified system of agricultural subsidies. When America and other major economic powers in the West promote enterprise as the answer to poverty and talk about state reforms as the key to increased trade, they need first to look in the mirror. Currently, rich Western nations spend $1 billion a year encouraging agricultural progress in the developing world while they spend $1 billion a day subsidizing their own domestic agriculture. A UN report referred to protectionist subsidies and tariffs as a system of "perverse taxation" on the world's poor.

Lifting trade barriers for Third World farmers and entrepreneurs would have a major positive effect on growth. Estimates for the number of poor people who would be raised out of poverty by the completion of the Doha Development Round of trade negotiations run into the hundreds of millions, while $200 billion could be added to developing economies annually.

CHAPTER FOUR

From Aid Bureaucracy to Civil Society: Participation and Partnership

> We have a heavy emphasis in AID now, in our democracy and governance programs, on decentralization. There is a growing awareness in the developing world that stronger local institutions with citizen participation and election of local officials may be one of the central governance reforms that will strengthen the institutions of democracy in the country.
>
> ANDREW NATSIOS[1]

SECRETARY OF STATE Condoleezza Rice has introduced a new term into the international development policy debate: "transformational development." This term suggests a departure from the status quo in approaching poverty reduction. Transformational development measures success in results on the ground.

The previous chapter discussed the great aid debate itself: whether America has been generous or stingy, and whether traditional aid has been effective. This chapter looks into the attitudes and tendencies within the foreign assistance culture that often generate counterproductive strategies for confronting poverty. It also considers how the paradigm of centralization, along with the attitudes and habits it cultivates, is yielding to an entirely new set of institutional arrangements.

If the paradigm for the past was monolithic systems designed and operated by governments, the paradigm for the future is pluralistic structures, partnerships with the private sector, and the widest possible participation by the people themselves. Alliances and partnerships will involve NGOs, faith-based charities, volunteer groups, and universities. Web-based partnerships will disseminate technical knowledge and products privately and at no cost. Top-down, command-and-control bureaucracy will be replaced with bottom-up innovation and flexibility.

After decades of dominating international development programming, aid agencies are naturally inclined to see themselves as the principal source of expertise and wisdom, with credentialed professionals to design and dispense services for the world's poor. Given their long monopoly on policy and resources, aid professionals tend to develop the attitudes and habits of hierarchy and control. Now they must deliver results and prove their competence in a decentralized and horizontal world in which control is elusive and bureaucratic expertise loses its edge.

Only a decade ago, USAID was basically in control of almost all international development policy and programming. Today it must share this role with dozens of agencies eager to share their expertise with the world. Most agencies eventually become connected to their counterparts overseas and find opportunities to work in partnership. In fact, nearly all of the most powerful domestic cabinet departments—Energy, Labor, Commerce, Treasury, Agriculture, and Environmental Protection Agency, to name a few—have international policy staff and are engaged globally in their fields of expertise.

USAID's health care programs and resources can't begin to compete with the extensive resources of the Department of Health and Human Services (HHS). If hospitals are to be built in Afghanistan, HHS will likely play a key role in providing funds and expertise. When the need becomes fighting HIV/AIDS, a policy "czar" is placed under the secretary of state so that resources and talent from across the entire U.S. government can be mobilized. When the possibility of an international global health pandemic materializes, such as the recent threat of avian flu, the lead is given to HHS, which controls numerous large agencies focusing on medicine and health such as National Institutes of Health, the Food and Drug Administration, and the Centers for Disease Control.

The proliferation of actors is challenging old monopolies and driving competition over ideas. Sharing of responsibility results in a wise and cost-effective leveraging of the assets of the U.S. government, which translates into far more assistance to the Third World needy. But it also means more fragmentation in U.S. policies and programs.

The only way USAID can cope in this new environment is to carry out a major overhaul of its organizational culture. Moving from the commanding heights of managing all U.S. assistance abroad to, in some cases, being a minor partner in projects means surrendering habits acquired in the command-and-control culture and learning new skills of collaboration. It also means that to be relevant, USAID must be politically skillful at assembling and guiding large inter-agency teams in response to international need.

If learning the skills of collaboration with competing governmental agencies is difficult, it is even harder to maintain leadership and direction over a nongovernmental sector that is exploding in size, wealth, and capacity to project power and influence policy. Describing this new situation in his testimony before the House of Representatives in May of 2001, Secretary of State Colin Powell noted that "over the past 20 years, a growing number of new actors has arrived on the scene: NGOs, Private Voluntary Organizations, foundations, corporations, the higher education community and even individuals are now providing development assistance. As a result, the U.S. government is not the only, or perhaps even the largest, source of American funding and human resources being applied to the development challenge."[2]

The post-conflict recovery period in Iraq presented major challenges of collaboration and coordination for the government at all levels. The military system, which had its own internal conflicts to manage, also had to share power during the occupation with a civilian command structure, often with blurred boundaries and obligations. Both military and civilian commands had to coordinate with a divided government in Washington, while the civilian structure (the

Coalition Provisional Authority) had to rely on staff who were drawn from many of the domestic agencies listed above, whose loyalties were often to their own bureaucracies.

The response to the tsunami in the Indian Ocean exemplifies how America's mobilization after a disaster depends on partnerships between agencies and with the private sector. During the early period of the crisis, USAID took the lead through its mission office in Indonesia and its emergency relief agency, the Office of Foreign Disaster Assistance. But even during this phase, USAID's resources were no match for the U.S. Navy and Air Force, which operated massive airlift and relief operations. Soon, the coordination of tsunami recovery policy was assigned to a task force at the State Department. At the same time, the U.S. government had to act as a minor partner in the effort when private assistance totaling $1.6 billion was pouring in, mostly sidestepping all government channels and going directly to NGOs, many of which had their own intentions in the region and were not always keen on coordinating their efforts with others. The business community, which supplied $560 million in donations, asked to coordinate with the State Department because they were not confident that USAID, being a foreign aid bureaucracy, had the savvy or clout to work effectively with the business community.

In his testimony before the House of Representatives, Secretary of State Powell heralded a bold vision for how foreign assistance is to be conceptualized and implemented. The new model would resemble a business, focusing on customer-friendliness and innovation. Powell made it clear that the old preoccupation with bureaucracy and budgets would yield to a strategy of decentralization, using existing governmental resources to leverage greater involvement by the private sector and civil society.

Secretary Powell was announcing that the government monopoly of resources, experience, and expertise would come to an end. Government aid programs would continue to play important roles, but they would serve primarily as catalysts, becoming minor partners in development if necessary. Official aid agencies would join forces with nongovernmental entities, whether corporations or indigenous humanitarian organizations, marrying their talents to create a force multiplier for larger systemic change.

In this new environment, the participation principle emerges as paramount. Implicit in a strategy centering on civil society is the recognition that most citizens possess both latent capacities and a strong desire for improvement in their social and political circumstances. The chief ingredient in human development in the twenty-first century is people themselves.

A common and persistent criticism of foreign aid establishments is that all too often the answers to Third World needs are presumed to exist inside development bureaucracies. Whether the challenge is promoting economic development or government reforms, the process has traditionally been dominated by the policy planning staffs of aid bureaucracies. Here, professionals trained in policy planning at elite universities apply the latest arcane theories and programming research to the design of new initiatives that are then delivered to "the field." Having worked inside USAID, I can confirm that much of the inner workings and products of these development "policy shops" are shrouded in technical concepts and hundreds of acronyms that serve mostly to insulate the bureaucracies, to shield them from other bureaucracies that might encroach on their powers, or even from their own aid workers on the ground in poor countries.

Much of this technically driven development programming is losing its relevance. Even government aid workers assigned to USAID's mission offices abroad report finding the Washington bureaucracy irrelevant and even burdensome to their work. Much of the practitioners' time is wasted in satisfying Washington's voracious appetite for documentation and reporting. When the bureaucracy hamstrings people on the ground who are best acquainted with their communities, aid agencies lose ground.

"Large-scale crash programs, especially by outsiders, often produce unintended consequences," according to Bill Easterly. He adds, "The simple dreams at the top run afoul of insufficient knowledge of the complex realities at the bottom."[3] In short, the helping hand can hurt.

Perhaps the chief failing of the top-down, outside-in approach to development is that it rarely accounts for the factor of local culture. A major shortcoming of the Iraq occupation during the early period was a failure to appreciate the extent to which life was dominated by tribal customs. Whereas we tried to understand reality at the superficial level of what was visible in the streets and at official meetings, real daily business was being conducted at the level of family and tribe as well as religion. This was a world that few of us knew much about and that could truly be known only from the inside—access to which had been denied to outsiders by decades of dictatorial rule.

A culture so alien presented complications in our efforts to work through problems. For example, seeing how Muslim families and tribes look out for each other, we might conclude that a particular activity involves corruption and nepotism, whereas they view the same activity as grounded in deeply revered principles of loyalty and honor. We may even be technically or legally right in our conclusions about such practices, but unless we start with an understanding of their traditional context, we are not likely to make headway in bringing about improvements.

In tribal cultures there is a popular motto that says: "I and my brother against my cousin; I, my brother, and my cousin against the outsider." As Americans in Iraq, we were the outsiders whose presence unified the brother and cousin. Unless the outsider is admitted into a relationship of trust and is able to maintain that trust, chances for positive results are poor.

FROM AID BUREAUCRACIES TO CIVIL SOCIETY: PARTNERSHIPS AND PARTICIPATION

The new model for development focuses on the power of civil society and its many functions in building stronger communities and nations. It recognizes the vital role that citizens and local nongovernmental organizations play in improving social and economic conditions. The formula for sustainable development as well as for the expansion of democratic participation is the wider inclusion of citizens in identifying and solving problems.

The key principles in this emerging model of Third World development are partnership and participation—building partnerships with the widest array of new nongovernmental actors on the development scene, and promoting the widest possible participation of the poor themselves.

The new approach recognizes the limits of distant institutions in today's electronically connected and rapidly changing environment, and seeks to tap into the resources of the poor themselves, making their aspirations and energies the guiding force of development. One answer to the failures of foreign assistance is simply to shift resources and programming further away from bureaucracy, changing the emphasis from what we can do for people, to what those people can do, and want to do, for themselves.

In many tribal cultures there is a tradition that one must go first to the village elders. Whatever is to be accomplished in that village will probably not occur without the mediation of the community's leaders and wise men. They alone have the prestige and means to make a project succeed. They already have given much thought to their own situation, and while they may not have the most advanced technologies, they have wisdom in abundance.

Perhaps the least-discussed and least-appreciated principle in Third World development is the power of relationships. Programs and projects are too seldom preceded by an honest attempt to develop genuine relationships with the poor and their village elders based upon a spirit of mutuality and genuine respect.

This is essentially the approach that President Bush chose to follow in both domestic and international social programming. When he unveiled his package of domestic initiatives he said, "Go first to the neighborhood healers." Don't go first to the experts in distant, glistening bureaucracies, even though they too have a contribution to make. In the most blighted and destitute communities, whether in

America or sub-Saharan Africa, there are antibodies at work fighting social viruses, and they cannot be bypassed.

Embracing civil society offers a possible path from traditional assistance to community-based, sustainable human development. Aid is directed less at treating symptoms of poverty than at building healthy communities and nations. Social programs that incorporate the participation principle can also help cultivate political skills among the poor. The civil society approach, in other words, simultaneously promotes economic and political empowerment, strengthening the forces of democracy and freedom around the world.

This approach requires thinking of the poor as citizens who are capable of independence—an idea that doesn't always come naturally to government officials and development professionals. Officials from donor nations tend to think first about working directly with governments because their business is bilateral relations. Professionals trained in international development come to think they can change Third World conditions from a distant capital. The poor thus become victims of an international aid system that doesn't see a need to treat them as citizens and vital stakeholders, capable of managing more choices on their own.

Democratization will probably not be brought about by governments alone or sustained by political parties and politicians alone. What needs to be done, say Keith Henderson and Juliana Pilon, is to "bring civil society—that is, voluntary organizations such as churches, unions, charities, professional and business associations and human rights groups, etc.—into the process." This involves "informing these groups of what reforms the governments in question have agreed to undertake."[4]

Governments don't reform themselves apart from outside pressure. As the experience of the past several decades confirms, it is all too easy for governments to make verbal commitments or display superficial evidence of political will, while managing to continue with the status quo. Grass-roots civil society organizations should be invited to partner with donor countries to monitor and hold accountable the ministries that have been charged with reforms, including the time frames they have committed themselves to act within. Why assign responsibility for tracking progress to development agencies thousands of miles away, when indigenous watchdog organizations are on the scene and have a stake in the outcome? Approaches based on partnership and participation carry the assumption that the poor and their own civil society advocates can be trusted to know their own best interests and pursue them.

FROM CLIENTS TO CITIZENS

If governments are unable to reform themselves apart from the people, neither are they likely to develop effective social and economic programs for the poor unless the poor are directly engaged in the planning and implementation. Perhaps the chief untapped resource in development programming is the creativity, knowledge, and motivation of local citizens.

Stephen C. Smith, a professor of economics at George Washington University and author of *Ending Global Poverty*, maintains that far too little is known about the poor. Much research has been directed toward understanding poverty reduction programs and policies, but little effort has been made to study the poor themselves and their daily lives. If the poor are to be given ownership of the programs that serve them, more must be known about them, and "genuine authority must be given to organizations *of* the poor, not just those who would like to work *with* the poor."[5] Smith adds that "to escape from poverty requires empowered people within a community that is empowered to function within the wider world. Communities of the poor must be collectively empowered."[6]

When the reigning concept of the poor is that they are helpless, powerless, and lacking in potential, the identities of poor individuals are shaped by whatever needs brought them into the consciousness of the helpers. The relationship is then governed by power and position: the poor person is identified mostly by his inadequacies, while the helper stands in the superior position of power to remedy those in-adequacies. Often, the result is that the poor are seen as clients, not citizens.

What is lacking in so many antipoverty programs, says Kirk Magleby, is a realization that the poor are just like us. Although they must endure "the brutal daily indignities of mind-numbing poverty," they are motivated and naturally resourceful. They do not wish to be poor "any more than they wish to be crippled, senile or malnourished." The poor, Magleby continues, "are survivors. They are adaptive. They are fashion brand and value conscious. Given the chance, they can learn readily and adopt modern technology enthusiastically. The poor can be tenacious when they sense an opportunity. Given a favorable environment, they can quickly become informed consumers and efficient producers in the global economy." The poor, he says, "are just people in acutely constrained circumstances."[7]

The poor do not lack their own resolve or insight. What they lack, says C. K. Prahalad, is "access to resources, capacity to enforce contracts, dignity and self-esteem." They are victims, he says, of a "huge asymmetry" of information and choices.[8] At every turn they find obstacles to their own advancement.

Americans are idealistic and have a commendable desire to share what they have with those who struggle in underdeveloped nations. They are confident that their values, their economic and political solutions, and their institutions are the answer to poverty everywhere. What Americans often do not appreciate is that even if our solutions are superior, they will never be adopted if the poor themselves do not take ownership of them, and if the solutions we offer aren't adapted to deeply ingrained patterns of life shaped by religion and local culture.

Legions of development projects have gone awry because big plans were just "parachuted in" to poor communities from distant bureaucracies. Blueprints were designed by development experts with advanced degrees who failed to take account of local attitudes and preferences.

Aid critic Tom Dichter tells of a project designed to apply the model of the agricultural extension program in Mali so as to raise agricultural standards to the level of farms in the American Midwest. The problem was that none of the capacity that is taken for granted in the American Midwest was present in Mali. Immediately, the program ran into a series of obstacles: government competence and capacities were minimal; many workers were illiterate and couldn't absorb the information; farmers lacked land tenure and irrigation; and even if products were produced, they couldn't be sold because of an absence of marketing and transportation services. The project failed.

A similar story involves the Peace Corps working on a project to improve chicken production in Morocco. The intent was to apply better breeding science in order to develop a chicken that was plumper and more nutritious. Experts working for USAID suggested that the best replacement was a Rhode Island Red chicken. The project proceeded nicely until it was discovered that no one was buying the chickens. Although the science may have been right, the experts discovered that this breed of chicken was poorly suited to Moroccan cooking methods. The Rhode Island Red took four hours to stew properly and then it tasted like mush. The project collapsed.[9]

The Moroccan story illustrates a basic problem that is common to Third World development projects: when we use power instead of partnerships, when we lead rather than listen, we end up alienating the very people we sincerely hope to help. Hostility toward America arises partly from a vague perception that we are more concerned about having our way with the world than we are concerned about the world itself. The irony is that many of the Third World poor harbor a genuine longing for the best of what we call the American way. Too frequently the problem with the American way is the American way of presenting and delivering it. In short, it is too much about us.

★ ★
★

Building Social Capital through Indigenous Civil Society

Effective development strategies begin with the realization that the poor possess assets and capabilities of their own, and that the voluntary networks already operating in poor communities generate a wide array of social goods and perform numerous tasks that only they can do. Each community has a unique social fabric and civic bonds. Foreign aid often ignores or inadvertently disrupts the local patterns of problem solving.

Foreign aid workers may arrive in a country with projects and ideas in hand, and quickly discover that the path forward will require dealing with local history. There may be no prior experience with self-governance, or there may be patterns of ethnic or religious conflict or domination of one group by another. This may lead aid workers to think that broad cooperation is not possible, when in reality a well-conceived initiative geared toward participation, such as a citizen council, can often draw diverse groups together and begin to shape a new interest in peaceful cooperation and pluralism.

A little-known feature of the postwar rebuilding program in Iraq was an extensive effort at decentralized decision making led by Chris Milligan, a career democratization specialist from USAID. Milligan developed a strategy for training all frontline reconstruction officials in how to encourage citizen participation in developing programs and services. The program was based upon three core premises: that "the consent of the governed begins at the bottom"; that efforts to start "nation-building from the top are likely to fail"; and that the existing authoritarian system and culture had to be dismantled.

Milligan believed it was not enough to remove "the head of the snake"; the entire body of authoritarian practice had to be destroyed. This would not be easy, especially in the face of an urgent need to restore services by means of the previous centralized system. But without immediate efforts at decentralization, the old authorities would likely remain dominant and a new culture of participatory democracy would be harder to cultivate.

A plan was implemented to fund citizen advisory councils in many Iraqi towns and cities. The purpose of these councils was to enlist citizens directly in the process of establishing community priorities and delivering services. Decentralized national ministries and more autonomous local governments would help curb abuse of power at the top. People who are focused on local and small-scale democratic arrangements would be less susceptible to the kind of nationalistic appeals that demagogically exploit internal divisions, such as Saddam Hussein used. Many of these endeavors were lost in the rush to address more urgent needs such as security, but there can be little doubt that participatory democracy in Iraq got a significant boost from USAID-led efforts to encourage citizen input on local decisions.

Improving an individual's capacities and deepening his or her participation in civic life through informal voluntary associations serve to generate social capital—the habits and attitudes that build democratic citizens. Outside interventions that see the completion of development projects as the only goal may actually deplete social capital.

Aid agencies tend to think of civil society mostly as large service-delivery NGOs, not as small-scale indigenous associations. The reason for favoring large humanitarian organizations or contractors is obvious enough. They are professionally run and usually have proven track records of managing complex projects involving tens of millions of dollars. They can be counted on to meet government standards of transparency and accountability.

Unfortunately, big private institutions that partner with USAID are often indistinguishable from the government itself in their philosophy and practice, and they are funded in large part by public resources. Many large USAID-supported NGOs now receive a very small percentage of their budget from private donors. In many cases, the staff is drawn from aid agencies and shares the view that expertise and well-managed programs are the keys to Third World development. The result is that they often employ the same flawed strategies as the official aid agencies to which they are closely aligned.

USAID as a Broker of Public-Private Partnerships

Can our current programming—using either contractors or nongovernmental organizations—more effectively nourish indigenous civil society within developing countries? In recent years, USAID has recognized the need to redirect some of the resources and power that have traditionally flowed from our government to Third World governments or to large intermediary NGOs, using them instead to expand the capacity for self-help and local problem solving.

A growing portion of USAID funds has been going to a host of nongovernmental organizations ranging from for-profit firms to nonprofit civic, youth, and social service organizations. There are now hundreds of examples of effective partnerships with indigenous civil society groups.

For example, in order to sustain progress toward transparent and accountable government in the Balkans, USAID organized the Balkan Trust for Democracy in partnership with American philanthropic foundations, the governments of Greece and the Netherlands, and the German Marshall Fund. This partnership has created a trust of $27 million that provides annual grants to civil society and pro-democracy groups for civic education and advocacy.

Another example: One of the chief impediments to development that USAID has identified is the failure to provide basic education and critical thinking skills to 114 million school-age children throughout the developing world. Working with in-country education experts and local producers, USAID has coproduced local adaptations of *Sesame Street*, a series that focuses on basic literacy and numeracy along with cognitive development. In places as diverse as Russia, Egypt, and Bangladesh, the Sesame Street Alliance is reaching as many as 90 percent of children.[10]

A frequently untapped American resource is colleges and universities, many of which are increasingly serving international students and offering programs in international business or development. USAID has created a Partnership to Cut Hunger and Poverty in Africa, headed by Michigan State University. The alliance combines the technical knowledge of universities with the power and resources of numerous multinational companies to promote trade, technology transfers, training, and infrastructure improvement.

USAID can also encourage countries that receive aid to partner with their own indigenous civil society at the national, regional, and local levels. USAID programming can do more to cultivate youth, educational, and religious organizations that, with a little capacity building, may be able to contribute more effectively to community development. Large NGOs, which are the recipient of generous USAID grants or contracts, can do more to subcontract with local civil society groups that reflect the culture and ethnic composition of the community being served.

At the center of this civil society agenda is a full-orbed vision of citizenship, in which individuals have the capacity, inclination, and right to participate fully in the life of a community and a nation.

Business as a Strategic Partner

Business entrepreneurs have moved forcefully into the arena of international development in a variety of ways, bringing financial resources, knowledge, and entrepreneurial talent with them. In some cases, businesses just want to practice good corporate citizenship by including philanthropy and service goals in their operations within a given country. In other cases, they may want to improve the business environment so as to expand markets and gain customers. Often there is a combination of objectives.

In recent years, an international movement consisting of major grant-making foundations, business associations, and civic organizations has been promoting volunteerism and philanthropy globally.

Those who are fixated on the problems of economic globalization should realize that multinational corporations with a firm commitment to social responsibility are bringing new resources, knowledge, and entrepreneurial talent to the challenge of international development.

Regardless of who wins the great aid debate and what levels of funding result, USAID will always have limited resources. Increasingly, USAID is replicating the behavior and principles of a private firm, turning to unconventional methods to leverage additional resources and institutional power. USAID's strength may reside less in its capacity to deliver resources and expertise than in its ability to serve both as a catalyst for worldwide economic and social development and as a broker for a host of partnering arrangements.

The flagship partnership initiative of USAID is the Global Development Alliance, launched in 2001. It represents the clearest departure from the government-always-knows-best model of development assistance. Heralded as "USAID's business model for the twenty-first century," GDA is promoting "a fundamental reorientation in how USAID sees itself in the context of international development assistance, in how it relates to traditional partners and in how it seeks out and develops alliances with new partners."

With the GDA initiative, USAID seeks to lessen its domination and even direct sponsorship of all development activity. Rather, it aims to use "its resources and expertise to assist strategic partners in their investment decisions and will stimulate new investments by bringing new actors and ideas to the overseas development arena." Much as with a private investment model, USAID called upon GDA to find "opportunities where relatively small amounts of risk or start-up capital can be prudently invested to generate much larger benefits in the achievement of the overall objectives."

This is not how foreign assistance has been done traditionally, nor how it is done by most European nations today. It is a characteristically American approach, based on the widely held assumption that America's comparative advantage is not public bureaucracy but private business, not government but civil society. GDA was tasked with finding synergies between and within sectors, and between actors across all levels of government.

By the end of 2004, GDA reported forging nearly three hundred alliances with foundations or corporations. The public contribution of $1.1 billion to these alliances has leveraged a total of almost $5 billion in resources for development, according to GDA documents. In each case, USAID was able to marry its core strengths of expertise, resources, and global presence—in over eighty Third World countries —with the resources and core competencies of private sector groups. Many GDA partnerships involve cash, but they also include human capital development and the transfer of a wide range of technical capacities.

The strategic partnering that is occurring with the business community represents significant opportunity to expand the role of U.S. business in the developing world while passing along valuable resources and know-how. The American business community has never had a larger presence around the world, and it can broaden its own markets by helping build more viable local and regional economies.

Increasingly, USAID is engaging in creative partnerships with American and multinational companies to the benefit of poor nations. To promote more economic growth in Latin America, the GDA forged a Remittances for Economic Growth Alliance, which is bringing improvements to the system of transferring private remittance payments to Mexican families. The alliance is training poor Mexicans in financial services and enhancing the capacity of private financial institutions. The result has been a 50 percent reduction in transaction costs for remittances.

Partnering with Cisco and Hewlett Packard, USAID helped create a multimillion-dollar global e-learning endeavor that resulted in the creation of 239 academies with strong local control in sixty Third World countries, with 700 instructors training 10,000 students.

By collaborating with forty-four commercial partners, mostly major health care companies or businesses operating in Africa, USAID formed a public-private partnership to reduce malaria across Africa.

Called NetMark Alliance, the partnership was able to overcome limitations on donor resources by combining private dollars of commercial partners with nonprofits, ministries of health, and other local institutions to expand the use of bed nets as protection against mosquito-born infections.

In Angola, where two million people were displaced by a twenty-seven-year civil war, an Enterprise Development Alliance involving USAID, Chevron, and the government of Angola is providing agricultural training and microenterprise development to rebuild the shattered economy and restore livelihoods.

In much of the Third World, the greatest health crisis is a shortage of clean water. Nearly 20 percent of the world's population, 1.2 billion people, lack access to clean water. Most of the deadliest health threats that take millions of lives each year—such as diarrhea, blindness, and worm diseases—are water-related. Responding to this crisis, USAID partnered with the Conrad Hilton Foundation, World Vision, and several other international organizations to form a West Africa Water Initiative, which is working to increase the supply of safe and clean water, to improve sanitation, and to provide training in better hygiene throughout Ghana, Mali, and Niger.

Another destructive trend that is undermining long-term prospects for the poor is deforestation and the gradual degradation of land and other natural resources through neglect and overuse. Working with numerous NGOs and American food companies, USAID forged an alliance to promote environmental responsibility. The Rainforest Alliance helps create markets for food produced through environmentally sound farming and forestry practices. A similar initiative, the Sustainable Forest Products Global Alliance, combines the commitment and interests of NGOs like the World Wildlife Fund and companies like Home Depot to train logging companies in sustainable forestry practice, to curb illegal logging, and to open up markets for products produced legally.

Working with the Starbucks Coffee Company and agricultural cooperatives, USAID forged a Finance Alliance for Sustainable Trade in Latin America and East Africa to help farmers improve and stabilize their production with better management and access to credit. Through cooperative services, farmers are able to guard against market volatility and better provide for their families. In 2002, four thousand small farmers in Latin America were able to improve their operations through loans provided by the alliance.

If partnerships fall short of their promise, it is often because of the inherent differences between business firms, governments, and NGOs. According to Erik Peterson of the Center for Strategic and International Studies, "the future of business engagement in global development could meet one of two fates: promise, in which business, governments and NGOs blend their unique competencies to define new areas of cooperation, innovation and creativity, or peril, in which the organizations experience a 'clash of civilizations' and the inability to tear down the cultural walls that sometimes separate them."[11]

The U.S. Chamber of Commerce's Business Civic Leadership Center has encouraged all three sectors to communicate more effectively with each other, giving equal decision-making capacity to partners as they work together, and making shared values the cornerstone of cooperation. According to the BCLC, collaboration would also be enhanced by a shared commitment to helping countries improve "rule of law, governance, education and training skills, infrastructure development, and business values."[12]

AMERICAN BUSINESS AND CIVIL SOCIETY AS A FORCE FOR REFORM

A common misconception of globalization is that whenever large American or multinational corporations move into a developing country for purposes of doing business, the benefits are entirely one way, with the poor gaining little. A closer look, however, suggests that whenever an attempt is made by business to improve market conditions for itself, the enabling environment is improved for all. Poor access to markets and numerous policy constraints cripple the development of low-income enterprises. Organized business is in a position to address this problem by lining up firmly behind reforms in governance.

Businesses in alliance with civil society groups can be a powerful motor driving economic and political liberalization. But to flourish, civil society needs a policy environment that permits and encourages independent civic life. The reform of government policies must be a central part of any strategy to promote development via civil society. Freedom to gather and express opinions is essential, as is a thriving entrepreneurial sector. Attention must be given to the areas of law that affect the economic and social sectors, including property and contract rights, freedom of speech and association, tax codes, regulations, and anticorruption law.

In many locations, the very idea of an independent sector consisting of numerous voluntary associations is relatively new and is viewed with skepticism or distrust by politicians with entrenched interests. Authoritarian governments have often acted with deliberate hostility toward the nongovernmental sector in order to preserve their power and avoid accountability. Local governments may resist granting wide latitude to civil society organizations for the same reason.

While flawed policies can weaken civil society, private voluntary associations are the chief means for beginning the process of reform. Actors from business and civil society can join forces to organize reform movements and supply the tools for effective governing, accountability, and open public debate. Among the policy reforms to be encouraged is a transfer of authority from the central state downward and outward, to widen the decision-making circle and create more space for citizen participation.

THE FUTURE OF AID BUREAUCRACIES: WHERE FROM HERE?

As previously noted, traditional assistance programs are facing unprecedented challenges and are perceived by many Americans as costly and bureaucratic engines of dependency. In order to generate wider public support, American development policy must therefore rely less on large governmental or NGO systems and more on a sense of shared responsibility within the host country.

To organize and apply the strengths of American resources and power, development policy is increasingly focusing on five core strategic principles.

1. *From Clientelism to Citizenship*

Whatever is done for the poor must start with the poor themselves. Citizens must have a voice, but even more, they must have a central part to play in their own development. This may require creating new institutional mechanisms to secure the participation of local stake-holders in programming. One approach is to build requirements into existing programs to ensure that expertise is being transferred to indigenous individuals and groups. More grants can be made available to intermediate organizations that specialize in training NGOs in areas of management, budgeting, fundraising, information systems, strategic planning, and donor or volunteer recruitment. Such grants can be used to train frontline development workers and indigenous NGOs.

2. *From Giantism to a Human Scale*

Scale matters. Large systems tend to be more top-down, bureaucratic, and rule-driven. These traits can drive away volunteers, crowd out smaller programs, and contribute to a sense of alienation from public life.

Organizational design and management in the twentieth century stressed the advantages of large, centralized service-delivery systems. Recent trends in both public attitudes and social policy suggest that more can be accomplished by decentralizing program delivery, placing it in the hands of community-based organizations and private enterprise.

3. *From Credentialism to Civic Capacity Building*

A hallmark of development policy has been an exaggerated faith in the ability of credentialed professionals to provide remedies for social problems, some of which can be solved only by collaboration among individual citizens. Development assistance must deliver more than American dollars and technical expertise; it must leave communities with a greater capacity to transform their own conditions.

On-the-ground development takes more than financial capital and visiting experts; it requires the cultivation of social capital, which involves networks, collaboration, institutions, trust, and shared values. To build programming around this model, aid workers need to incorporate the principles of community organizing with the goal of strengthening the local civic networking that accompanies development activity.

Expertise matters, but a greater effort should be made to link experts to community-based volunteers. With appropriate accountability built into the programming, more funding could be directed toward "civic seed planting," aiming to increase citizen participation and enhance the competence of volunteers.

4. *From Fragmentation to Integration*

A misplaced focus on professional expertise often brings a compartmentalized and fragmented approach to programming, commonly referred to as "stove-piping." Development programs are often organized by professional specialization—education, health, infrastructure improvement, education, and so on. This only reinforces the perception that development has no role for local nonprofessionals, who are likely to look at problems more holistically. Aid programs should involve studying the integrated patterns that communities use to solve problems.

5. From Aid Bureaucracies to Civil Society

The fifth principle sums up the previous four. Moving beyond clientelism, giantism, and credentialism can lead to an integrated strategy for curing poverty that is grounded in civil society.

CHAPTER FIVE

Wealth, Poverty, and the Rise
of Corporate Citizenship

To solve poverty the world needs tens of millions of profitable
locally owned small businesses creating employment and providing goods and services tailored to emerging markets in the
developing world.

KIRK MAGLEBY[1]

IN SEPTEMBER OF 2005, the biggest-ever summit of world leaders
took place at the United Nations for the purpose of assessing progress
on goals that had been established at a similar gathering of world
leaders five years earlier. The goals that were set in 2000, called Millennium Development Goals (MDGs), involved specific targets for
eradicating extreme poverty, delivering universal primary education,
and improving material health, among other goals, by the year 2015.

To no one's surprise, progress thus far toward the ambitious goals
was disappointing. Most private sector leaders observe these large
global conferences, filled with development experts and awash in
professional jargon, and wonder where they fit in. Often, the subtle
message has been that the role of business is simply to sign on as minor
partners in large government-sponsored development schemes, engineered and managed entirely by development agencies and the United
Nations. Until recently, the relevance of business, entrepreneurship,
and trade has been treated mostly as an afterthought.

Fortunately, that is rapidly changing. The preponderance of

planet's education, health and environmental problems." According to the article, over one thousand corporations now annually publish "sustainability reports"—up from zero ten years ago—each detailing how business growth can be combined with policies to promote better labor practices and protect the environment.[3]

Many businesses have sprouted up for the sole purpose of finding new solutions to global social problems, or to take proven concepts or technologies into the developing world. Steve Case, the cofounder of AOL, poured $500 million into Revolution, a for-profit venture dedicated to "building businesses that change the world." Revolution invests in innovative startup firms that are confronting Third World problems from health to water quality to literacy. Another entity, Brain Trust Accelerator Fund, makes equity investments in companies that are working on therapies for brain diseases and other health conditions. Case describes the growing practice of "sector blending," whereby for-profit and philanthropic entities work in complementary ways toward the same ends.[4]

The Acumen Fund, a nonprofit venture capital fund, is an example of sector blending at work. The nonprofit is investing in low-cost mortgages in Pakistan and health clinics in Kenya. It has received a large donation from for-profit Google and shares an office in New York. The entire microlending phenomenon also illustrates the power of sector blending, as nonprofits provide loans and technical support to small enterprises, which often grow into commercially viable ventures.

Most companies, aware that many developing countries will languish without a major investment in education and human capital, are now making social investments too numerous to catalogue. IBM is sponsoring a global "reinventing education" program to tackle some of the toughest education problems. Similarly, ExxonMobil is developing education and literacy programs.

Many more companies are simply trying to reach the poor by cultivating customers in emerging markets. Throughout the developing world, where the poor buy consumer items such as soap, shampoo, and diapers mostly from local mom-and-pop stores, Procter & Gamble is scaling its products to be viable in low-income markets. The consumer product giant is building a distribution and sales force to take affordable products into the most remote areas, hoping to grow sales by 5 to 7 percent annually in emerging markets.[5] Procter & Gamble now distributes products in 180 countries.

Those countries fortunate enough to join the upwardly mobile category of "emerging market" countries are typically placed on the receiving end of enormous capital investment and attention from American private equity investors, a wide array of commercial franchise firms, a boom in private health investments, and commercial banking. "This is the era of the developing world and of emerging markets," says GE's chairman and CEO, Jeffrey Immelt.[6] GE expects revenues from emerging markets to expand by 30 to 40 percent by 2010.

Banking services, long targeted at the richer residents in low-income regions, is shifting markedly toward the poor and the middle class. In mid-2007, Citigroup announced the launch of a major "down market" banking presence throughout emerging markets in Asia. In Malaysia, Citigroup will partner with a telecommunications company to enable foreign workers to send money home over cell phones. In India, the firm will install ATMs with biometric thumbprint recognition for the lower-income class. In Indonesia, they will provide consumer loans in partnership with the post office. Like many other institutions, Citigroup is discovering that the future is with the emerging consumer class, or the "mass affluent," not the elite.[7]

New customers, new markets, and new partnerships with large firms result in the cultivation of smaller firms, linking them as suppliers and distributors to globally connected firms. Developing countries are building local stock exchanges, enabling local firms to raise capital from the considerable untapped pool of local wealth, which in turn allows poor citizens to own stock and use their capital to generate wealth. A leading business journal reported that the relatively young stock market in Colombia experienced a fourteen-fold increase over the past several years.[8]

In a study noting the rise of public-private partnerships and the positive effects of globalization, the U.S. Chamber of Commerce reports that "there are public-private partnerships on every continent, spanning an array of issues, from community safety and healthcare to education, environmental care, and small business development." While critics of globalization focus on outsourcing and the disruption of communities and traditions, there are also benefits, including "accessibility to new cultures, new technologies, new ideas and new products and services."[9] The report describes "a new way of thinking about wealth creation and global development," along with unprecedented interest in helping the poor. "Old patterns that focused on budgets and pre-determined line items, and imposed outside nostrums on domestic decision-makers, are becoming obsolete."[10]

Many companies tailor their corporate citizenship projects around their core products or services, often involving a combination of philanthropic giving, technical assistance, and on-the-ground organizing. Pharmaceutical firms, for example, are known to release huge volumes of product for lifesaving purposes.

Numerous health care firms are taking on the HIV/AIDS pandemic in Africa. Others combine new investments with local humanitarian projects. When Marathon Oil acquired production interests in Equatorial Guinea, they discovered that malaria was a chief concern among local residents and set out to develop a comprehensive project to eradicate it.

Merck & Co., in partnership with the Bill & Melinda Gates Foundation, is donating two of its antiretroviral (ARV) medicines to Botswana. Abbott Laboratories is modernizing hospitals in Africa. JPMorgan Chase is working on developing homes for children orphaned by HIV/AIDS. Working with dozens of government and nonprofit partners, Merck is donating the product Mectizan to prevent the transmission of onchocerciasis (river blindness), which is spread by a common fly.

In many rural communities, the poor are forced to rely on unsanitary sources of drinking water. The Fairmount Minerals Company has identified a new market for filtration sand that will provide a solution to a scarcity of potable water in many communities, and is partnering with a nonprofit to make the technology available in Kenya.

Technology firms are working to get life-improving innovations into just about every activity in the developing world. One such technology company, Voxiva, provides real-time disease surveillance with data sent by cell phones to a central database, which allows health officials to slow the spread of disease.

E+Co, an alternative energy company, is developing solar power systems for rural households in Uganda that would not otherwise have access to electricity. A variety of firms are working to introduce affordable huts made of durable composite materials, and are using discarded freight containers for portable health clinics. Few applications of American ingenuity are escaping the attention of today's globally aware social entrepreneurs.

THE RISE OF CORPORATE CITIZENSHIP

Global economic integration has been ongoing for over a century, but never before have events around the globe affected daily business operations so directly, continuously, and significantly. When IT services are outsourced to a place like India, for example, the distance between a company's headquarters and an Indian city such as New Delhi is no greater than the distance to a local town ten miles away. When American manufacturing draws component parts from a global supply chain, business firms are compelled to care about daily developments in remote places.

Global realities have changed the way business views the world, and they have changed how business operates. The larger a company's radius of operations, the greater the number of stakeholders who factor into that company's success and whose interests have to be kept in sight. Contrary to the claims of antiglobalization forces, the wider a firm's span of operations, the less feasible it is to disregard people for the sake of profit. Companies operating internationally face pressure from the media, international institutions, stockholders, and host nations, who demand transparency, codes of ethical conduct, better labor standards, and help in promoting human rights. The result is that businesses must now specialize in building relationships of trust with governments and nongovernmental organizations alike.

As the entire world becomes a potential marketplace, companies have unprecedented opportunities to combine altruism with entrepreneurialism. There is a growing realization that American businesses can help meet the needs of the poor while advancing their own interests at the same time. In this "new era in corporate citizenship," businesses that recognize the benefits of ethical practice will gain major advantages. Putting a priority on the real worth of people results in a firmer basis for trust and cooperation, which becomes a major strategic asset in itself.

THE INDIVISIBILITY OF BUSINESS AND COMMUNITY

Businesses today are facing pressure from within and without—from workers, communities, and a variety of stakeholders—to operate in accordance with well-articulated core values. Many business managers are discovering that their firms are not working at full potential unless they have a clear vision or philosophy, a mission or a sense of purpose. In many cases, a company's mission is closely tied to a vision for community health. Most entrepreneurs hope that their legacy will bring about prosperity for others besides themselves and their co-investors. Most companies recognize that they have a role to play in improving economic and social conditions.

"Business no longer operates in a vacuum," says John Sullivan of the Center for International Private Enterprise. "There is today an indivisibility of business and community" involving expectations and mutual dependence. "For good or bad, we live in a world in which far more is expected of business than merely succeeding from a profit making standpoint." Today's companies "carry the expectation of social responsibility." They are "no longer purely economic but also civic entities."[11] Corporate citizenship is essentially an outgrowth of core values. Businesses not only consume the social capital that is available in communities, they play an important part in regenerating it.

Corporate charity has long been motivated by an unstated rule that the community must be compensated by the business for the privilege of operating there. Businesses were expected to "give something back" to the community as a form of conscience repayment for what they "took out" in the course of creating wealth. Generally, business and philanthropy were viewed as two separate functions: first the company made a profit; then it turned around and tried to figure out how to "make a difference" to society.

Today, social concern is being made an integral part of a company's mission. What was formerly a firewall separating business from philanthropy, says Stuart Hart of Cornell University, is now "transforming into a host of new and creative approaches to combining the two through corporate partnerships with nongovernmental organizations, strategic philanthropy, and other forms of social innovation."[12] The business function is being stretched in order to support complementary capabilities in the social sector.

THE NEW PHILANTHROPY

One of the numerous ways in which businesses and business leaders are becoming more socially engaged is a new phenomenon in philanthropy (described in greater detail later). Companies today are increasingly expected to develop a clear vision for service and philanthropy and build it into their business culture. When the president and two former presidents spearheaded a public campaign to raise private money for tsunami relief and reconstruction, major business institutions such as the Business Roundtable and the U.S. Chamber of Commerce joined in, while companies were encouraged by management peers, workers, suppliers, and customers to display generosity.

Philanthropy offers opportunities for businesses to become partners in solving social problems while improving their public profiles.

Over the next few decades, philanthropy will emerge as a far more consequential factor in solving social problems, as tens of trillions of dollars will be transferred from one generation to another.

Many philanthropists today believe the world of philanthropy could be more effective if it learned some basic principles of business. They want to apply the ideas that produce the most entrepreneurial success to social problem solving. According to the *Economist*, the world of philanthropy has even adopted the jargon of business. For example, "philanthropists now talk about 'social investing,' 'venture philanthropy,' 'social entrepreneurship,' and the 'triple bottom line.'"[13]

Entrepreneurs want their profit-making savvy to be applied directly to nonprofit causes. Today's philanthropists think in terms of giving money away in the same way they made it—through small, flexible institutions with lots of personal, hands-on involvement and with a strong emphasis on outcomes. In many cases, they adopt a single cause and stay with it for many years.

A distinct category of corporate giving to emerge recently is *strategic philanthropy* or *venture philanthropy*, which replaces casual giving with a highly targeted form of giving that often reflects the company's core values or mission. Strategic philanthropy results when a business has a specific issue it cares deeply about and believes it can help address, or alternatively when a company wants to tie its giving more directly to business objectives. Whether designed for altruistic purposes or for corporate objectives, venture philanthropy leads to effective synergies between business operations and social purposes.

One objective may be simply to improve corporate reputation and branding. During a decade of fairly damaging corporate scandals, many companies have turned to social marketing and cause sponsorships in order to woo customers and boost employee loyalty. There are a variety of ways in which targeted philanthropy can benefit business, according to the U.S. Chamber of Commerce, such as "relations with important constituencies, including customers, employees, investors, regulators and community leaders."[14] For a growing number of firms, the company name is synonymous with a particular civic commitment.

Most defenders of strategic philanthropy will acknowledge that the activity is not purely philanthropic, but argue that it nevertheless serves critical social purposes. Writing in the *Harvard Business Review*, Mark Kramer and Michael Porter stated without hesitation that the purpose of strategic philanthropy should be to "give corporations a leg up on competitors." They added, however, that "true strategic giving addresses important social and economic goals simultaneously, targeting areas of competitive context where the company and society both benefit because the firm brings unique assets and expertise."[15]

Strategic philanthropy can lead to long-term improvements in education and health services, among other social factors that are crucial to successful market economies. For example, IBM has concluded that technological literacy is good for its own sake as well as for IBM. The company has provided over $75 million for international training and education to extend research, technology, and expertise to schools worldwide. The program matches up company experts with teachers and administrators throughout the Third World in order to transfer the latest technological skills and knowledge. Similarly, the Microsoft Corporation has channeled hundreds of millions of dollars in cash along with computer products to nonprofits. A variety of other grants to cover training and a curriculum to support computer proficiency at community centers have been offered as well. In both these cases, the philanthropic activity serves a real community need while also enhancing the market for the company's products.

SOCIAL ENTREPRENEURSHIP

The so-called social entrepreneur is a whole new kind of business role model, who engages personally in a civic venture. A social entrepreneur may incorporate a social goal into the mission of his or her business, or adopt and underwrite a social cause. In some cases, this means leaving the business altogether to start a nonprofit organization. For the social entrepreneur, business is placed in the service of a larger social or humanitarian mission. The combination of financial support and hands-on business savvy provided to a civic enterprise often means that the organization can be dramatically scaled up and made more effective.

Ariana Eunjung Cha, a writer for the *Washington Post*, reports that five years after the high-tech bust, venture capitalists are leading an effort to remake Silicon Valley as "a center for a new form of social entrepreneurship and venture philanthropy, a place where you can make good money by doing good." Cha writes that there has been a surge in investments aimed at "solving some of the world's most formidable problems."

Billboards along the 45-mile stretch of Highway 101 that runs through Silicon Valley once read "eGain.com" or "Excite.com." Now, they display such banners as "End World Hunger." [16]

Social entrepreneurs want to do more than make money; they want to make a mark. In particular, they are eager to lend their skills of innovation and technical knowledge to taking on poverty and underdevelopment. For almost every poverty-perpetuating problem, there are known remedies and successful models of implementation.

For example, firms are combating killer diseases by tackling water and sanitation problems with innovative and inexpensive new techniques. One former Internet entrepreneur is working on low-cost, low-energy methods of purifying water. Another is developing a system for more efficient delivery of water. Still another firm raised venture capital to help stop the spread of waterborne disease in underdeveloped countries. Companies are building filtration systems that purify water from almost any source. Procter & Gamble has pioneered a chemical treatment technology that is affordable and transportable to any community in the world.

Agriculture is also undergoing a major transformation thanks to private enterprise. Research firms have completed genetic mapping of the rice plant, making it possible to develop seeds that are more drought-resistant and can grow in colder climates. Firms are developing new techniques for irrigation, planting, and cultivation, and new methods of restoring nutrients to crops.

A startup company in New York called Fingerlakes Aquaculture is attempting to capitalize on the problem of overfishing in natural fisheries by developing a system to raise fish indoors in a cost-effective way, avoiding the pollution problems associated with pond fishing.

A growing number of firms are attempting to meet the challenge of environmental degradation by pursuing new technologies that will produce renewable energy and biomaterials. Through new "green technologies," environmental protection strategies are relying more on market forces. Companies such as Shell and BP that have traditionally profited from extracting petroleum products are now investing in wind and solar technologies. Firms and nonprofits are searching for energy-efficient and affordable means to deliver electricity to the rural poor so that fewer rely upon costly, dangerous, and environmentally dirty forms of heating and light, such as kerosene.

Corporate philanthropy and social entrepreneurship are spawning a cottage industry of firms that are bringing hands-on expertise to everything from disaster relief to low-cost housing. Others are figuring out how to lend their core competencies to nonprofit organizations. One company was founded to produce and sell online ads for corporations in order to offer the same services to nonprofits free of charge. Accenture, a for-profit firm, is donating supply-chain management services and advice to Global Relief Network, a nonprofit that allocates surplus food, clothing, medicine, and other relief materials to local NGOs.[17]

In Lancaster, Pennsylvania, Jeff Rutt wanted to put his home-building success to work in promoting housing and economic opportunity globally. He decided to dedicate a portion of his time and income as a contractor to a humanitarian organization called Hope International, which incubates small businesses through microfinance. Much of the organization's budget is raised by constructing several homes a year entirely with donated supplies and volunteers. This is a classic example of creating synergy between business and an allied nonprofit.

Rutt considers himself a "half-timer," a term coined by Bob Buford, a retired entrepreneur who authored a book by that name. The term describes the phenomenon of business owners in midlife who want to "trade in money for meaning" and spend part of their remaining years in humanitarian activity.

Scott Harrison, a physician who built a successful medical care company, decided to investigate how he could use his medical and entrepreneurial skills internationally. As he traveled in Africa, the sheer number of children who suffered from crippling deformities moved him. Many had no medical care at all, and many were hidden away by mothers ashamed of having children with obvious defects. Today, twenty years later, Harrison presides over a growing network of teaching hospitals that care for physically disabled children throughout Africa and Asia, developed by a nonprofit he founded, Cure International. By offering care for the disabled and training locals in treating the poor, Cure is developing indigenous capacity that will serve needy children for generations to come.

Rutt and Harrison are among thousands of entrepreneurs who have redefined their purpose and have turned from making dollars to making a difference.

CORPORATE CITIZENSHIP'S BOTTOM LINE

Those who still see entrepreneurial success as separate from social engagement might consider what businesses say about the rewards of being civically minded. In a survey of over five hundred companies of various sizes conducted by the U.S. Chamber of Commerce and the Center for Corporate Citizenship at Boston College, most accepted that businesses have responsibilities beyond making money, creating jobs, and paying taxes. Regardless of the size or type of the business, a majority of firms reported regularly providing cash, volunteer time, or donated goods for local communities.[18]

According to the study, eight out of ten companies believed that corporate citizenship helps the bottom line. Additionally, 59 percent of companies cited a concern for their public image. Many felt a need to design strategies for managing not just business risks but also reputation. Three-quarters of the companies surveyed were socially engaged because of their own traditions and values. What they did was in keeping with who they are.

Studies show that investors and financial analysts are interested in companies that are socially committed. These companies are able to attract more capital and borrow at lower costs. According to the Center for International Private Enterprise, "Companies that have an active corporate citizenship strategy are able to improve access to capital, build up brand image and corporate reputation, reduce business risk, and most importantly, improve their bottom line."[19]

CORPORATE SOCIAL RESPONSIBILITY

Critics of this bold call for more business engagement point to a variety of problems associated with economic globalization. At the top of the list are the dangers of environmental degradation linked to reckless capitalism. Critics supply evidence that forests, streams, oceans, and soils are in trouble. If natural systems have already come under unprecedented strain, how can anyone call for more exploitation of resources?

Those who oppose corporate globalization also point out that the real instruments of international business power today are not mom-and-pop firms, but multinational corporations (MNCs), which now produce over 25 percent of the world's economic output, even though they employ less than 1 percent of the world's labor force. The ten largest MNCs have annual sales that exceed the GNPs of the one hundred smallest, poorest countries.

The global economic, cultural, and political power of MNCs is undeniably a matter of concern. They can pose threats to the sovereignty of weak and poorly run countries. Divided nations and vulnerable indigenous cultures are hardly a match for the power of wealthy companies. Professor Stuart Hart of Cornell refers to "a worldwide commercial monoculture" based upon the values of consumerism, "bringing with it the decline of local cultures, products and traditions."[20]

"Global capitalism now stands at a crossroads," says Hart. "Without a significant change of course, the future of globalization and multinational corporations appears increasingly bleak." What is required, he suggests, is a "new, more inclusive brand of capitalism" that brings in more people, more voices, and the concerns and needs of four to five billion people—fully two-thirds of humanity—who have been ignored. The corporate sector, he says, can "become the catalyst for a truly sustainable form of global development—and prosper in the process."[21]

In the end, Hart argues, business is the solution. "Corporations are the only entities in the world today with the technology, resources, capacity and global reach required." In fact, business should be taking the lead, with both governments and nonprofits serving as collaborators. Only business, Hart says, can "lead us toward a sustainable world" in the years ahead, and only business knows how to harness the profit motive to produce economic transformation.

Less than one percent of the world's population participates in global financial markets as stockholders, and thus more than 99 percent have virtually no voice in the operations of MNCs. Hart suggests that corporations "become indigenous" with respect to the places they operate in by widening "the corporate bandwidth" and admitting voices that have long been excluded. Corporations should become more *transactive*, not merely *transparent*.[22]

Figuring out how to meet the needs of the four billion persons at the bottom of the economic pyramid represents significant growth potential for many businesses. Globalization is inevitable and irreversible, and along with new social pressures it has brought unprecedented opportunities for businesses to make a positive difference. Governments and NGOs expect that firms operating in the global marketplace will subject their activities to standards that contribute directly to improving social conditions in the communities where they operate.

Companies are being asked to support human rights, to ameliorate labor conditions, and to address a host of environmental concerns in the course of doing business. Food and agricultural firms are being encouraged to support land and water conservation policies and sustainable forestry practices. There is new pressure to avoid investing pension funds in ways that are considered socially unsound. Firms are being asked to take a hard line on corruption by applying new standards of transparency to their business practices and supply chains. They are expected to promote ethics in their corporate governance.

Carrying forward these social values is a movement loosely called Corporate Social Responsibility (CSR), which involves a set of corporate goals and practices that go well beyond altruistic purposes and philanthropy. According to the International Organization of Employers, which is attempting to coordinate a common approach for business, "corporate social responsibility is driven as much by competitiveness as it is by philanthropy and encompasses general principles of ethical behavior as well as environmental, economic and social responsibilities."[23]

At the core of the corporate social responsibility movement is the recognition that profitability and social improvement go hand in hand. Corporate social responsibility can be an important tool in promoting sustainable development because it is helping to build the legal and ethical infrastructures of market-based economies.[24]

Governments and NGOs have taken an interest in the CSR movement because it represents an opportunity to curb the negative aspects of global corporate influence and can be used to harness businesses for social goals. But the purpose of CSR should not be to challenge or change the core mission of business. To do so would make it less successful. The International Organization of Employers stresses that CSR is about "initiatives by companies to voluntarily integrate social and environmental concerns in their business operations and in their interaction with their stakeholders."[25]

A key to the successes of the CSR movement is its voluntary nature. Businesses are engaging in socially responsible activity because it makes perfect sense to do so, not because they are coerced by government or pressured by NGOs. Many have elected to join precisely because there is flexibility to integrate social responsibility objectives into business operations.

Real corporate social responsibility, says Stuart Hart, is not about "mere philanthropy to compensate for the damage done by conventional business strategies." It is about adopting new business strategies altogether, combining the strengths of established business firms with the potential of businesses at the bottom. A vision of social responsibility aimed at helping the poor and not merely improving corporate reputations will link the technical capability and resources of the formal economy with the "indigenous knowledge, human face, and cultural understandings of the informal sector."[26]

GOVERNMENT AND BUSINESS: UNDERSTANDING ROLES

Few doubt that the best thing that could happen to the Third World would be for countries to generate their own economic growth. And the best thing American business can do to advance both its own interests and those of the Third World poor is to help cultivate small businesses to employ people who, in turn, become new customers and participants in a global trading system.

But the emergence of business as a force for Third World development has deepened the debate over the causes of poverty and prosperity. There are many mysteries surrounding the development of communities and nations, and perhaps the most basic question is why businesses form and prosper in some locations and not others. What explains economic success or failure?

Certainly there are many factors, including infrastructure, soil and climate, access to ports, and the state of human development as measured by levels of education and general health. But even taking these into account, there are nations with almost no natural resources that have evolved into economic giants, such as Japan.

In *The Mystery of Capital*, Hernando De Soto dismisses the tempting thought that poverty has something to do with the poor themselves. There are many variations of the blame-the-poor attitude. If they have failed to prosper despite all the excellent advice they receive, he says, people suspect that the reason must be that "something is the matter with them." For instance, "They missed the Protestant Reformation, or they are crippled by the disabling legacy of colonial Europe, or their IQs are too low."

According to De Soto, the suggestion that culture explains the success of diverse places such as Japan, Switzerland, and California, or the relative poverty of equally diverse places, "is worse than inhuman; it is unconvincing." [27] De Soto says the cities of the Third World are teeming with entrepreneurs. What they lack is the lifeblood of capitalism —which is capital itself. They are lacking in the right to own houses or land with proper titles, and in laws that encourage the formation of business. A consensus has emerged that the principal obstacles to business development are not primarily physical or geographic, but legal and political.

During the summer of 2005, when a major drive was under way among the world's leading Western democracies to "make poverty history" by canceling Third World debt and making more foreign aid available, Kurt Hoffman, who directs the Shell Foundation, argued that the real answer to persistent problems of underdevelopment is capital. "The moral question of our time," he stated, "has little to do with public money and everything to do with private capital." Hoffman continued, "The calls for rich taxpayers' money to eliminate poverty, either as debt relief or as aid, drown out the whoosh of billions of dollars of private capital that is circling the globe, looking for a place to land and multiply." [28] The tragedy, he added, is just how little of this capital lands in proximity to extreme poverty. Less than one percent makes its way to sub-Saharan Africa.

Many people make the mistake of assuming that large numbers of businesses will somehow overcome their risk-aversion and invest in Third World economies against all logic. But capital, as is often remarked, is cowardly. It will search for places that are hospitable to growth, avoiding locations that involve high levels of social or political risk.

Capital is an impersonal and amoral force, indifferent to its impact on a given community or country. It falls to responsible authorities in government and responsible voices among NGOs to push for the kind of systemic reforms that will make the poorest countries attractive to capital investment. And this is where government, NGOs, and business become necessary collaborators.

But if this partnership is to succeed, an effort must be made to establish a clear understanding of the distinct missions of governments and companies. Each must perform its vital functions without encroaching on the other. Government and business can have legitimate expectations of each other, but those expectations must be realistic. Creating wealth is not the job of government. Establishing rule of law is not the job of business. The mission of business is to generate products and services in response to customer demands, and in the process to generate wealth and jobs. That is its contribution to society; any other achievement is secondary and optional.

Business is often lectured on the need to "put people above profits," as if it were possible to separate the two. But succeeding in business is a service to humanity in itself. The measure of success for business is its ability to make a profit and employ people, which is hard enough. There is no need for private enterprise to apologize for this. Of all the contributors to society, it is the entrepreneur who is not rewarded for his time and investment unless he succeeds at pleasing customers.

While only the drive and innovation of risk-taking entrepreneurs creates economic growth and jobs, there is much that governments can and must do. If the error of the past several decades was the assumption that government bureaucracies have all the answers to global poverty, it would be equally misguided to believe that business entrepreneurs are the only actors. Where business operates without rule of law, crony and corrupt capitalism is almost inevitably the result. The mission of government is to maintain a stable political and legal system that enables citizens to pursue economic and social progress in a safe environment.

BARRIERS TO BUSINESS FORMATION

The greatest impediment to the development of a small-business sector in Third World countries is the long and often exasperatingly difficult process of obtaining legal permission to operate. Common barriers to entrance involve permits, licensing requirements, and an assortment of regulations that often consume large portions of the startup capital and frequently require bribing officials. These barriers to indigenous business constitute the most basic form of risk for American businesses that might consider partnering with or investing in new enterprises.

India is often cited as a country that has shown a lot of potential for market-based development but is struggling to improve its legal and regulatory environment for business startups. New Delhi started liberalizing its economy in 1991 in a much-touted move to throw off socialism and embrace markets. The problem, according to Amit Varma, was that much of the economic liberalization "was half-hearted and didn't address the systemic barriers to business formation."[29] Even though manufacturing was poised to take off, well supplied with labor and raw materials, it faltered. What gained momentum instead were service exports that could function better in the poorly licensed service sector. The result was that small local firms that were not part of the large export-oriented service sector were ignored, and thus it remained "excruciatingly difficult for most Indians to start a business or set up shop in India's cities."[30]

India has made world headlines as an emerging economic superpower, driven largely by its ability to capture a large portion of business involving the outsourcing of IT services. Yet to start a business in India, entrepreneurs can expect to go through eleven steps, taking an average of eighty-nine days, which is a heavy drain on startup capital. That compares with two days for Australia, eight days for Singapore, and twenty-four days for Pakistan.

Many find it impossible to get a legal permit to operate a business and end up working in the informal economy, where survival requires frequent bribing of police and municipal officials. Says Varma, "they are trapped in a cycle of enforced illegality and systematic extortion by authorities, which results in a tragic wastage of capital. It serves as a disincentive to entrepreneurship, as well as to urbanization, the driving force of growing economies."[31]

The case of India also illustrates how democracy and development are compatible over the long term, although the democratic process can actually be used to stall economic reforms. Prime Minister Manmohan Singh defends the pace of change: "We are often criticized for being too slow in making changes in policy, but democracy means having to build consensus in favor of change."[32] Fourteen years after economic reforms began, 30 to 40 percent of the economy remains in the informal sector, which employs 90 percent of the people, according to Marun Mitra of the Liberty Institute in New Delhi.[33]

Governments cannot create business enterprise, but they can and must secure the best possible "enabling environment" for private enterprise to flourish. This requires establishing a basic system of law, starting with simplified licensing requirements and regulations. In order to attract foreign investment, Third World governments must also do more to protect intellectual property rights and reduce corruption.

Business in the Vanguard of Social Reform

Hernando De Soto estimates that upwards of $9 trillion in equity exists in the hands of the world's poorest, but it cannot be used effectively to leverage business development because of insufficient banking institutions, property titles, and laws protecting private enterprise.

Business firms in the developed world have entirely ignored 80 percent of humanity. Professor C. K. Prahalad of the University of Michigan asks, "What if we mobilized the resources, scale and scope of large firms to co-create solutions to the problems at the bottom of the pyramid, those 4 billion people who live on less than $2 a day? . . . Why can't we mobilize the investment capacity of large firms with the knowledge and commitment of NGOs and the communities that need help?"[34]

How can the trends in corporate citizenship described above be harnessed to develop indigenous markets in the Third World? At the present time, the corporate social responsibility movement does not have a coherent and compelling strategy. It is mostly about promoting ethical corporate practices and supporting conventional development projects. Energy should be refocused on actions that would contribute directly to prosperity for the poor. By redefining its agenda, the CSR movement can become a major force to promote better governance and new markets for the poor.

The greatest act of social responsibility would be for American and multinational firms to create a worldwide network of businesses and business associations committed to the rule of law, strict curbs on corruption, and a variety of other badly needed state reforms. Corruption is said to add 10 percent to the cost of doing business in many parts of the world, and may be the single greatest factor blocking opportunities for the poor and for businesses seeking to invest.

Business should be at the vanguard of improving the "enabling environments" of Third World countries by encouraging the reform of laws and policies. Writing in *Foreign Affairs*, Ben Heineman and Fritz Heimann suggest that corporate leaders "create a culture of compliance that brooks no winks and nods and no double talk and that fosters the desire to 'do the right thing.'" They encourage corporations to disclose evidence of bribery that they uncover, and to work with governments to establish sound auditing and accounting procedures, corruption hotlines, and whistleblower protection laws.[35]

NGO and civil society groups have not hesitated to point out problems in corporate behavior and demand that companies take social and environmental concerns into account. But NGOs should direct some of their attention to the policies and practices of Third World governments that systematically and often willfully stymie opportunity for the poor.

Companies, for their part, should evaluate their policy alliances and humanitarian partnerships for evidence that a particular NGO is promoting the rights of poor entrepreneurs. Firms should direct financial support to the many fledgling indigenous think tanks and Third World social and political movements that are advocating rule of law, property rights, and microenterprise.

Corporate foundations can do a better job of using their philanthropic dollars to build capacity within the entrepreneurial sector of the Third World. Kurt Hoffman of the Shell Foundation believes that the hopes of the whole African continent rest entirely upon the entrepreneur; and while foreign aid isn't the answer, neither are entrepreneurs operating completely on their own. Many small to medium-sized enterprises need assistance in presenting better business plans and improving management capacity in order to raise the confidence of investors. This, Hoffman believes, presents an opportunity for firms or foundations to provide mentoring and technical assistance.

In Africa, Shell is piloting "commercially viable ways of channeling mentoring and financing to large numbers of smaller companies" in need of capital. According to Hoffman, banks across Africa are flush with money but refuse to lend it to the millions of small-scale African entrepreneurs who could help lift the continent out of poverty if only someone gave them a chance. Capital is not being released into the African economy by either domestic or foreign banks, and this feeds the perception that investing in the African economy is all risk and no reward. The Shell Foundation's mentoring and technical assistance, Hoffman believes, will "help bridge the gap between the millions of small-scale African entrepreneurs who already understand risk and return and the millions of dollars in the accounts of risk-averse local banks."[36]

Other companies could follow Shell's lead and fill gaps that the private sector cannot fill on its own. Too little effort has been made by the business community to catalogue and quantify the steep "transaction costs" associated with entering Third World markets. Once compiled, this information could be taken to government authorities and international bodies for review and action. Some of those transaction costs have to do with the peculiar social and political characteristics of a given country. Many of those costs and barriers are simply a function of too little information available to outside investors. Business associations could create resource centers that organize and disseminate vital information on the financial, legal, and political details of particular Third World communities.

American business is still searching for more ways to contribute to market-led growth in the developing world through its own philanthropy, through social entrepreneurship, and through governance reforms. Undoubtedly, the shift in international development strategies from traditional aid to growth led by the private sector will continue to present opportunities for business leaders who want to use their resources and skills to improve the world.

CHAPTER SIX

Microenterprise: Tapping Native Capability at the Bottom of the Pyramid

> Capital is the force that raises the productivity of labor and creates the wealth of nations. It is the lifeblood of the capitalist system, the foundation of progress, and the one thing that the poor countries of the world cannot seem to produce for themselves, no matter how eagerly their people engage in all of the other activities that characterize a capitalist economy.
>
> HERNANDO DE SOTO[1]

THE GREATEST HARM that can be done to the poor is to ignore them altogether. While they weigh on the minds of humanitarian workers and religious charities, they have been largely overlooked by business firms and financial institutions, the most powerful actors in the global market economy. How is it possible that 80 percent of the world's population can be so invisible?

The world's poor are regarded as the concern of large international aid agencies or as wards of the state, possessing minimal intrinsic talent or creative power. But in reality they are customers, entrepreneurs, and producers, waiting to enter the global economy.

Fortunately, global trends are unlocking opportunities that could not have been imagined a short time ago. Many advocates for the poor are moving beyond failed foreign aid and charity models to promote a range of growth-producing strategies, including village banking, microenterprise, microfranchising, and partnerships between established companies and fledgling Third World businesses.

Occasionally a concept comes along that transforms the way a particular problem is understood. Professor C. K. Prahalad looked with dismay over fifty years of failed attempts to eradicate poverty by sincere and well-intentioned people at places like the World Bank, government aid agencies, and even civil society organizations. Why, he asks, with all our technology, investment capacity, and managerial know-how, have we been unable to create a more "inclusive capitalism" and reverse the disenfranchisement of the poor?

Prahalad decided that a new approach was called for, one that would start with a "clean sheet of paper" and would see the poor through fundamentally different lenses. In his book *The Fortune at the Bottom of the Pyramid*, Prahalad calls for an enlightened development strategy that starts not with the United Nations or aid agencies in Europe or Washington, D.C., or even with the resources of multinational corporations, but at the bottom of the pyramid (BOP). The process, he says, must start with respecting individuals at the BOP as consumers and problem solvers.[2]

Prahalad laments that the poor are not regarded as a pool of potential consumers. The dominant view is that the poor have no purchasing power and therefore do not represent a viable market; that gaining access to the poor is very difficult for large firms; and that the poor are not particularly brand-conscious or interested in the products of major companies.[3] Another common assumption is that the poor are too isolated and too technologically unsophisticated to be important to the world economy. These assumptions either are inherently wrong or are becoming outdated by technology. For example, the proliferation of wireless devices among the poor is enabling BOP consumers to communicate efficiently with each other and with the outside world, which in turn is affecting consumer attitudes and purchasing habits.

"Poor nations," says Prahalad, "are incubating new business models and innovative uses of technology that in the coming decade will begin to transform the competitive landscape of entire global industries, from financial to telecom services to health care and car making." Western corporations, he says, are at risk of being usurped by a "new breed of super competitive multinationals" that are now completely off their radar.[4] Contrary to popular perception, there is significant potential buying power among the poor and far more potential for new markets and business development than is commonly assumed.

Traveling with Prahalad in Bombay, *Business Week* writer Pete Engardio saw streets clogged with belching vehicles, beggars and hawkers—images of poverty and desperation that fit Western perceptions of major Third World cities. Yet "behind those familiar images of poverty there are very positive trends," Prahalad tells Engardio. "Just about everyone is engaged in business of some kind, whether it is selling single cloves of garlic, squeezing sugar cane juice for pennies a glass, or hauling TVs." On every block, there are "intriguing enterprises tucked into the nooks and crannies." With the world's cheapest telecom rates, says Prahalad, "all you need here is a phone and a $20 card to start a business."[5]

This is the future of entrepreneurial ingenuity that will come from places "many executives don't even think about because they have been considered too marginal."[6]

ECONOMICALLY INTEGRATING THE POOR: BEYOND CHARITY

Much is known in development circles about programs and strategies for poverty reduction, but until recently not much was known about wealth-creating capacities among the poor themselves. The poor are not usually viewed as capable managers of capital. Many of the institutions and laws that brought economic advancement to the developed world over the past century have left the Third World poor behind.

Hernando De Soto believes that policy leaders in the West have been so successful at integrating the poor into their own economies that "they have lost even the memory of how it was done, how the

creation of capital began."[7] The reason that the aspirations and energies of common people were channeled into economic productivity
in the West, says De Soto, has a lot to do with the legal systems that
were built by Western governments. The key to integrating today's
poor into the mainstream global economy is to revisit the process that
brought America's poor into full participation in economic life. The
assets, property, and labor of the Third World poor require legal protection so the capital that already exists in their hands can be used to
generate wealth.

The world economy now generates over $40 trillion in annual
output, but large majorities of the world's poor have not benefited
from the staggering growth of global wealth. The gap between the
world's richest and poorest has widened into a huge chasm over the
past several decades and continues to expand each year. In 1960, the
richest 20 percent accounted for 70 percent of global GDP; today
they account for 85 percent of global GDP, with the poorest 20 percent owning a mere 1.1 percent.[8] Today, a few hundred millionaires
own as much wealth as the world's poorest 2.5 billion people.[9]

Or consider the gaps among nations: in 1820, the GDP ratio
between the richest and poorest countries was 3 to 1; by 1950, it was
35 to 1; and by the twenty-first century, it was 72 to 1.[10] The GDP
of the poorest forty-eight nations when taken together is less than the
wealth of the world's three richest people combined.[11] Of the world's
one hundred largest economies, fifty-one are not countries, but companies. However one analyses the data, the long-term trends point to
a continued widening of the global wealth gap.

Discussions about the inequality of global wealth tend to degen-
erate into disputes over questions of fairness and justice. Is the wealth
of the rich in any way responsible for the poverty of the poor? Are the
rich obligated to take care of the poor? Would the redistribution of
wealth away from the rich make a significant difference? Would the
poor be any better off if there were fewer millionaires in the world?

For most people who study the issue, the answer to these questions
is no. Though enormous sums of capital are owned by a relatively

small number of rich persons, it is not idle capital. It is part of the global pool of resources that is directed toward profitable use in the form of credit, loans, charitable gifts, or investment, which often directly help the poor. The wealth of the West also generates much of the demand for consumer products exported from the Third World. Slumping Western demand for these products would have a deleterious effect on Third World economies.

But these basic economic facts hardly settle the vexing issues of morality that gnaw at people's consciences. The wealth of the rich may serve socially beneficial purposes, but that has not prevented the glaring inequalities from emerging, or from worsening year by year. The reason for this is that most global economic activity simply bypasses the poorest of the poor. According to Stuart Hart, much of the direct foreign investment occurs either within the richest countries or in those poor countries that are believed to be emerging markets. Even there, he says, most of the products made by multinational corporations are "aimed at the wealthy, elite customers or those in the rising middle class segments of the market."[12] The top one-fifth of the world's people in the richest countries enjoy 82 percent of the expanding export trade and 68 percent of foreign direct investment; the bottom fifth, barely more than 1 percent.[13]

The reasons for this maldistribution of wealth and opportunity are complex, but the most sobering fact is that the economies of the poorest nations have been flat-lined or declining for the past decade. And virtually no attention "has been paid to serving the needs of those at the base of the economic pyramid," says Hart. Corporations must learn how to "open up to the world" and "take account of the entire human community."[14]

The next big wave in international development recognizes the potential for business when the world's poor are brought into the mainstream of the global economy. The more they earn, the more they are able to purchase. When a customer base is developed at the bottom of the wealth pyramid, the benefits are not merely to the poor, but to business as well.

Another step forward involves partnering with native capability to create products. "The objective is indigenous enterprise, co-creating technologies, products, and services to meet local needs and building local businesses from the bottom up," says Hart. This means that multinational corporations need to "understand and nurture local markets and cultures, leverage local solutions, and generate wealth at the lowest points on the pyramid."[15]

Writing for the *Washington Post*, John Lancaster describes a powerful trend at work in India. The country is experiencing an economic boom, but its 8 percent annual growth rate has been mostly an urban phenomenon, driven primarily by service industries that have largely overlooked the rural poor. In rural India, most families still farm and malnutrition rates are higher than in sub-Saharan Africa. According to Lancaster, "poor roads and inadequate electricity deter outside businesses from seeking new customers and opportunities outside of cities and larger towns."[16]

This is about to change, however, as major companies find ways to spread the consumer culture to the vast hinterlands of India, where two-thirds of the nation's 1.1 billion people live. Hindustan Lever Ltd., the Indian subsidiary of the Dutch consumer products giant, is looking to reach into some of India's 638,000 villages through unconventional sales and marketing schemes that will bring the poor directly into the company's distribution system. Hindustan Lever is enlisting about 20,000 poor and mostly illiterate women to peddle products such as Lifebuoy soap and Pepsodent toothpaste in villages which, according to Lancaster, were "once considered too small, too destitute and too far from normal distribution channels to warrant attention."[17] The money these women earn is miniscule, from $16 to $22 per month, but the added cash represents on average a doubling of their monthly income and in many cases is making education for their children possible for the first time.

Hindustan Lever is among a growing number of companies that see the potential for doing good while doing well in rural India. According to economists and business experts, urban markets are becoming saturated, forcing companies to retool their marketing and distribution systems to target rural consumers who may have tiny incomes but collectively represent huge growth potential. Those products include anything from shampoo packets selling for a penny to motor scooters that are sold for monthly payments of $4.50. In many cases, banks are joining the trend by offering savings accounts and credit to first-time customers. The economist Rajesh Shukla says that "in four or five years the rural market will be a major sector that is well beyond anyone's imagination."[18]

LEGALIZING CAPITALISM FOR THE POOR

The key to capitalist success among the poor is the same as with the rich: *capital.*

Professor Stephen Smith of George Washington University describes the numerous traps into which the poor fall, such as illiteracy, illness, debt, and joblessness. But more than these poverty traps, he says, it is a lack of credit that thwarts success. The poor have too little net income and too little capital to scale up beyond whatever entrepreneurial capacity they might presently have. Smith tells the story of a woman in Ecuador who sold used American jeans door to door, but could maintain an inventory of only three pairs, which severely limited her ability to match up styles and sizes with customer needs. With modest amounts of credit, this woman could acquire a larger inventory and boost her profits.[19]

But something so simple as capital is not simple at all when one considers the wide range of legal and institutional barriers that prevent the poor from gaining access to it. "Imagine a country," says Smith, "where nobody can identify who owns what, addresses can't be easily verified, people cannot be made to pay their debts, resources cannot conveniently be turned into money, ownership cannot be divided into shares, descriptions of assets are not standardized and cannot be easily compared, and the rules that govern property vary from neighborhood to neighborhood and even street to street." Smith continues,

"You have just put yourself into the life of a developing country."[20]

Hernando De Soto, widely known for his work to advance legal rights for the Third World poor, describes how his research team decided to open a garment shop on the outskirts of Lima, Peru. The team set out to meet all the legal requirements, which necessitated long bus trips to central Lima, waiting in line, and filling out registration forms. They spent six hours a day at this and finally registered the business 289 days later at a cost of $1,231—all for a garment shop that would employ one person. Obtaining legal authorization to build a house on state-owned land took more than six years, requiring 207 administrative steps in fifty-two government offices. Obtaining legal title to the land took 728 steps.[21]

This is the exasperating process required to conduct business legally, so onerous and irrational are the demands of bureaucracy. It is even harder to remain in the legal economy once arriving there. Many end up returning to the underground economy, at which point whatever minimal legal protections they might have gained are gone. Often they fall victim to corrupt government officials or economic tyrants who practice a form of predatory capitalism that robs, rather than empowers, the poor. Third World economies are teeming with people who profit off the poor—such as corrupt officials, moneylenders, and middlemen—and have a vested interest in keeping them poor.

At the same time, in every Third World country that De Soto's team examined, the entrepreneurial ingenuity of the poor "has created wealth on a vast scale—wealth that also constitutes by far the largest source of potential capital for development."[22] Third World cities are home to numerous skilled workers and entrepreneurs who, in spite of the odds, are creating entire industries through clandestine connections. In many cases they are thriving, but not generating the jobs and prosperity for their communities that would be possible in a legal system for business.

According to the UN's International Labor Organization, 85 percent of all new jobs in Latin America are created in the "extralegal sector." Because much of the economic activity in poor countries is extralegal, actual commercial resources, property, and assets remain largely out of sight. This is what economists call dead capital: because it cannot be legally used to expand enterprises, it represents minimal utility for producing general prosperity.

ASSET-BASED DEVELOPMENT

According to Hernando De Soto, poor inhabitants of the world—fully five-sixths of humanity—do have things, but "they lack the process to represent their property and create capital." He continues, "They have houses, but not titles; crops but not deeds; businesses but not statutes of incorporation." This, he says, is "the mystery of capitalism." [23]

Whether the neighborhood is an American urban slum or a poor Third World village, the starting point in generating wealth is to identify the assets that the people already have, and then begin building upon them. The poor are not likely to have steady or reliable jobs, savings, credit, or land. But they do have skill and means to produce something of value in a market, however limited.

With the help of credit, a poor person who fishes for a living may be able to sell the portion he doesn't need to feed his family into the local market. A poor family might have goats or a cow and would be able to make small amounts of excess milk available for sale. A poor woman might produce exquisite crafts that would appeal to urban customers or tourists, if she could find the means to transport and market the goods. A poor man may be a skilled mechanic who can repair car transmissions, but he needs more advanced tools if he is to expand his service.

Seemingly minor assets can be leveraged into larger revenue-generating enterprises. Modest improvements in capital, production capacity, or market expansion can make the difference between living in extreme poverty and being only moderately poor. A little bit of credit can go a long way in magnifying the value of such basic assets as tools, draft animals, or small tractors to cultivate larger plots of land.

The asset with the greatest potential for the poor may be land.

When surveyed, the poor frequently identify land as key to their own development. They either need more land to live on and make a living, or they need legal control over the land they do claim so it can be treated as an asset for purposes of securing credit. A UN study found that half a billion people survive by farming land that they do not securely own. They may be sharecroppers, tenants, or squatters with some access to the land for subsistence, but because they lack secure land tenure rights, they lack collateral to access credit necessary for creating additional wealth.[24]

In Haiti, one of the poorest and most dysfunctional Third World countries, 68 percent of the urban poor and 97 of the rural poor live in housing without clear legal title. Untitled real estate in Haiti is valued at $5.2 billion.[25] In the Philippines, the value of untitled real estate is $133 billion, four times the value of the 216 domestic companies that are listed on the country's stock exchange. A major breakthrough for the poor would come if more were able to own their homes and count their properties as assets, which could then be used as collateral. In some of the worst slums in the world, where the poor are stuck in conditions of extreme poverty with inadequate sanitation, the landlords are often government officials and politicians. Ownership in such cases would represent a significant shift in power.

Most of the poor depend on natural assets in their living environment, such as forests, agricultural land, or streams and rivers, which in many locations are depleted or polluted. According to Stephen Smith, "the poor are both victims and also unwitting perpetrators of environmental degradation."[26] For example, when the poor are compelled to destroy woodlands for firewood to cook meals or stay warm, as is common, they are depleting natural resources, which in turn diminishes the prospects for sustainable development.

The greatest need of the poor may be simply to have more control over their time, a critical asset in itself. More efficient delivery of essential daily services and supplies, such as water and fuel, can free up time that might be used to produce goods for sale. Timesaving technologies are becoming great aids to the poor as they cope with daily necessities. Cell phones are the biggest timesaver, sparing the need to trek long distances to conduct business that could just as easily be done by phone. Women with cell phones can do business during their daily trips to the river for water. High-tech devices are already a part of poor people's lives, according to Gautam Ivatury, writing for *The Banker*. In Africa alone, the number of mobile phone subscribers has reached 76.8 million, growing by 58 percent annually over the past five years. In many cases, mobile phone subscribers are able to sell airtime to other users, dramatically expanding the availability of phone service.[27]

CREDIT-BASED CAPITALISM FOR THE POOR

Standing between extreme poverty and the first rung of the economic ladder may be something as simple as a small loan.

Sources of capital for poor people are often very limited. Even local and national banks in Third World countries frequently refuse to make money available to the poor because of perceived credit risks. Studies show that 90 percent of small entrepreneurs are excluded from financial services in their countries. In the vast majority of cases, banks simply prefer to put their reserves in a Western bank, a pattern that exacerbates the severe problem of credit flight in much of the Third World.

The local moneylenders who do offer loans to the poor are often corrupt, charging outrageous interest rates ranging as high as 1,000 percent per month. Such usurious rates can completely consume the borrowers' profits, defeating the entire purpose of extending credit to the poor. Too often it is moneylenders who reap the rewards.

One of the most promising antipoverty initiatives to arise in recent decades has been the microfinance movement, which provides small loans along with financial services to the poor. It has become so powerful an antipoverty tool that the United Nations declared 2005 to be "the Year of Micro-Credit" and called upon Third World countries to address the shortcomings of their credit systems. The U.S.

government has stepped forward and is currently providing $155 million annually in loans and capacity-building funds to over 3.7 microenterprises worldwide.

Small loans enable the poor all over the Third World to make consequential purchases of equipment, expand product inventories, and make modest upgrades in their business operations. Loans can also enable poor entrepreneurs to obtain training, get better nutrition and health care, or improve the condition of their homes or facilities.

Microfinance clients are generally low-income persons who have no other access to financial institutions, but have some means of self-help and can do far more for themselves with a little capital. In rural areas, that usually means small farmers or those involved in food processing or trade. The purchase of a draft animal or a small tractor can dramatically improve a farmer's productivity. In urban communities, loans typically go to shopkeepers, street vendors, artisans, or service providers. For a seamstress, the ability to buy a sewing machine can make the difference in whether her family is fed and educated.

The stories of microcredit success reveal a latent energy and ingenuity among the poor that is waiting to be harnessed. Consider these stories from recipients of Hope International loans.

In China, Niu Jun received three loans, which he used to expand his coal delivery business by developing a unique product to meet the heating needs of local customers. Jun purchased coal powder and converted it into honeycomb-shaped blocks that proved to be efficient heating fuel. This product quickly increased local demand. Through his additional profits, Jun is enabling his children to receive an advanced education.

Also in China, Wu Ai Ying used a microloan to take a struggling dairy business to a new level. The fresh capital enabled him to provide a higher quality of feed for his animals, dramatically improving their health and raising levels of milk production. The healthy cows also bore healthier calves, promising even more future milk production. Ying used a second loan to purchase bottles for delivering the milk to market.

In Sri Lanka, a fisherman named Melius lacked the equipment to feed his family adequately, much less make a profit from his unpredictable daily catch. His children were forced to leave school because of the family's financial difficulty. Through a small loan, Melius was able to purchase a boat and expand both his hours and his fishing options. His family is now well fed and his children are back in school.

Rajeev, also from Sri Lanka, had lost everything when his family's business was destroyed in a local conflict. When he received a loan, he was able to purchase a hundred hens and build a chicken coop. Rajeev's plans succeeded enough that he is moving to double his flock and is beginning to sell chickens into a wider market. He is using the surplus cash to pay for university training.

Colette, from Rwanda, had no work and her husband's income was not sufficient to provide for their seven children. Through a microloan, Colette was able to open a booth in the local market and begin selling children's clothing. She also managed to purchase a small house to rent to a local family and to provide home-cooked meals for twenty local factory workers each day.

These stories reveal the true promise of microfinance. Viewed through the eyes of the prosperous West, the level of economic production in each of these cases seems miniscule. Yet in the context of the developing world, the advances these loans brought for the families and communities involved were major. In each case, sufficient income was generated for children to be fed and educated, and in some cases for additional workers to be hired, building general prosperity by small increments.

Although microfinance programming dates back as far as thirty years in countries such as Bangladesh and Brazil, it gained momentum in the 1980s and has flowered into the dynamic global movement it is today.

The program operating the longest, and perhaps most frequently cited as a model for broad-based economic development, is a financial services program in Bangladesh started by an economics professor, Muhammad Yunus. Motivated by the conviction that each person is born with some capacity for entrepreneurship, Yunus set out to confront what he found to be the primary obstacle to economic opportunity—the lack of credit. He created Grameen (which means "rural" or "village"), a nonprofit economic development organization that today serves over three million poor borrowers through two thousand branch offices.

When Yunus began his program in 1976, he had to overcome skepticism that the poor had any ability to manage credit and repay their loans faithfully. To prove the skeptics wrong, he designed into his program the means to instill trust and a sense of ownership among the poor. For one, the Grameen program relies heavily on what Yunus calls "the collateral of peer pressure," which describes the practice of requiring borrowers to jointly guarantee and cosign each other's loans. This group solidarity provides strong social incentives for loan repayment, but also social support for those who fall behind.

In 1983, when he chartered his program as a public cooperative bank, Yunus determined that the borrowers themselves would own 75 percent of the bank's stock. Each borrower is entitled to stock ownership after arriving at a certain level of borrowing. As the program diversified into a wider array of financial services, Grameen emphasized the importance of home ownership, offering loans at 8 percent interest, an astonishingly low rate for a microfinance program.

The Grameen program has demonstrated the power of allowing the poor to guide their own development. Increasingly, loans are directed toward farming activity that the Bangladeshis themselves have identified as meeting consumer needs. For example, given that fish is a major part of the local diet, entrepreneurs discovered that building fish farms with high-yielding fish stock is a profitable method of providing food for the poor.[28]

Today, microfinance institutions, or MFIs, serve more than eighty million poor people in developing countries with over $7 billion on outstanding loans. Microfinancing is offered by numerous entities, including credit unions, NGOs, and commercial banks. The potential worldwide market among the poor for microfinance programming

ranges as high as five hundred million people. Women in particular—
who constitute 70 percent of the world's poor—benefit from micro-
loans because they are able to grow home-based enterprises while
caring for children, which often improves their children's chances of
completing school.

According to Peter Greer of Hope International, "most of the
poor have untapped entrepreneurial qualities of self-development.
Through access to credit (as little as $50) at a reasonable rate of inter-
est, they can start up or expand their business, free themselves from
poverty, and participate in a free market economy." Greer stresses that
the key is to promote real business development, involving profits and
real employment, and not merely focus on the humanitarian objective of poverty reduction.

Too many well-intentioned credit programs have proved to be
unsustainable because their operating goal was the vague notion of
"alleviating" poverty. The evidence suggests that for the poor to break
out of poverty, they must become acquainted with the practice of
generating real economic activity in the free market. Microlending
programs recognize that "the poor are creditworthy and 'bankable,'"
says Greer, and that the promotion of self-employment through microenterprise is not only the most effective way to reduce poverty, but
the surest way to put the poor in charge of their own future.[29]

Whereas most humanitarian programs involve providing some
form of service to the poor from outside, microcredit initiatives place
the emphasis almost entirely on people's capacity to help themselves.
Except for the financial credit, everything else that is to be accomplished is up to the poor. Few antipoverty programs can compare to
microfinance initiatives in demonstrating just how capable the poor
are of helping themselves, or how responsible they can be in meeting
their obligations. Repayment rates on microcredit loans are in the
neighborhood of 95 percent.

Unlike traditional banking, where borrowers are expected to put
up collateral to cover loans, microcredit programs often rely on peer
group supports, or "social collateral," as in the Bangladesh experience.

Loans are often taken out by groups of up to eight people, who then work together to make sure the loans are repaid in a timely way in order to prevent a penalty for the entire group.

One leading organization, Accion, combined the provision of credit with a focus on developing skills among the poor to make them better at combating credit risks and thus more eligible for loans. Accion offers a business curriculum covering a variety of topics including marketing, pricing, and quality control. The poor are even shown how to develop a business plan. The organization's affiliates have made $5.8 billion in loans available to 3.2 million poor entrepreneurs over the past ten years, and have a repayment rate of 97 percent.

Adding greatly to the expansion of credit services to the poor is the spread of affordable communication services. Personal digital devices and PC kiosks are opening up the world of information and credit to the poor. Farmers are finding information on markets from the Internet, which helps them determine when to sell a commodity. According to C. K. Prahalad, "chat rooms are full of activity that none of us could have imagined." He cites the example of fishermen in Kerala, India, who use cell phones to check prices at various fish markets before directing their boats to a landing site at the end of the day.[30]

The hope among microfinance practitioners is that programming will continue diversifying to include new sources of credit and many variations in the institutional delivery system; that it will become one facet in a larger integrated approach to economic development. Given that microfinancing has rates of return that compare favorably with mainstream commercial lending, it would appear likely that more and more for-profit banking operations will move to provide small loans to the poor, particularly as consumer capitalism makes its way into small rural communities. The more sources of credit for the poor and the more competition among credit providers, the more access poor families will have to credit.

Part of that diversification will likely be supplied by other powerful development trends, including remittances. The flow of money earned by immigrants back into Third World communities is strengthening local credit institutions and promoting indigenous financial sectors.

Increased localization remains critical to success. Like many services provided by outsiders, microfinance programs may fail to adapt to the local culture or may inadvertently discourage local initiative and ownership, becoming just another source of dependence on external solutions. It is possible that local institutions controlled by the communities themselves will increasingly replace much of the current funding of microfinance programs by philanthropies or governments.

Others stress the importance of shifting from credit supplied by lenders to savings by the poor themselves. Perhaps a better strategy for advocates of local market-led growth is to focus more on "lump sum" payments from savings pools, which would enable the poor to purchase outright the things they need to produce more income. The problem is not merely that the poor don't have access to credit; it is that they don't have a secure place to deposit their savings.

Jeffrey Ashe of the Institute for Sustainable Development at Brandeis University maintains that generating local savings practices and institutions is essential. After several decades, microfinance has not reached deep within rural villages or reached sufficient numbers of clients to transform entire regions or countries because it has not relied on the locally controlled organizations that already exist in virtually every village.

In countries where microfinance has enjoyed the greatest success, local saving institutions, or "revolving credit and saving societies," were mobilized to deliver financial services more effectively.[31] These local saving societies operate entirely through member deposits, with no external loan funds. Ashe believes that local saving and credit groups can perform far more tasks in the community with a little help in capacity building. "What would happen," he asks, "if these groups with their empowered and prospering members became platforms for literacy, health education, business literacy and sustainable agriculture training, and even candidates for bank financing?"[32]

Most advocates of expanding credit to the poor are aiming to extend credit to the most remote areas of the developing world, where the lack of basic infrastructure such as roads and reliable electricity has traditionally presented insurmountable obstacles. Advocates of microfinancing are not waiting for safe roads and electricity to arrive. They are looking for ways to "bypass the infrastructure problem," according to Gautam Ivatury, by using simple cell phones to bring banking to villages. Here's how it works: Mobile phone operators partner with small shopkeepers in rural areas and take cash from customers, transferring an equivalent amount electronically to the customer's bank account at a remote location. "Could rural shopkeepers become banking points and make bank branches obsolete?" Ivatury asks. "It is hardly a rhetorical question."[33]

Microenterprise development represents a major breakthrough for poverty reduction. But as even its advocates will concede, microfinance is not a panacea for poverty. The problem of poverty is multifaceted and not susceptible to a single solution.

MICROFRANCHISING

Another "bottom-up" approach to promoting economic growth and job creation is the introduction of the franchising strategies of small-scale enterprise to poor Third World villages. Microfranchising, a recent concept, is based upon the proposition that the poor, with the right incentives, are capable of developing local markets for desperately needed goods and services. Small franchises operating in their own self-interest will achieve far more than centralized command-and-control bureaucracies. Hundreds of products essential to health and welfare are affordable and could be made accessible to the poor through incentive-based systems.

There is significant evidence to suggest that lifesaving products are more effectively distributed among the poor when they are sold than when they are given away. The best example is the distribution of bed nets for malaria prevention in Africa. One survey found that when free nets were distributed in Zambia, 70 percent of the recipients didn't use them. In Malawi, where nets were sold at affordable prices, there was nearly universal use.[34]

Scott Hillstrom was another successful entrepreneur who arrived in midlife not knowing what he would do with the rest of his life. He was troubled by Third World poverty and not impressed by conventional strategies to alleviate it. Like many in the private sector, Hillstrom believed that top-down bureaucratic approaches were simply not capable of reaching the poor with solutions, and that even if public health funding were doubled, government programs would still fall far short of meeting the need in most poor countries. Convinced that "it is within the grasp of most Americans to reach out and make a lifesaving difference to someone, somewhere in the world," Hillstrom searched for his cause.

He was radicalized by a report he heard that twenty-five thousand children in the developing world die each day—nine million a year —for lack of medicine that costs less than a cup of coffee. Hillstrom discovered the little-known fact that infectious diseases such as malaria, dysentery, and respiratory infections that strike down 70 to 90 percent of these children could be prevented or cured by inexpensive generic drugs. He kept thinking about having to encounter the corpses of twenty-five thousand children each day, and the recurrent image in his mind appalled him.

Hillstrom sold his business and decided to experiment with the application of market principles to the distribution of basic lifesaving drugs. He founded what today is called the HealthStore Foundation, which has emerged as a successful franchising model for selling and distributing basic medicines to the poor. The program relies entirely on incentives and profit-making opportunities for the poor to get medicines to those in need. Operating in fifty-four locations in Kenya, the HealthStore Foundation provides basic training to community health workers who own and operate a franchise outlet store. The basic idea is to allow them to make a modest living by selling medicines to the poor at prices that the majority can afford. The clinics are now treating forty thousand patients per month.

Hillstrom hopes that commercial franchising can be applied widely to poverty reduction across the globe, and that it can be used as an instrument to enforce three core principles on all government aid activity: the program must have quality controls; it must be scalable; and it must reduce the cost of delivery as it grows.

Franchising has emerged as a leading business model for small to medium-sized businesses in Africa. The African Development Bank has studied the performance of microfranchising enterprises and has found that they have many advantages over other kinds of business. Among these advantages is that they allow small operators access to the products and market strength of larger firms, which in turn keeps startup and overhead costs down and offers long-term durability. In South Africa, for example, failure rates for franchise businesses were 15 percent, compared with 80 percent in independent small to medium-sized enterprises.

MARKETING THE POOR'S PRODUCTS

Among the questions that are asked about the role of microfinance are: What must be done to help the very small entrepreneur graduate into the category of small or medium-sized firm and become a real driver of economic growth and jobs? What, in other words, lies beyond microenterprise?

Assisting small entrepreneurs to take steps forward is important, but it can do only so much to lift families out of poverty without broader social and economic development. Small loans can often help poor persons modestly scale up their enterprises, but without the necessary infrastructure and modern services such as electricity and telecommunications, microenterprise will be limited. According to Koenraad Verhagen, a microfinance consultant, "with all of the attention that micro-finance has garnered, the tendency may be to view it as a universal remedy, suggesting that access to credit and to the market is all that poor people need, which can further contribute to governments denying responsibility they have to secure access to basic services such as health and education."[35] And as mentioned earlier, governments in the West brought the poor into the economic mainstream mostly because they developed modern institutions of law and government.

Microfinance and small-scale enterprise development are ultimately limited by external realities, including macroeconomic policies, infrastructure requirements, and perhaps most importantly the need for entrepreneurs to be linked to the global economy.

One of the biggest impediments to economic integration of the poor is that they so often live in remote and inaccessible places. Local markets served by microenterprise can quickly become saturated, resulting in an oversupply of goods and services combined with weak demand. Isolation makes it difficult for microenterprises to enter larger markets, regional or international, and they remain essentially invisible to investors and financiers who might otherwise identify economic potential. Many Third World businesses must survive within a very small radius of potential sales and distribution because of deficiencies of infrastructure and marketing capacity.

What can be done to help small enterprises trade beyond the small circle of the village? Scaling up small firms and markets usually requires the assistance of larger organizations with greater capacities and geographic reach. Programs that build cooperatives for farmers and entrepreneurs can often link up small producers with large firms and markets that lie beyond their reach. Such programs also present opportunities to businesses, large and small, in the developed world.

One nonprofit, Business Professional Network (BPN), has seen the frustrating limits that stifle many entrepreneurs in the developing world, even those with training and expertise, and has come up with an innovative solution. BPN is interested in doing more than just assisting small entrepreneurs with loans of $50 to $100. They find investors in the West who will offer interest-free loans to a revolving national funding pool, which in turn provides small to medium-sized enterprises with loans ranging from $1,000 to $20,000 at moderate interest rates. The key is to establish strong partnerships that combine coaching in general business know-how with connections to market opportunities that would not otherwise be available.

Nonprofits have also stepped forward. One model program, called Ten Thousand Villages, is run by the Mennonite Central Committee, the relief and development arm of the Mennonite Church. Ten Thousand Villages helps expand export opportunities for Third World producers of handicrafts by providing outlets for their products in the United States. In many cases, these are products that would otherwise not make it to American markets. They are available for sale via the Web or at one of their 180 stores.

A host of international volunteer groups specialize in delivering technical knowledge to business and government institutions in the developing world, thereby creating important people-to-people linkages. For example, the Citizens Development Corps helps build the local capacity of firms in order to improve the manufacture of innovative products and to expand local and regional economics. CDC achieves its purposes through a base of expert volunteer advisors who want to use their business or professional training and expertise to help promote economic growth in the Third World.

Similarly, the Financial Services Volunteer Corps recruits volunteers with various technical backgrounds in the financial service sector to provide assistance in anything from improving banking services, to training regulatory staff, to developing capital markets and stock exchanges.

As part of the administration's agenda for volunteerism and service, President George W. Bush launched the Volunteers for Prosperity Initiative, which links up skilled professionals with international service opportunities in the hope of building prosperity. This initiative, housed at USAID, operates through a network of nonprofit partners to recruit and mobilize volunteers.

Building Blocks International is working with major American corporations to develop what it calls a "corporate peace corps," which will offer corporate service fellowships to professionals willing to serve anywhere from a month to a year in providing help in anything from computer services to the construction of schools.

CHAPTER SEVEN

The Great Tsunami of 2004
and America's Generosity

FEW EVENTS HAVE done more to illustrate the future of the private sector's role in relief and development than the massive earthquake and tsunami that struck several nations in the Indian Ocean on December 26, 2004, leaving some 230,000 dead or missing and hundreds of thousands more homeless and jobless. The staggering relief and reconstruction challenge left by the receding waves was met with the largest combined response to a natural disaster in world history.

As the director of private sector coordination for tsunami reconstruction at the State Department, I was able to witness America's response to the disaster from the inside. I was also able to travel in the region and see the full power of a mobilized NGO community. That much of the affected area was fairly remote, underdeveloped, and in some cases politically repressive and unstable (such as the Banda Aceh region of Indonesia), didn't matter at all. If the Acehnese had no preparation for the tsunami disaster, neither were they prepared for the tidal wave of NGOs, humanitarian workers, and volunteers who poured in by the tens of thousands. One aid worker joked, "This place went overnight from being North Korea to being Woodstock."

Many people deserve credit for the massive and rapid response, including UN agencies and dozens of governments. America's own USAID and military performed impressively. USAID coordinated a massive emergency relief operation and later implemented a generous congressional aid package providing shelter, livelihood restoration, health services, and capacity building.

Airmen operating C-130 Hercules aircraft rushed food, clothing, and temporary shelter supplies to survivors across the region. The U.S. Navy deployed USS *Abraham Lincoln* and a medical treatment facility aboard USNS *Mercy* to provide emergency care throughout the area. Sailors aboard the *Abraham Lincoln* worked around the clock for thirty-three days using helicopters to deliver nearly six million pounds of relief supplies, saving many lives and preventing epidemics as well as widespread malnourishment. Through these mobile response systems offered by America's fighting forces, more than ten thousand patients received medical services ranging from primary care to complex surgical procedures.

The response of the American government inspired many. A fact little known to the American people, however, is that the majority of support from the United States came from them, the people, working through the private sector. Almost immediately following the first horrific television images of massive waves wiping out seafront villages, Americans from all walks of life and in thousands of locations mobilized. Kids, university students, churches, businesses, and service organizations were moved to sponsor fundraising projects. Assisting them were TV networks and Web-based companies, celebrity entertainers and athletes. The result was the most generous outpouring from American soil ever.

The great Indian Ocean tsunami of 2004 generated waves that destroyed life, property, and livelihood, but it generated waves of a different kind as well. A variety of factors combined to drive giving to stratospheric levels, which in turn produced the first major test of a new electronically connected private donation system that had been evolving since the terrorist attacks of 9/11. Donations poured in at an unprecedented rate because individuals, businesses, and charities used marketing savvy, informal networking, and high-tech know-how as never before.

By the time the giving peaked, a Pew poll found that fully one-third of Americans gave to tsunami relief, with 36 percent getting involved in relief efforts through a church or other religious group. The American Red Cross stopped accepting money when it felt that more was coming in than could be managed or effectively absorbed for emergency assistance in the region. When Doctors Without Borders realized that it had more money than needed, it offered donors the option of having the money returned or used elsewhere.

THE WONDERS OF WEB-BASED GIVING

Thanks to a boost from global TV and Web connections, citizen-based philanthropy surged in response to the tsunami, proving that civil society today is globally integrated across the traditional distinctions of language, nation, and creed. Citizens from nations in Europe and Asia with little prior experience of supporting religious organizations poured hundreds of millions of dollars into groups such as World Vision that were both American and faith-based.

For the first time, numerous Web-based companies got into fundraising activity on a large scale by building systems to direct donors to newly created relief funds or to familiar charities. According to an online source, "a gaggle of news sites, search engines and corporate home pages," ranging from America Online to Yahoo! established direct links to major charities. Within two days of the disaster, Amazon.com had established a donation system that generated 187,000 individual contributions almost overnight.[1] The eBay auction site used its interface to allow sellers to donate a portion of their proceeds to charities.

Similar to the Internet companies and often in partnership with them, big retail chains—by using their daily contact with millions of shoppers—emerged as major players. According to a *USA Today* account, "when the disaster hit, an army of retailers and banks—

including Best Buy, Costco, Kmart, OfficeMax and Washington Mutual—immediately started accepting Red Cross donations on their websites."[2] Wal-Mart made an immediate contribution of $2 million and also created collection sites at all of their stores, enabling customers, workers, and suppliers to contribute cash.

Almost every organization with customers or subscribers thought of some way to help. *New York Daily News* subscribers sent in $100,000 to the paper's tsunami relief effort in a single day.

Meanwhile, a new generation of "citizen journalists" emerged, publishing frontline reports and constant updates on weblogs. This added another level of exposure for tsunami victims—often of the most personalized kind—to the saturation coverage in the mainstream media. Bloggers combined eyewitness accounts of devastation with visual images fed by digital cameras to large electronic networks, which motivated large audiences to help out.[3]

Web-based philanthropy increased the speed of fundraising and dramatically enhanced the creativity of fundraisers. Some Web companies set up their own relief funds, while others formed links with recognized charities. Money moved from credit cards to bank accounts to operations on the ground in Asia with remarkable efficiency. As one online fundraiser put it, "when the roar of the deadly tsunami subsided, the clicking began. From laptops and desktops, from offices and internet cafes, shocked people around the world sought and found an impressive way to help: go online, click and give."[4] The great advantage brought by the Internet is that donors can act on their decision immediately. Fundraisers can capture donations as the news and TV images flood into people's homes—when interest is at a peek. According to Ted Hart, president of ePhilanthropy.org, a foundation that promotes online giving, "the ease and immediacy of making gifts online is unprecedented."[5]

Some doubted that Web-based giving would win the trust of donors. The tsunami disaster demonstrated that there is a high level of comfort with online giving. According to a survey of humanitarian organizations, as much as half of the hundreds of millions in donations that came in during the early period arrived by way of the Internet. Fully $350 million arrived via Internet donations in the first month following the disaster.

Many charities appealed to their own electronic databases within days, even hours, of the tsunami. Of the $168 million that came into the Red Cross during the first month, fully $71 came in via their own website.[6] Three of the largest humanitarian organizations—Save the Children, CARE, and Oxfam America—reported receiving 31 percent, 38 percent, and 80 percent of donations, respectively, via their websites.[7]

CITIZEN-DRIVEN PHILANTHROPY

Many of the major philanthropies have large fundraising staffs that spend much of their time making calls on high-net-worth individuals or writing proposals for grant-making foundations. What was remarkable about the tsunami response was how the generous works of an entire society were spawned and multiplied at the grass roots, in many ways bypassing official channels.

The range of community activities seemed endless. One committee of citizens organized a "Story Tsunami" project, which hosted fifty-eight storytelling performances in various locations featuring creative writing on the tsunami, raising in excess of $50,000. A painting produced by an elephant at the Fort Worth Zoo raised $7,000. Concerts were held in Nashville featuring country music stars, an event called "Music City Comes Together for Tsunami Relief."

KIDS COUNTED

Too often, the business of caring for suffering in the world fails to capture the attention of the young. Not in the case of the tsunami. Many children made donations directly to their favorite charity, and many more worked through their school, place of worship, or service organization to sponsor projects.

The National Service-Learning Clearinghouse, which serves schools with information and advice on community service, offered online resources for schools to sponsor projects and provided up-to-date information on the many ideas being tried in schools. There were plenty of standard fundraising drives where people were just invited to make donations. There were pizza sales, bake sales, and even fashion shows. Every imaginable marathon was tried: walkathons, dance-athons, and even a read-a-thon that raised $7,000 for the Red Cross.

There were photography shows and silent auctions. Ordinary chores such as housework were turned into opportunities to generate donations. A six-year-old parlayed 16 cents that he found on the floor into $6,000 through a community-wide fundraising campaign, and another produced $1,200 in pennies, nickels, and dimes in a spare-coin collection project. One group of students made and sold friend-ship bracelets for a dollar each, raising $1,000.

Thousands of projects emerged to solicit donations of school sup-plies, backpacks, and gifts for kids. Twenty students from Cincinnati Hills Christian School organized thirty-five pallets of relief supplies for orphanages in India and then boarded a Boeing 747 for a two-week trip to deliver the supplies to kids. Some combined donations with an effort to adopt a specific school, sending personalized condo-lences, photos, and friendship bracelets along with supplies in the hope of building a long-distance bond.

College students were no less energized or inventive. Several cam-pus groups at Princeton teamed up to create a "Making Waves" cam-paign that involved folding origami waves to memorialize victims of the tragedy, which were sold by the thousands for $1 each. Students at one Cal State campus sponsored charity bowling events. University of Michigan students organized three pallets of relief supplies.

Students at the Harvard Business School raised $40,000 by an Internet campaign. Baylor University students organized a "Bear the Burden" campaign, raising $58,000. Others organized pool parties, sold CDs and bracelets, and set up collection boxes at various places on campus. Many sent small teams of volunteers directly to the affected countries to help construct temporary shelters. Many more simply dedicated previously scheduled annual events to raising relief money.

No prior disaster yielded as deep or broad a response from the world of celebrity music and entertainment. Rock superstars as well as lesser-known bands produced songs and organized concerts. Steven Spielberg, Sandra Bullock, and Leonardo DiCaprio each made donations in excess of $1 million; Ellen DeGeneres donated a new car to be auctioned on eBay; and Jay Leno donated an autographed Harley-Davidson. Others donated gowns from famous TV sets for auction.

Also joining the effort was the professional sports community, from race car drivers to golfers to football players. The NFL and the NFL Players Association teamed up to raise awareness. Along with owners and fans, they raised $4 million. The New York Giants sent their quarterback and a wide receiver to Indonesia and then partnered with AmeriCares to raise funds at ballgames. Professional golf established the U.S. Golf Tsunami Relief Fund and teamed up with former Presidents Bush and Carter in a fundraising drive.

THE PRIVATE SECTOR PRE-EMINENT

The earthquake in the Indian Ocean also displayed a seismic shift in how emergency relief and development is being done. The private sector response of $1.6 billion far exceeded the $657 million in public monies appropriated by Congress. What's more, that figure understates the actual amount of private sector donations because it does not include the hundreds of millions that flowed into American NGOs from international donors, nor does it include amounts raised by religious congregations or denominations sent directly to partners on the ground.

Two decades ago, 70 percent of the resource flow to developing countries was official development assistance, whereas today, over 80 percent of all outflows come in the form of private philanthropy, remittances, and foreign direct investment. The accusation of American stinginess misses this point. Neither does it account for the full range of nonfinancial support that flows to the needy from American schools, universities, and religious organizations in the form of knowledge products, technology, and powerful NGO partnerships. The nonmaterial aid in response to the tsunami was as impressive as the cash donations. Thousands of volunteers left jobs and journeyed to the region, companies offered technical assistance and product donations, and congregations partnered directly with their own contacts on the ground.

BUSINESS BLURS BOUNDARIES

Like no other event, the tsunami disaster showed that future success in all areas of global development will require the use of creative partnerships between government and the private sector. Demonstrating just how powerful the trends in corporate citizenship have become, American businesses donated over $560 million in cash, products, and services, an unprecedented sum for a foreign disaster, with 130 major corporations giving over $1 million each. The next-highest showing of business support for disaster relief outside our borders was $70 million after Hurricane Mitch in 1998.

In today's globally connected "new economy," where speed and efficiency are at a premium, services and donated products and equipment frequently move faster to the front lines of a disaster through private delivery mechanisms than through the hierarchical world of bureaucracy. In some respects, both NGOs and businesses proved more nimble-footed than government in the initial response.

Companies also demonstrated that they have core competencies to bring to disaster assistance and reconstruction beyond making cash and in-kind donations. Companies with subsidiaries or partners in the region mobilized operating units, released employees whose expertise had previously been catalogued in volunteer databases, provided assistance in shipping and logistics, and helped restore communications services.

Some companies experimented with bringing an entire emergency response system into the region. For example, GE assembled a team within forty-eight hours of the tsunami that worked around the clock to provide clean, potable water. They deployed two 52-foot Mobile Water purification systems that assisted more than 220,000 tsunami victims. After ninety days of operating the system and producing 500,000 liters of fresh water daily, GE handed over ownership to the Indonesians.

Similarly, in addition to providing generous financial support through direct grants and employee matches, Motorola donated an estimated 1,600 mobile phones along with other equipment and technical assistance. HP supplied notebook computers, printers, and digital cameras that were used to identify victims and file insurance claims, and helped establish an IT infrastructure in Aceh, Indonesia.

Companies that engaged from a distance typically donated supplies and equipment that met a specific need on the ground, in addition to financial gifts.

Johnson & Johnson contributed antibiotics valued in the tens of millions, as did Pfizer. Abbott Laboratories provided drugs and other health care supplies. Baxter International provided nearly 200,000 units of IV fluid sets. Eli Lilly and Company provided supplies of insulin and antibiotics. Bristol-Myers Squibb donated $7 million worth of antifungal drugs and other medical supplies.

Transportation companies offered road, rail, and airlift assistance, including helicopters and heavy equipment. Ford provided $1.5 million in donated vehicles and Caterpillar provided moving equipment. FedEx offered free shipping of relief supplies.

Not to be outdone, business and trade associations mobilized their entire constituencies to help. The agriculture industry in North Dakota organized farmers to donate money from their spring crops. The National Association of Realtors sent mailers to its roughly one million members asking for donations to a disaster fund. The National Restaurant Association spurred its constituent members to organize benefit events such as "Desserts for Disaster Week" in New Mexico and Illinois, "Cooking for a Cause" in Massachusetts, and "Dine Out for Disaster Relief" in Maryland.

Some companies that played a direct role in the emergency relief phase extended their commitment into the reconstruction phase, sponsoring their own projects to rebuild schools and clinics, provide housing, and retrain workers. In Indonesia, a country with a rapidly expanding consumer market, businesses proved that corporate social responsibility and market development can go hand in hand. More and more companies understand that in order to develop markets they need to help build a more productive global workforce, which means promoting improvements in health and education.

BUSINESS AND NGOS: AMERICA'S CHIEF EXPORT

The sense of potential created in the business community by its experience with tsunami relief and recovery led the Business Roundtable to consider how to make a more enduring commitment to emergency preparedness in the private sector. The Roundtable started a new initiative, Partnership for Disaster Relief, for the purpose of integrating the capabilities of several business sectors—including health, technology, financial services, transportation, and communications—into one disaster-relief planning system. According to the Roundtable, the basic idea was to achieve better collaboration within the business community "across sectors, industries and borders" in order to ensure that the private sector's disaster preparedness is operating at full potential.

The tsunami response also demonstrated that civil society has become one of America's most consequential exports. U.S.-based voluntary organizations have proliferated over the past ten years and are delivering American democratic values, along with compassion, to the most remote and underdeveloped places on earth.

Gifts from the American people to their favorite NGOs have enabled organizations to make multiyear commitments to the disaster area, becoming in effect a private army delivering aid on behalf of the

American people. The number of NGOs in the worst-hit areas of Indonesia was so great that they were "overaided." From my travels in the region, it appeared that the ratio of private NGO workers to official development staff was easily twenty to one. Responding to the dominant presence of well-funded NGOs in the region, one government aid official commented to me: "They used to beg us for money; now we beg them for help in coordination."

While rebuilding communities and restoring livelihoods is the priority in places like Banda Aceh, NGOs are also a catalyst for democratic reforms and good governance. The influx of American and international NGOs has led to a mushrooming of local civil society organizations, which ensure that the Acehnese people have a strong voice in the reconstruction of their own communities. The result is an unprecedented experiment in village-based planning and participatory democracy. Empowered in this way, indigenous civil society becomes a powerful internal force for advancing human rights, building democratic institutions, and implementing new concepts in sustainable development. No amount of official lecturing on the importance of anticorruption standards compares to the impetus for transparency and accountability represented by hundreds of NGOs working with local civil society on the ground.

In both Indonesia and Sri Lanka, where governments had to cope with separatist rebellions, international and local civil society organizations worked together to encourage peace settlements. Not surprisingly, when reactionary elements moved to crack down on NGOs, local civil society spoke up to defend the presence of American NGOs.

Perhaps the greatest discovery of all after the tsunami is just how powerful the compassion of the American people is in the war to win hearts and minds. In a world where foreign policy professionals often appear helpless to curb a virulent anti-Americanism, the tsunami response proved that American citizens, working through their charities, schools, and congregations, are their own best ambassadors of good will. In Indonesia, the world's most populous Muslim nation, favorable opinion of America stood at 37 percent in early 2004. One year later, after America's great outpouring of compassion, 66 percent had a favorable opinion of America and a comfortable margin supported America's leadership in the war on terror.[8]

Speaking in Indonesia, Secretary of State Colin Powell referred to the impact that U.S. assistance was having in a country with a history of terrorism. In addition to meeting need, he said, this assistance is "in our best interest and it dries up those pools of dissatisfaction which might give rise to terrorist activity."[9] One leading expert on terrorism in the region commented on the many powerful images at work in America's rescue operation. The refrain, he said, was that the United States and the West are losing the war of ideas, especially in the Muslim world. Countering that perception were "images of U.S. helicopters bringing aid to places like Aceh, delivering something that insurgents can't."[10]

TESTING TRI-SECTOR COLLABORATION

America's response to the tsunami disaster is an inspiring story of a whole nation acting in compassion through its organizations and institutions, including government, business, and civic philanthropy. This response demonstrated the comparative advantage of the private sector in a variety of areas, for example, in how quickly and flexibly they could mobilize resources and get donations and personnel to the region. The success of companies in using their subsidiaries and supply chains and databases of employee experts will likely be studied and replicated.

While the tsunami response represented a high-water mark in American generosity, it also presented an invitation to focus on lessons learned, such as the need for collaboration among business, civil society, and government sectors. The relief and construction operation was a major test of public-private partnership, and also of how well business and NGOs can function together. The great bulk of the business relief money passed from corporate to nonprofit hands, and the working assumption has long been that the former give financial aid and the latter deliver it. These two sectors have not had the best of relationships. Due to a variety of factors, including mutual distrust and the emergence of business in a more direct role in the delivery of aid, the tsunami may have widened the gulf between business and NGOs.

Business has long been disinclined to coordinate with, much less place its money into, large mechanisms created by the U.S. government, the United Nations, or multilateral institutions. This has meant that donations generally do not go into government coffers where emergency officials on the ground can channel them. Many of the same attitudes are now being directed toward large charitable institutions that have not always had the best record of managing funds and are often seen as indistinguishable from the government itself. The private sector will always prefer working through private sector channels.

The tsunami disaster also displayed how the private sector response of both financial and in-kind donations can be somewhat piecemeal, leading to problems of coordination. Donations may not match a particular need, or they may not be distributed fairly and rationally across the affected area. In some cases they are unwelcome for cultural or practical reasons. With the private sector playing a dominant role, there are almost certain to be gaps, bottlenecks, and logistical challenges.

Another lesson is that in the rush to send checks to the front lines, far more money than needed may arrive in a particular area, and money may not be distributed rationally across needs or countries. Indonesia has some of the poorest rural regions in Asia, and many island provinces unaffected by the disaster were heard asking: "Does it take a tsunami to get emergency aid?" This kind of environment puts pressure on NGOs to stretch their missions or spend money on purposes beyond the scope of activity for which it was raised.

These are manageable challenges that are already being addressed. None of these factors significantly diminish the impact that the American private sector had on tsunami recovery and will likely have again in the future. Official government aid agencies will continue to welcome the money, brainpower, and technical products of business as well as the enormous energy and commitment of NGOs.

CHAPTER EIGHT

Conflict or Collaboration?
Religion and Democratic Civil Society

America will always stand firm for the non-negotiable
demands of human dignity: the rule of law; limits on the
power of the state; respect for women; private property; free
speech; equal justice; and religious tolerance. America will take
the side of brave men and women who advocate these values
around the world—including the Islamic world—because we
have a greater objective than eliminating threats and contain-
ing resentment. We seek a just and peaceful world beyond the
war on terror.

GEORGE W. BUSH
State of the Union Address, 2002

When it comes to the common rights and needs of men and
women, there is no clash of civilizations. The requirements of
freedom apply fully to Africa and Latin America and the entire
Islamic world. The peoples of the Islamic nations want and
deserve the same freedoms and opportunities as people in every
nation. And their governments should listen to their hopes.

GEORGE W. BUSH
Speech at West Point, June 2002

We are engaged in a struggle to defeat terrorism. I have no
advice on how to win that struggle, but I have some thoughts

as to why it exists. It is not, I think, because Islam is at war with the West or because Palestinians are trying to displace Israelis. The struggle exists, I think, because the West has mastered the problem of reconciling religion and freedom, while several Middle Eastern nations have not. Reconciling religion and freedom has been the most difficult political task most nations have faced.

JAMES Q. WILSON[1]

AMERICA'S PUBLIC DIPLOMACY challenge at this time permits no evasion of the topic of religion and culture as substantial factors in global affairs. But most career foreign policy officials today, not to mention the professors who taught them, were trained and have served during a time when religion could be relegated to the sidelines. For much of the twentieth century, American foreign policy was engaged in confronting the ideologies of Nazism or Soviet totalitarianism. In most elite institutions it was assumed that secularism would soon triumph over religion. That assumption no longer holds. Many of the regional conflicts and civil wars of the world today have something to do with religion.

Conversely, much of the best work on conflict prevention and reconciliation is influenced by religion, as is the most effective humanitarian work globally. Many of the world's worst humanitarian crises—involving malnutrition, human trafficking, HIV/AIDS, and persecution—are being boldly confronted by faith-based organizations. Those grass-roots civil society groups that are most effectively promoting sound development along with democracy and good governance throughout much of Asia, Africa, and Latin America are frequently inspired by a spiritual vision.

Yet while America is an exceptionally religious country, its foreign policy establishment has been deeply secular in outlook. Disposed by training as well as temperament toward the strictest notions of church-state separation, it is struggling to comprehend the influence of values, culture, and religion in world affairs. It has had neither the language nor the intellectual framework to deal with religion and culture abroad. This shortcoming has been a handicap particularly when it comes to the Islamic world, where religion permeates all aspects of life.

Many in the foreign policy establishment are uneasy about the notion of officially fostering alliances with moderate Muslim voices as a means of confronting Islamic extremism. Encouraging moderate Islam seems tantamount to promoting religion, which is something the U.S. government does not do.

Many would prefer to avoid the subject altogether. I was serving at USAID during the post-9/11 period, when there was a huge scramble to review and revise American programs operating in Muslim-majority countries. Lack of development was not the only or even the principal factor in the rise of Islamic terrorism, but promoting development was what we understood, so it was to development strategies that we turned.

Coordinating much of that work was an interagency planning team that took on the informal name "Engaging Islam." The name provoked debate about how appropriate it was for American officials to take an interest in matters of religion, not to mention the delicate matter of focusing on Islam. Some participants awkwardly suggested that perhaps we should consider *all* religions and their part in conflict. Others suggested making economic and political issues the focus. At the least, some strenuously argued, we should call it something other than "Engaging Islam."

But the name survived for the simple reason that to call it anything else would have been to live in denial of reality and to trivialize what Muslim spokesmen themselves said about their religion being taken hostage. The inescapable fact was that in the wake of 9/11, and with the global war on terrorism that followed, America's predominant problem was not with specific nation-states. The struggle, unlike perhaps any that had come before, was in fact with political Islam, or Islamism, a violent ideological movement driven by Islam's most extreme elements, who loudly announced their intentions to bring down America and the West.

Being religiously illiterate and insensitive has been a general hindrance in American foreign policy. When confronted with the menace of Muslim extremism, our foreign policy establishment often advocates official secularism, which is an understandable tendency. But promoting secularism as an alternative to officially supported Islam may be the least effective antidote to extremist thinking, because it only confirms the suspicion of many Muslims that America is antireligious generally and opposed to their religion in particular. Further complicating the matter are programs of the U.S. government that overtly attempt to modify Islamic practices in the area of women's rights, lifestyles, birth control, and the family—a policy which, not surprisingly, reinforces the perception among many Muslims that America is thoroughly secular, anti-Islam, and out to change their culture.

Religion was one of the most awkward issues for Americans to deal with in the early phases of the Iraq operation. Many of my colleagues could be heard talking enthusiastically about wanting to build "a secular Iraq," without appreciating what that term meant in Iraq, where well over 90 percent of the population were Muslims of various stripes.

For many Americans and for most American officials, "secularism" is a word with positive connotations, representing a host of democratic values that we cherish, including tolerance, pluralism, freedom of expression and assembly, and minority rights. For American officials, use of the term "secular" was comforting because it fit their view that religion is a personal matter, something to be compartmentalized and kept in its place. It meant that we would value the right to practice religion, as we do at home in the United States, but religion would remain wholly private, not a force for shaping society, much less the state.

But Iraqis by and large didn't see things that way. I remember meetings in which Iraqis registered visible irritation when the term "secular" was used. Even for those Iraqis who were comfortable using the word—for example, the Kurds and many secularly trained academics and officials in Baghdad—it didn't carry the same meaning as when Americans used it.

The Iraqi perception that America was interested in partitioning Islam off from the affairs of state made our job harder. Public pronouncements often contained references to our respect for Islam, but our official policy was committed to secularism. As we were eventually forced to conclude, this approach would never work in the thoroughly religious environment of the Middle East. Religion would be officially embraced; it was only a question of how.

On numerous occasions the issue of religion proved challenging to navigate. For example, it is commonplace for Muslim nations to have a Ministry of Religion, and this was true even under Saddam Hussein, who by all accounts was not especially friendly toward ardent Islamic belief, particularly if it got in the way of his power. As the postwar planning team gathered in Kuwait City during the five weeks it took for the Coalition military to liberate the country, every ministry was evaluated and had a team assigned to it except the Ministry of Religion. For several weeks before and after our arrival in Baghdad, the working assumption within our planning circles was that the Ministry of Religion would be made extinct. One career diplomat was heard whispering, "We don't do religion," suggesting indifference or hostility to religion and implying that Iraq was ours to remake in our own secular image. He further commented that, depending upon how things went, we might do away with the ministry altogether or subsume it within the Ministry of Culture. The implication was that religion fits under culture, not the other way around—a common approach to religion by American secularists.

To be fair, Americans were very reluctant as non–Muslims to be seen as wrongly using the Ministry of Religion and thereby causing offense. But as I listened in on conversations, just as great a factor was American hopes of planting a new secular state in the heart of the Muslim Middle East. An alternative approach to the Ministry of Religion might have been to place a well-respected Muslim American or Iraqi exile at the helm as a transitional measure and assign him to engage religious and other factions of Iraq to promote trust and reconciliation. Bringing the diverse and fractured tribes, ethnic groups, and religious factions together would probably not be possible by methods that were entirely secular.

The topic of religion hung over just about every discussion of what the new Iraq would look like. Would the constitution allow Islam to be merely one influence, or would the tenets of Islam hold veto power over all that conflicted with them? Clearly, the ultimate outcome of that debate would be highly consequential. Few Americans wanted to read that their investment of life and treasure to liberate the Iraqi people from oppression was resulting in a theocracy without minority rights or freedom of conscience. Most Iraqis did not want an Islamic state patterned after the one in Iran, with clerics as politicians and the mosque effectively running the state; but they did want an Islamic republic where all institutions are very accommodating of Islam.

We were surprised to discover that many of the most fervently devout Muslims were students of political philosophy, especially the young intellectuals around the Grand Ayatollah Ali al-Sistani. They had read Aristotle, Plato, Madison, and Jefferson. Many had their own Islamic sense of differentiating between the state and civil society, and of safeguarding religion from the kind of state abuses that often come with theocratic systems. Their thinking was not so far removed from the principles of America's own constitution, which, as founder John Adams stated, was "made for a moral and religious people and inadequate for any other."

If American officials were more alert to this philosophical affinity, they could reach back into their own history and recommend for translation and distribution a variety of Western texts on social and political philosophy—texts which, as Paul Marshall of Freedom House put it, treat "divine revelation and divine law as foundations for human freedom and human rights." By contrast, much of contemporary political thought in the West is antipathetic to religion in public life, which would likely alienate Muslims further.

Rather than promote secularism, a more palatable and potentially effective strategy would be to empower the more enlightened Islamic elements, while honoring and respecting Islam itself. There is a profoundly important debate going on within Islam that addresses the difference between separating mosque from state, on the one hand, and separating religion from society or politics, on the other. As many Islamic reformers will point out, the answer comes in embracing civil society, a public space that, unlike the state, is generally free of coercion. The outcome of this debate could affect Islamic practices, and in turn the political realities of the entire region, for decades to come.

As the experience with Iraq demonstrates, efforts to promote secular social and political results can be counterproductive. The United States will likely have to settle for a government ruled by parties that are at least nominally Islamic, hoping that those parties are inclined toward tolerance and pluralism.

HONORING ISLAM, CONFRONTING ISLAMISM

The greatest foreign policy challenge for America today is the need to confront the terrorist threat. Meeting this challenge requires a frank assessment of the enemy. While broad-based strategies to improve America's image and reputation abroad are likely to have some positive consequences, they will not make a significant dent in a terrorist threat that is rooted in radicalized Islam. That is a different challenge altogether.

Any effort by Americans to confront Islamic extremism must begin with an expression of respect for Islam and sympathy for those overwhelming majorities of the Muslim faithful who are not responsible for the destruction that is carried out in the name of their religion. For Christians or Jews who are slow to comprehend this point, they need only to imagine their response to hearing mention of their own religion in connection with extremism or terrorism on a fairly regular basis. Most people might prefer to avoid linking discussions of terrorism to the religion of Islam, but it is quite obvious that acts of violence are being perpetrated in the name of, and in obedience to, a particular vision of the Islamic faith.

While the enemy is not Islam itself, as must be repeated, the enemy does emerge from a deep conflict playing out within Islam. Robert Satloff of the Washington Policy Institute describes Islamic radicals, or Islamists, as "a relatively small but still sizeable, intensely ambitious, and disproportionately powerful subgroup of Muslims who do indeed hate 'who we are.'" At the deepest levels of belief and intention, they have declared themselves determined enemies of Western democratic values.[2]

Islamists, Satloff says, "reject modern notions of state, citizen, and individual rights and instead seek to impose a totalitarian version of Islam on peoples and nations around the globe." Within this group, there are subgroups who seek power through violent or revolutionary means and others who seek it through nonviolent or evolutionary means. According to Satloff, "while the former are unabashed terrorists, it is equally true that the latter can never be democrats."[3] These are not people who are likely to be influenced by more positive images of America or wonderful stories of American freedom at work. For them, Western-style freedom is the problem.

It will take all the resources of civilized society to defeat this group of sworn enemies. Richard Holbrooke, former under secretary of state, notes that while stopping terrorism must include first-rate intelligence and use of military force, the struggle is fundamentally a "war of ideas," which necessitates "a more aggressive, direct attack on those ideas, and the men behind them." Terrorism, Holbrooke says, constitutes a movement with "goals, gurus, ideologues, myths and martyrs," of which suicide bombers are "merely the expendable, deluded cannon fodder." Thus the counteroffensive must focus heavily on destroying the movement's myths and ideologies.[4]

Satloff agrees that the battle in which we are engaged with extreme Islam is fundamentally ideological and that much of our programming abroad could be counterproductive unless we realize as much. "Those who dismiss this as a public relations challenge and not a potentially cataclysmic life and death struggle are wrong," he asserts. The battle is "a fight being waged by Muslims against Muslims, within each society," even though "the United States cannot avoid its role as a central player."[5]

Because this is a battle within Islam, it is not, for the most part, work that governments can do on their own, except in aligning themselves with the right movements within civil society. As many people are learning, the possibilities for direct government action are very limited. Mark Leonard and Conrad Smewing point out that "Arab fear of western Islamophobia is so strong that even when western governments do positive things, they are presented as a threat." Consequently, "it is time to think big and involve millions of people across the region in people-to-people diplomacy rather than oiling the wheels of bilateral relations among authoritarian regimes."[6]

The U.S. government will need to rely upon partnerships with effective nongovernmental organizations that are on the front lines of promoting human rights, democratic reforms, and open societies. An example of this strategy at work is the recently created Middle East Partnership Initiative, funded at $129 million annually, to strengthen ties to indigenous organizations in Muslim and Arab societies, in some cases using U.S. civil society organizations and businesses.

But if more savvy public diplomacy is not a sufficient response to extremism, neither is an exclusive focus on building civic and democratic institutions. Those who promote civil society as a means of encouraging democratic objectives must admit that building institutions is not enough; it matters greatly what values take root in those institutions. In fact, Islamic extremism travels in large part via private voluntary associations, whether madrassas or corrupt Islamic "charities."

Much of our democracy programming abroad is geared toward building local institutions, with an emphasis on political parties, independent local journalism, and model parliaments. These are all important, but there are dangers in a simplistic focus on democracy. As Robert Satloff points out, "focusing on the abstraction of the institution rather than on the people who occupy that institution can lead to the absurd situation of U.S. funding of Islamist radicals—Islamist parliamentarians, Islamist educators, Islamist editors, and so forth." He concludes that "our outreach to Muslim societies should not be so fixated on form that it is blind to content."[7]

This leaves public diplomacy having to engage in multifaceted strategies, always with an eye toward defeating the ideas within extremist movements. Public diplomacy, according to Satloff, should continue to sharpen America's image and promote America's interests, but it must invest in "indentifying, nurturing and supporting allies," a strategy that becomes vastly more important in a post-9/11 environment where the critical new element is an ideological battle against extremism.[8]

Fighting an ideological war against Islamism may call for re-examining a variety of foreign assistance and development strategies adopted by the U.S. government. Satloff suggests that the need to win this ideological war is so great that we should concentrate on doing fewer things and doing them well. The government should leave traditional development activity such as health and clean water to other donors and channel our resources into education: "curricular reform, teacher and media training, schoolbook provision, new scholarship, English-language initiatives, and so on."[9]

Many will disagree with the idea of relinquishing traditional development activity—especially people like myself who have worked at USAID and see the value in humanitarian programming both for moral reasons and for improving perceptions of America. But Satloff is certainly right in saying that priorities need to be established.

DEVOUT MUSLIMS, DEVOUT CHRISTIANS: COLLABORATION OR CONFLICT?

The emergence of radical Islam onto the world stage on 9/11 was only the most dramatic manifestation of alien and threatening forces that had been gathering strength for decades but were mostly ignored. In fact, a thesis devoted to the centrality of culture (and religion) has been in circulation since the end of the Cold War, put forward by Professor Samuel Huntington of Harvard in *The Clash of Civilizations and the Remaking of World Order*, published in 1996. Huntington maintains that world divisions today are no longer rooted in the East vs. West ideologies that characterized the Cold War era; they are grounded more in ethnic and religious differences, with the West still overwhelmingly Christian, at least in its foundations, and the East predominantly Muslim.[10]

Huntington's "clash of civilizations" thesis, placing the epicenter of conflict at the intersection point of Islam and the West, gained wider acceptance after 9/11. But this analysis doesn't entirely capture the complexity of the dynamics. For one thing, the cultural divisions that separate the Muslim East from the more secular West have echoes within Western culture itself. An alternative view is that the major divide in the world today is not so much between different religions as between religious traditionalism generally and secular modernism. In other words, the religiously devout may have much in common when it comes to the social debates occurring around them.

Professor Philip Jenkins of Penn State, an expert on religion, remarks that secular analysis has long assumed that the religiously devout everywhere will eventually succumb to the challenges of secular dominance in the political, legal, and cultural spheres. In this conventional view, "traditional faith is under assault by the forces of modernity," and religious organizations will survive or fail depending upon their willingness to "come to terms with the modern world." Contrary to predictions, however, Jenkins sees a shift in what many assumed was the natural direction of history. It is secularism, he suggests, that "appears to be a beleaguered ideology, with faith in the ascendant." There is evidence that religion has gained adherents *because* of secularism's failure to provide order and meaning for society and its unrelenting assault on religion over the previous century.[11]

Paul Marshall remarks that 87 percent of the world's population professes some religious adherence, and that "the growth trend for Christians, Muslims and Hindus, as well as some small religions, is higher than the trend for global population as a whole." Both Islam and Christianity are making substantial gains around the world. Just as globalization has minimized national borders and broken down economic and cultural barriers, it has also reconfigured global religious dynamics. Yet few of the major books on globalization address the subject of religion and its impact on societies and nations. Thomas Friedman's popular book on globalization, *The World Is Flat*, gives no attention to religion. In Marshall's critique, "we do not face Thomas Friedman's choice between a Lexus and an olive tree; instead we face people who drive to their olive groves in Lexuses with religious symbols."[12]

The East vs. West framework for understanding religious conflict breaks down in view of how Christianity, once largely identified as Western and specifically European and American, is making its greatest gains in Africa and Latin America. Similarly, while Islam originated in the Middle East, it now claims majorities in fifty-two countries stretching from North Africa to Asia. With this geographic expansion comes a shift in social and cultural attitudes, as well as in global politics.

Philip Jenkins adds a North vs. South dimension to the East vs. West theory of conflict. On cultural and moral issues, he says, the older "religious ideologies of the west" are often closer to Western secularism than they are to the "newer religious ideologies emerging from the global south." As a prime example, he points to the tilt in vitality and influence within the Anglican Communion from Europe to Africa, where social attitudes and beliefs are far less accommodating of the secular ethos of Europe. The secularizing tendencies of the recent past in Europe and America are facing resistance from new religious movements in the Southern Hemisphere.[13]

Many people, especially secular analysts, assume that the most basic conflict is between Christianity and Islam. When a natural antipathy is taken for granted between devout Muslims and devout Christians, the possibility for Christian-Muslim dialogue and collaboration seems remote. Among the more extreme Muslim elements there is clearly a deep hostility toward all Americans, including religious believers. But evidence suggests that all but the radical fringe of Muslims respect sincere believers in other faiths, especially Christians, even though Muslims rarely get positive images of religious faith from the American entertainment industry.

A surprising reality is that Americans with traditional religious inclinations may have less in common with the secular materialism of their own cultural elite than with the values of moderate, peace-loving Muslims. The potential exists for better Muslim-Christian relations for the simple reason that each group holds a sacred as opposed to a secular worldview. Theological differences are often played up in a way that eclipses the common ancestry of Islam and Christianity in the Abrahamic tradition of the Old Testament. In other words, Christians and Muslims are essentially first cousins, who may have more natural affinity than might be possible with other belief systems such as Buddhism or Hinduism.

Sibling relationships can be characterized by warm regard or by the most intense rivalry, as Philip Jenkins and Paul Marshall observe in an essay titled "Sibling Rivalry among the Children of Abraham: Global Conflict and Cooperation between Islam and Christianity." Jenkins and Marshall acknowledge that the border between Islam and Christianity "is obviously one of the world's dangerous places," and warn that if "the 'siblings' cannot learn to get on with each other, prospects for the future are very disturbing." Of the twenty-five most populous nations, twenty will be either Christian or Muslim or some mixture of the two religions. As many as eleven of these countries will have a majority that is either Christian or Muslim, with a substantial minority of the other faith. If these populations "cannot learn to maintain a civil relationship between the two faiths, the likelihood of future violence and warfare is alarming," say Jenkins and Marshall.[14] They suggest that both faiths take a deeper interest in simply knowing more about the other in hopes of discovering the shared aspects of their history. "For so many reasons," they state, "the two religions should be working together—they have so many natural affinities."[15]

Often overlooked is how key elements of the Christian story are woven into Islam. Few Christians know, for example, that Jesus receives respectful treatment in the Koran, although never rising to the level of divinity as in Christian belief. The Koran says that when the last day comes, it is Jesus whose appearance will usher in Armageddon. For Muslims, Jesus is the greatest prophet of Islam apart from Mohammed. The figure of Christ rarely presents a barrier to Christian-Muslim conversation, and can actually aid it. Although Islam clearly does not recognize the Old and New Testaments as authoritative, Christians can nevertheless find in the Koran, as Marshall and Jenkins put it, "old friends on every page." There are stories of Moses, Aaron, John the Baptist, and Jesus, while Mary gets more attention in the Koran than in the New Testament.[16] The Koran presents Christians as the "nearest among men in love to the Muslims, because amongst them are men devoted to learning and men who have renounced the world, and they are not arrogant."

While many Muslims are quick to criticize the vulgar and materialistic tendencies of American society, they also recognize that America is home to some of the most religiously devout citizens, however incongruous that may seem. According to Mustafa Akyol, "Muslims who recognize this fact make a distinction between 'righteous Westerners' and other ones."[17] Akyol offers as evidence this statement from a popular Muslim website called The Final Jihad: "Western secular materialism takes us from our prayers, takes us from our Islamic culture . . . gives us a society of crime, violence, drug abuse, alcoholism, prostitution, pornography, homosexuality, exploitation of the people and resources, and reduces life to a meaningless exercise in futility." But rather than issue a blanket condemnation of the West, the website makes a clear distinction: "It is important to realize that many good people in Western nations are trying to live right. . . . These people are not our enemy; they also are victims of Western secular materialism."[18]

The problem, says Akyol, is that not enough Muslims know much about America beyond what they "see . . . through its materialist pop culture." Thus when "Western ideas" are mentioned, "many Muslims do not think about Jefferson, C. S. Lewis, Lincoln, or Burke, but rather of Nietzsche, Freud, Marx, and Carl Sagan."[19] Akyol and numerous other Muslims recommend that American policymakers work harder at trying to convince Muslims that much of Hollywood's portrayal of American life in film and television is simply not representative of society at large. In particular, if more Muslims knew about the many Americans who are religiously devout, their opinion would be more favorable.

At the present time, Akyol says, Muslim radicals who want to attack America "have to de-Christianize it" in their own minds first, "and this is exactly what they do—with a big assist from the entertainment and news media of the United States itself." [20] While it is true that Muslims in parts of the world are attacking local Christians and preaching hatred toward Christians and Jews, the extremist ideology that fuels this violence grows in large part from a general hatred of American cultural influence as a threat to Islam.

Just how difficult might it be to forge stronger sympathies between these "cousin religions," and how might that be facilitated? There are obstacles, to be sure. Both Islam and Christianity are proselytizing faiths, and to varying degrees resist allowing the other to seek converts across the religious divide. Muslims are known to raise strong barriers against any kind of proselytizing among their members. Islam has a different concept of political community, with religion going much further in shaping the state than most Christians would support.

Muslims know too little about real Americans, and most Americans have a distorted view of the social attitudes and beliefs of Muslims. Each assumes that the mutual distrust is rooted in religious differences alone. But a shared religious worldview may in fact provide for common ground on issues of ethics and morality. Illustrations of this commonality can be found at the United Nations and at world conferences, where Evangelicals, Catholics, and Muslims frequently express similar views on issues such as family planning, AIDS, and genetic engineering.

During my work at USAID and in the Middle East, I had many unforgettable conversations about values with Iraqi Muslims. Wherever you go in the Middle East, it doesn't take long to appreciate that

Arabs and Muslims take family life and the elaborate rituals, holidays, and symbols associated with it very seriously. On many occasions in Iraq, conversation turned immediately to children and how to protect them.

In one such conversation, the Iraqi expressed his worries about corrupting influences on youth that were coming into their once tightly controlled community. What was striking to me was how his concerns so closely paralleled the concerns voiced by parents in traditional communities in America. I informed my Muslim friend that when I returned to the United States, I would arrange for him to visit Washington on official business, and on the weekend I would take him out to an Amish farm near the community where I was raised in Lancaster, Pennsylvania. I also made the prediction that within five minutes of their meeting, the Muslims and the Amish would be sympathetically sharing stories about how difficult it was for traditionally minded people to shield their families from the worst of the surrounding culture. This happened just as I predicted. There was no evidence that religious differences were a factor at all in that encounter.

I had the pleasure of hosting Iraqi delegations who came for official business and to visit America. In each case, Iraqis reported being overwhelmed by the commitment to work, faith, and family they found among Americans, and they didn't seem to notice that most Americans' faith was not the same as their own. When Christians and Muslims encounter each other, they often find that as human beings they have at least as much in common as in conflict.

ISLAM AND DEMOCRATIC CIVIL SOCIETY: ARE THEY COMPATIBLE?

The debate over religion and democracy may be somewhat recent, but the role of religion in shaping civilizations of East and West alike is well known. It should thus be unsurprising that the most pivotal force in the next phase of Arab and Islamic-world development is Islam. Attitudes about the most basic foundations of society, such as the life of the mind and the role of knowledge, the place of reason and revelation, freedom and pluralism, the individual and community, work and profit-seeking, are all deeply shaped by religion.

The forces that drive nations to either succeed or stagnate, to chose modernization or reaction, are linked directly to religious attitudes. Most historians acknowledge that both religion and science contributed to the success of Western civilization. But Christian culture had its Dark Ages, when religion and science, revelation and reason were in conflict, while religion and the state were too closely joined. New possibilities opened up in the West when reason and scientific progress were no longer considered antithetical to religion, and the pursuit of knowledge outside of religious dogma was affirmed. Another highly consequential development occurred in the West when work and vocation were described by theologians as having sacred value. As Max Weber showed in *The Protestant Ethic and the Spirit of Capitalism*, industry and the pursuit of wealth received enormous encouragement from reform movements within Christianity.

Similar issues are now being debated throughout the Islamic world. Many participants in those debates take a skeptical view of democracy's prospects in the Middle East. In the lead-up to the liberation of Iraq, many voices where heard remarking that there wasn't even a good Arabic translation for the word "freedom," a term that would define and justify the mission and was emphasized in its name, "Operation Iraqi Freedom." Neither is there in many Muslim countries a good translation for "citizen" or "referendum" or, for that matter, "democracy." Skeptics point out that the Middle East as a region is generally authoritarian, lacks a middle class, has had no recent experience with rule of law, and hasn't had a functioning model of democracy for 1,500 years.[21]

Debates over prospects for democracy in the Middle East have produced "a river of ink," says Professor Richard Norton of Boston University, with most observers seeing little chance of major advances for democracy in the immediate future. To the factors impeding progress already listed, Norton adds a set of "culturally imbedded" practices. These include tribal patronage that undermines popular participation in politics, the habit of "governments rich with oil buying off dissent," and Islamist movements that "deride democracy" but enjoy impressive popular support.[22]

Nevertheless, says Norton, "the pressures for change are formidable, and regional rulers intent on survival may find political reform irresistible." The region, he believes, is on the brink of "a momentous era of change," ushered in by powerful new forces of democratic civil society.[23] Norton predicts that a highly consequential struggle will ensue as naturally evolving communications and civil society networks force authoritarian governments to permit greater openness.

If a case for hope exists, it is usually grounded in the emergence of civil society as a seedbed for democratic reform. It is civil society that is becoming the principal means for opening up closed systems. Moreover, if channels for dialogue are going to be established within Islamic communities as well as with the West, the only available avenue, it is reasoned, may be through civil society. But strategies that rely on the expansion of civil society will be fruitful only to the extent that civil society can take root within the framework of Islamic faith and daily life. The Western idea of civil society, according to Jillian Schwedler, "applies itself incongruously to the Middle East for reasons involving history, religion and culture."[24]

For the West, civil society is generally regarded as the antidote to closed political systems, because by definition it involves space for uncoerced human association and action independent of the state, and even functions as a limit on the state. In America especially, civil society is thought of as prior to the state, as a voluntary order of life that restricts the dominance of government. Furthermore, the term connotes tolerance, pluralism, and free association.

Although the European view of civil society is more as an adjunct to the state, the American model gained ground following the Velvet Revolution inside Eastern Europe, when civil society movements proved instrumental in throwing off communist regimes. There is evidence that this concept of civil society—one that has the heft to resist repressive regimes—also gained currency in Muslim states across Southeast Asia and in the Middle East at the same time, and further with the debate that 9/11 precipitated.

In the post-9/11 environment, a veritable cottage industry of reform-minded initiatives emerged, including think tank projects, councils, and centers for the study of Islam and civil society. New organizations were founded by Muslims to promote discussion within Islam and to sponsor dialogue with non-Muslims, especially among the Islamic diasporas in the United States and Europe. Most Arab reformers assume that strengthening civil society movements within predominantly Muslim countries would, at a minimum, strengthen the pro-reform position of moderates. The longer-term hope is that civil society can serve as an incubator of democratic values such as pluralism and tolerance, and possibly become a building block for democracy itself.

Recognizing that Arab states will be slow to embrace democratic reforms if they are regarded as alien to the Islamic faith, Muslim reformers have focused much of their discussion on whether the principles of democracy are compatible with Islamic theology. There could be no more consequential debate than the one within Islam over this basic question. The main arena for this debate is not at conference tables where moderate Muslims and Western intellectuals gather, but on the streets and inside the mosques, where such theological matters are addressed each day.

Mosques may support or resist change, but they are one of the few institutions that authoritarian states cannot really touch. Whereas "independent parties, associations and clubs have been stifled by state controls," explains Richard Norton, "the mosque is much more difficult to police." While it is easy to outlaw a party, "the Muslim state can no more shut down a mosque than a North American or European government can lock the doors of a church."[25]

When government impedes the creation of autonomous forms of association such as political parties, unions, and professional groups, it cedes civil society ground to Islamic organizers. By refusing to allow populist dissent to be aired openly within civil society, Arab states inadvertently contribute to the domination of dissent by Islamists inside the mosques. But when the state opens up public space, "the blossoming of civil society, even if inchoate, is impressive," says Norton, and given the opportunity to mature, "these organizations not only lend vitality to experiments in open government but serve as counterweights to populist movements such as the Islamists." [26]

The development of civil society must be seen as a "gradualist endeavor," according to Norton. It will likely be aided by a variety of factors over which Islamic communities have only limited control, and all of which tend to introduce a measure of pluralism. Chief among these factors are greater access to modern communications technologies, which "inherently undermine vertical structures of control." [27] The proliferation of cybercafés, printing presses, and photocopy machines offers access to information beyond what is supplied by government-run publications. Another force of change operating in the Muslim world is the increased migration of people away from rural enclaves that have been essentially cut off from the outside world. Villagers and city dwellers traveling across borders in search of work "return with fresh images that often reflect poorly on the quality of life at home," says Norton, and they have more money "to support protest movements and collective self-help organizations." [28]

These forces will play a significant role in opening up closed Islamic societies. But the "gradualist endeavor" will also need to take into account the complexities of Islamic history, teaching, and experience.

Islam today is anything but a monolith. There are many schools of Islamic thought, and, unlike Catholicism or even Protestant denominations in the United States, there is no hierarchy or central place of authority. Thus the most basic challenge for American policy officials and institutions that wish to engage Islam positively is knowing whom to engage. "You can't understand the future direction of Islam without understanding who speaks for Islam," says Luis Lugo, an expert on religion. "Questions of legitimacy and authority bear on a wide array of policy issues facing the U.S. in its relations with the Muslim world—issues such as democracy, reform, public diplomacy and the battle against terrorism."[29]

In the earliest period of Islam, the governing idea was a single leader of all Muslims, but this idea had died off by the end of the ninth century A.D., according to Professor Roy Mottahedeh of Harvard. Divergent schools of thought emerged as clerics became freer to develop their own followings. This new class of religious experts, the *ulama*, "divided itself into certain discrete schools of law," with divergent teachings on matters of policy and practice The *ulama* attempted to maintain a measure of unity within Islam by preserving the uniformity of ritual observance.[30]

Of the world's major religions, Islam is probably the most decentralized, with wide theological divisions on matters such as the relationship of religion to the state and civil authority. Another division concerns the extent to which Islam should govern unbelievers as well as believers. Islamic doctrine can be used to justify capitalism or socialism, militancy or accommodation, ecumenism or exclusivism.[31]

Those who hope to encourage a renaissance in the Islamic world will need to give careful consideration to the tendencies within Islam that accounted for both the ascent and the decline of Islamic civilization in history. Scholars have wrestled with the riddle of why Islam produced an early flowering in all facets of life, including science and technology, commerce and higher learning, and why it later yielded social stasis and economic underdevelopment. Why have Muslim societies been slow to industrialize, and why does the Islamic world remain so poor in spite of its oil wealth?[32]

According to Bernard Lewis, the noted scholar of Islamic societies, "there is nothing in Islamic doctrine to oppose economic progress, though there is much in the social and legal practices of Muslims that needs careful reconsideration from this point of view." In early Islam, he says, leaders, intellectuals, and theologians were more or less free to develop answers to society's problems left unresolved by scripture and tradition. That freedom resulted in broad innovation, which became an engine for economic growth, and a fluidity of opinion on matters of commerce and experimentation. By the eleventh century, however, freedom of innovation and independent judgment were deemed impermissible.

The main barrier to progress in the Islamic world, says Lewis, was a system of education for the leadership class that taught people to embrace a finite set of ideas and information, rather than to "use their own judgment, exercise their critical faculties, and decide things for themselves."[33] In this view, Islam itself at least played a role in legitimizing these growth-inhibiting attitudes. Before long, education outside of religious instruction was devalued, while critical thinking and problem solving gave way to rote learning and memorization.[34] The result was a society-wide discouragement of inquisitiveness and invention in favor of social stability. If the objective is stability, numerous obstacles are likely to be placed in the path of modernization. In the post-Ottoman era, stagnation may also have been a consequence of regimes resisting development in order to preserve their power.

The narrowing of acceptable fields of inquiry within Islamic culture is perhaps the main explanation for a lack of development in the area of political theory. Specific teachings about public matters were absent in early Islam, writes Professor Mottahedeh, and a lot of the *ulama* were "incredibly quietistic," believing that religious doctrine was designed to foster piety in the believer but indifference to, and even separation from, the affairs of state. This view left open a "de facto secular sphere."[35]

This deficit in political theory was the vacuum into which literalist Islamic schools would eventually move. For example, many scholars have observed that the Wahhabi school, founded in the mid-eighteenth century, advanced unchecked for a long time because of the prevailing quietism around it. Wahhabism declares anyone who rejects Islamic monotheism to be an "unbeliever," and in some cases rejects the notion of logic. It holds the Koran to be the purest and fullest expression of God's will on earth, supplying all necessary answers to questions of conduct and governance. Wahhabism has thrived in part because of financial backing from Saudi Arabia. As Professor Mottahedeh explains, this school supplied "a succession of people leading up to Osama Bin Laden."

For reform movements to succeed today, they will need to confront the Wahhabi Muslims who "have the microphone" and are intent on projecting their vision of Islam not only onto all Muslims but onto the non-Islamic world as well. Reformers will need to challenge the wide perception created by Wahhabi elements that religion and government are necessarily united, and that the job of government is to enforce Islamic law on everyone—even though this was not the Muslim view for much of the religion's history.

Those who wish to plant the seeds of reform in the Muslim world will need to search Islam's Golden Age to find again the basis for intellectual development and freedom of conscience and association. The Islamic age of innovation was also an era of robust civil society, according to Imad-ad-Dean Ahmad. "The great achievements in the sciences, medicine, agriculture, urban growth, and international relations of all sorts were underpinned by a successful infrastructure that included that third sector," separate from the state. Many of the major institutions had independent charters and were not controlled by the state, and they received big endowments from financial institutions. Ahmad finds similarities between the civic and educational institutions of early Islam and the private foundations that play such a vital role in funding Western civil society today.[36]

The important question concerns what form an Islamic civil society will likely take. The Wahhabi example is evidence that civil society can be used for illiberal purposes. In a culture where even mainstream thought tends toward the unity of all human order, civil society can be used to encourage a return to traditional forms of solidarity against the forces of democratization and innovation.

Can liberal civil society find a home in Islam or is it alien to a religious system that is inherently and incorrigibly illiberal? Some argue the latter. An essay on civil society in relation to Islam published by the Institute of Islamic Political Thought maintains that the term "civil society," like "democracy" and "secularism," is an "intruder to Islamic political thought."[37] Others point out that civil society has always existed within Islam, although with a decidedly less pluralistic and tolerant cast than in the West. The broad assumption among scholars and Muslim observers is that Islamic civil society will follow its own path and not necessarily that of the West. As Jillian Schwedler remarks, the Western idea of civil society "applies itself incongruously to the Middle East for reasons involving history, religion and culture."[38]

Even so, both the early Islamic period and more recent experience in the Islamic world offer evidence that civil society and modernization may go hand in hand, and may draw from the same religious sources. Why, for example, are certain predominantly Muslim nations in Asia thriving socially, economically, and politically? There is much to be learned from the patterns of development found today in Islamic states of Southeast Asia, such as Indonesia and Malaysia, where civil society is identified with promoting rapid transformation of states and economies. The working assumption in these countries, according to Norani Othman, has been that development and modernization would bring "an attendant push within their societies for greater political liberalization and democratization." There is also evidence that civil society may function as a basis of social harmony and cohesion in countries such as Malaysia and Indonesia where Muslims constitute a majority but must live cooperatively with other faiths in multiethnic cultures.[39]

Understanding the possibilities of Islamic civil society requires distinguishing civil society as espoused by Westerners and even Arab secularists from the notions of society that emerge out of Islam. Ernest Gellner, a leading expert on civil society, defines Western notions of civil society as entailing "diverse non-governmental institutions which are strong enough to counterbalance the state" but do not prevent the state from "fulfilling its role of keeper of the peace and arbitrator between major interests."[40] By contrast, the Muslim world displays a strong tendency to establish a strict community that operates over all "based upon the shared faith and the implementation of its law."[41]

The most enduring concept of Islamic society, says Gellner, is "seg-mentary communities." The Islamic notion of community may pro-duce an identity that is distinct from central authority but which nevertheless firmly embeds the person in a tight social subunit. It may be a civil society that resists centralized power but still restricts indi-vidual freedom.[42]

In other words, the strictest interpretation of civil society can mean just another form of Islamic polity, in which all human activity is guided by religious doctrines. According to Chandra Muzaffar, civil society is roughly translated as "a vision of a polity of virtue guided by belief in God and based upon values rooted in the Divine—values such as justice, equality, freedom, compassion and dignity." This is civil society that operates under authority rather than the kind that embodies Western values of freedom and autonomy.

Some devout Muslims would argue that Muslim civil society can and will thrive once it is properly defined by a distinct Islamic vision. In a much-discussed speech on civil society to a 1979 Islamic Summit Conference in Tehran, Mohammad Khatami, then president of Iran, called on Muslims everywhere to dedicate themselves to "the realiza-tion of 'Islamic civil society.'" It would be "fundamentally different from the civil society rooted in Greek philosophical thinking and Roman political tradition," he said. It would be a homogeneous civil society "centered around the axis of Islamic thinking and culture," and embodying "the soul and collective memory of Muslims."[43]

Khatami went on to say that the two divergent concepts of civil society "need not be entirely in conflict and contradiction," and that Muslims "should never be oblivious to judicious acquisition of the positive accomplishments of the Western civil society."[44] Muslims could "live in peace and tranquility with other peoples and nations," but only after "taking abode in this common home." Neither would Muslims have to withdraw from the modern world. In fact, Islamic civil society would entail dialogue with other societies that enjoy a right to self-determination.

To a limited extent at least, this vision of civil society would cultivate such values as creativity, innovation, and independence. The goal was to enjoy Islam's "treasures and its doctrinal and intellectual traditions" along with a "sophisticated scientific and philosophical understanding of the modern world." The picture that emerges here is of a "thick" civil society strongly informed by Islam, which becomes "thinner" and more accommodating of divergent views as it engages with the wider world.[45]

Many Muslims would endorse a notion of civil society that, although less heterogeneous than the Western model, nevertheless mediates between the state, on the one hand, and the individual or the family on the other, and encourages self-sufficiency and independence from the state through education and enterprise. This vision of Muslim civil society was presented at an Arab-world symposium in Beirut: "Civil society as we understand it is the sum of the political, economic, social and cultural institutions that act each within its own field independently of the state to achieve a variety of purposes." The statement went on to define the range of those purposes to include political activity such as party participation, vocational purposes such as "those served by the trade unions to uplift the standard of professions and defend the interests of union members," cultural purposes such as those advanced by "unions of writers and cultural societies," and social purposes that promote development.[46]

Some Muslim leaders ask what is wrong with encouraging the development of civil society in their own way. After all, they aren't Westerners and shouldn't be forced to become such. Why, they ask, must Arab civil society conform to the demands of Western liberal thought in order to be respected? After all, Western liberal thought has its own faults, such as favoring individualism and devaluing the sacred, thus undermining social cohesion.

More secularized voices in the Arab world will challenge the idea that the Islamic community, or *Ummah*, must necessarily be so thoroughly shaped by religion. The concept of *Ummah*, they say, can be interpreted broadly to include other forms of social identity, based on voluntary cooperation rather than coercion. Such notions as freedom of religious conscience, expression, and affiliation appear to be making inroads among moderate reform-oriented Muslims, especially in the West. The more Muslims are exposed to real-world experience with religious pluralism and the benefits of peaceful coexistence, the more likely it will be that principles of tolerance and freedom of conscience take root in Islamic society.

The relationship of citizens to the state is a central issue in any effort to promote more liberty and openness in Islamic countries. By creating opportunities for individuals to exchange opinions and take collective action in the community, civil society may be the first and most essential step toward democracy. As Imad-ad-Dean Ahmad put it, "the history of democracies in the world suggests that a meaningful democracy cannot exist without a separate healthy functioning civil society that lies outside the political sphere, although it may interact with it." [47] But ultimately, for citizens to be politically empowered, the gap between civil society and political society must be narrowed.

In various Middle Eastern states, such as Morocco and Jordan, the emergence of an institutionalized and robust civil society has led to modest but steady progress toward political liberalization. Civil society was the means by which reform movements produced breakthroughs in human rights and eventually achieved political parties and elections in countries ranging from Turkey to Bangladesh, Malaysia, and Indonesia. In addition to their other functions, civil society organizations cultivate skills in democratic participation and promote values such as tolerance.

Civil society may provide the most realistic foundation for building democracy in Muslim nations. Yet democratization experts maintain that civil society is ultimately not enough. It is not the responsibility of civil society to control or direct the state; that job falls to political parties, candidates, and elections. Ivan Doherty of the National Democratic Institute warns that embracing "the development of civil society as a means of apolitical involvement in the internal politics of a country fails to recognize the limitations of such an approach." In fact, says Doherty, there is "grave danger" in encouraging civil society without a simultaneous effort to build reform-oriented political parties. "Strengthening civic organizations, which represent the demand side of the political equation, without providing commensurate assistance to the political organizations that must aggregate the interests of those very groups, ultimately damages the democratic equilibrium." [48]

Citing the experience of Morocco, Doherty insists that an abundance of "advocacy and citizen action groups" does not necessarily ensure that good governance actually occurs. Thousands of NGOs and advocacy groups had been active in Morocco for years, "but it was not until the development of political parties and their acceptance into the governing process that change occurred." While civil society "played a central role in bringing about these changes," he says, "it was the commitment of the political parties and their leaders that gave them effect." [49]

If freedom is to be advanced, it will come in small increments as the subjects of closed systems discover citizenship and begin making demands for liberalization from within. The means by which individuals join together to reform their governments is through the voluntary networks and associations of civil society.

fault of a single administration, but reflects deficiencies in the entire American foreign policy establishment dating back decades. The fact is that prior to 9/11, a foreign policy career in the Arab and Muslim world was not the path to diplomatic power or stardom because the focus of foreign policy for half a century was Soviet-backed totalitarianism.

The consequences became painfully obvious in the planning and execution of the liberation of Iraq. There were far too few country specialists available and far too few who spoke fluent Arabic. I rarely met a person who actually knew a lot about Iraq. Ambassador Paul Bremer was at least honest about his degree of knowledge, admitting openly upon his arrival in Baghdad that he knew very little about the country. The team managed to attract a few former ambassadors to the region, and they at least had some awareness of Muslim sensibilities and Arab ways. But that was pretty much the extent of it. Those of us who were planning the postwar reconstruction spent a lot of time reading intelligence reports, which were often disappointing.

Established relationships inside Iraq were largely nonexistent, owing largely to the closed nature of the totalitarian state under Saddam. The knowledge most of us acquired about the country was paper knowledge, not shaped by in-depth experience in Iraq. At the time of the invasion, all the frontline agencies—including the State Department, the CIA, and numerous others—were urgently trying to recruit and train more Arabic-speaking Muslim-world specialists.

If the official community was thin on Arab-world expertise, the American people knew even less. Most Americans have never met a visitor from the Arab Middle East. Nor is it likely that the vast majority of Muslims and Arabs have ever met an ordinary American. Their attitudes and opinions of America are a composite of various elements: bias fed by anti-American parties and politicians within Islamic countries, ugly images fed by the Arab-world media, images of vice and vanity from America's own popular culture, and a never-ending stream of rumors drifting around in a "whisper down the lane" local culture—all producing a near-paranoia about what America's nature and purposes actually are. What they encounter is the least appealing reflection of our nation.

From my experience, anti-Americanism is born of three things: one, disagreement with American policy; two, a natural suspicion, if not resentment, of America's global military, political, and economic power; and three, disdain for the worst aspects of American popular culture. Americans are understandably proud of their political and economic successes and are pleased to see American values exported. However, we often naively assume that what is being exported is our democratic values, respect for human rights, and entrepreneurial free enterprise, when what is increasingly viewed abroad as our dominant product is a popular culture that many regard as crass and tasteless. When many Muslims hear of American values, it is not Jefferson or Lincoln that come to mind, but rather a popular culture that makes Americans look vulgar and vain in the eyes of many abroad. The most toxic elements of American culture—the supercharged sexuality and the senseless violence—are arguably the chief factors thwarting efforts to export American values.

The Gallup organization has taken an interest in the huge gulf between the West and Islamic countries. A number of negative perceptions surfaced having to do with power: Muslims labeled America as arrogant, ruthless, and biased. But the more steeply negative attitudes had to do with our culture. According to Gallup, "the respondents have a deep-seated disrespect for what they see as the undisciplined and immoral lifestyles of people in Western nations." The report continued, "The disapproval extends not just to the sexual and violent content in movies and music, but respondents also hold the view that the West embodies the concept of an inappropriately relaxed culture, and that the West has lost respect for its own traditions and religion, extending even to a lack of respect for its elders."[3]

American officials are inclined to downplay, if not entirely dismiss, the complex political, historical, and cultural factors that play into the Arab world's alienation from America. Certainly America's friendship with Israel and its alleged imbalance in the Israeli-Palestinian conflict are factors, and America's relationship to the Arab people today would be nominally better without that complication. But there are a variety of other factors over which we have only limited control, including a history of foreign intervention and an unhealthy dependence by America's economy on the region's oil supplies.

Some of the negativity is a byproduct of America's overwhelming power in the world. Fairly or not, America is often seen as a bully. On a trip to Indonesia to finalize military cooperation with the world's most populous Islamic country, Secretary of Defense Donald Rumsfeld was lectured by the Indonesian defense minister about America's approach. The defense minister said: "As the largest Muslim country, we are very aware of the perception that the United States is over-bearing, over-present and overwhelming in every sector of life in many nations and cultures."[4]

The intentions of any unrivaled power operating in the Arab or Islamic world are bound to be viewed with suspicion. Russia, it must be recalled, had an extremely harsh reception in Afghanistan and was eventually ejected. Britain, which took upon itself the task of trying to cobble together Iraq as a modern nation-state in the aftermath of the Ottoman Empire's collapse, had troubles that bear an eerie resemblance to the circumstances that Americans and their allies faced in 2003. It is generally a tough region for foreign powers to operate in, especially a superpower suspected of having mostly selfish reasons for being there.

There is widespread suspicion that Americans don't like Arabs, and that whatever we may say about our interest in the Arab people, our words only gloss over our government's real objectives, which are perceived to be about safeguarding our supply of oil and protecting Israel. Even the agenda of bringing democracy to the region may be seen as merely the latest and perhaps cleverest version of an American power play.

Rather than appreciate the deeper realities of Middle East politics and social dynamics, American officials in recent years have instead treated anti-American attitudes as largely a public relations problem.

In my years of work in the foreign policy arena, I attended innumerable meetings involving legions of young, energetic staff who did what good press people do in response to a problem—work even harder and more creatively at getting their message out.

Frequently, the starting assumption of U.S. policymakers is that our positions and policies are unassailably in the best interest of the Arab people but they just don't understand it or haven't been properly informed. We conclude that either we aren't trying hard enough to get the message out, or that there must be some nefarious forces at work sabotaging the transmission lines. So the discussion is about managing messages and getting better access to media outlets.

Getting our message out more effectively is not unimportant. We would be foolish not to engage our embassies more creatively in better strategies of public diplomacy. We would be derelict not to avail ourselves of the proliferating media outlets in the Arab world, including TV and radio, the Web, bloggers, and numerous other venues for presenting factual information on American policy and interests.

After all, the business of diplomacy is to use official channels to convey U.S. policy objectives and interests. But to the Arab public, the least credible or persuasive source of information may be anyone representing our official government establishment. Finding the right messenger, and in some cases relying on indirect means of communicating, is vastly more important than just getting the message right.

It is very easy to get this wrong. We Americans are very confident in promoting our democratic system and our way of life. What we often fail to appreciate is that while most people around the world respect our democratic institutions and dynamic economic system in broad terms, there are a lot of details they would rather do without. Many people in traditional cultures, if informed that they could have our prosperity and free-wheeling lifestyles if only they would trade in their strong families and time-honored patterns of life, would respectfully decline the offer.

A policy of just talking can be counterproductive if we are oblivious to deeply ingrained attitudes about America's shortcomings as well as its strengths, and if it appears that we are talking down to the Arab world, as we often do. In many cases, we would do well to abandon talking strategies and spend a lot more time listening. The announcement of just such a policy by Karen Hughes, the high-profile under secretary of state for public diplomacy, was widely welcomed in the Arab and Muslim world.

However unfair or absurd we may find the sentiments emanating from the Middle East, there are reasons for them, and an attempt must be made to understand them. The Arab people simply have a hard time believing that the United States could have an authentic interest in them as people—in their culture, religion, and social conditions. Some of the worst poverty in the world can be found in the slums of major Arab cities. Yet while American opinion leaders, NGOs, and government officials can regularly be heard decrying poverty in Africa, Latin America, or segments of Asia, until fairly recently, concern for poverty and injustice has rarely included references to the Arab Middle East.

ARAB-WORLD CULPABILITY

Arab states themselves must take a significant portion of the blame for poor attitudes toward America. Arab rulers have proven quite clever at keeping themselves in power and their restive populations in check by promoting distortions of America to their constituents. Arab regimes, most of them autocratic, perpetuate their rule by using state-controlled media to manipulate attitudes toward the West on the Arab street, in some cases "pandering to the ideological extremes of their own threatening insurgency movements," according to one observer.[5]

The biggest problem by far in the Arab world is that too many regimes have failed to develop their own societies. Like closed societies everywhere, they have little need to heed the demands of their own poor for opportunity and justice. For major oil-producing states, revenues from petroleum have created a privileged ruling class that seems uninterested in sharing resources with or developing services for the poor. When an entire ruling elite makes itself comfortable off oil revenues, little energy is going to be directed toward building a more diversified business base in which those outside the power structure get to compete through small-scale enterprise. Oil has a hugely distorting effect on the economies and politics of many Arab states, reinforcing graft and corruption and suppressing inducements for reform.

Rather than develop long-term strategies to empower their own people, Arab states with few exceptions redirect street rage toward outsiders. According to James Fallows, Arab powers have long histories of diverting the attention of malcontents away from their own governments' failings by portraying the United States as a nation that will stop at nothing to harm and suppress Muslims by occupying their holy sites, opposing the rise of Islamic governments, and taking their resources.[6]

The result is that almost all major Arab cities now have massive urban slums teeming with restless and resentful males, many of them jobless, idle, and ripe for recruitment into extreme or terrorist movements. In these circumstances, it is not surprising that Osama bin Laden emerges as a folk hero to many Arab youth, even among those who would never sign up for a suicide bombing mission themselves. As Richard Holbrooke put it, "his ideas, no matter how insane they seem to us, appeal to many people."[7] Bin Laden has been clever at arousing hatred among alienated Muslim youth by portraying Western powers and the Middle Eastern regimes they support as infidels to an equal degree.

The United States is left in a lose-lose position. Oppressed Arab populations either believe the propaganda of their autocratic rulers and hate America as a great oppressor, or they reject the propaganda and hate America for its hypocrisy in supporting corrupt regimes. Glenn Kessler, a reporter for the *Washington Post*, identifies the Arab perception of American hypocrisy as a major factor in the plummeting of support for America. The United States, he says, is considered scary by many because of its military history in the region *and* hypocritical because the administration, while it calls for democracy, "funnels $2 billion a year to an autocratic government like Egypt."[8]

Many blame the invasion of Iraq for taking opinion of America to historic lows, but the most precipitous decline started a year and a half earlier, immediately after 9/11. In addition, the impact of the Iraq invasion and occupation on Arab world opinion is probably more mixed than is generally assumed. America's long effort to rebuild Iraq and bring democracy to its people has produced some of the most inspiring—as well as some intensively negative—images of America in the Arab community.

Particularly positive were the pictures of Iraqis from all segments of society braving the violence to cast votes and waving their inkstained fingers proudly in the air. The movement toward democracy in Iraq has undeniably generated positive dynamics across the region for those who want to see democracy spread. All of us who served there, including those most skeptical about prospects for an Iraqi democracy, were surprised again and again by the Iraqi people's preoccupation with the idea of casting a ballot and the jubilation among democracy advocates throughout the region in response to the January and August elections of 2004. Voter turnout and the broad enthusiasm surrounding the elections, especially among women, produced a virtual earthquake through the Middle East and a momentary optimism about the prospects for democracy in Iraq.

But the war and occupation also generated a relentless stream of negative images: of babies dying, of ordinary families having their front doors kicked in and their privacy invaded, of women being patted down; and also allegations of indiscriminate military operations in and around the many holy sites that dot the landscape.

I have never met a more courageous or committed group of Americans than the military men and women who served in Iraq, but even they privately admitted how difficult it was to prevent mistakes in an environment where differentiating between friend and foe on the streets was nearly impossible; where our own guys were being shot and killed by a surprisingly resourceful insurgency; and where the natural frustrations associated with operating in a completely alien culture would become difficult to bear. The best of intentions and the best of training would not be sufficient to prevent negative images of wartime mistakes from migrating electronically across the Arab world.

Most destructive by far were the prison scandals at Abu Ghraib. After serving in Iraq as a senior ministry advisor, I spent the following year in the Coalition Provisional Authority's office in the Pentagon, coordinating social programs and private assistance. The day the prison abuse story broke was the worst day of my two years working on Iraq. I was with the CPA Washington staff in our usual 7 A.M. meeting, and suddenly the graphic images of sexual sadism committed by an American soldier came across CNN. I looked around the room and saw the ashen faces of my colleagues as they caught the horrifying glimpses of sexual humiliation on the TV screen. A couple of colleagues dropped their heads to the table in disbelief. One murmured: "It's over. We're toast."

Most of us around the table had experience in the region and knew just how toxic the images were of an American female employed by the American occupation sexually humiliating a Muslim male in the heart of the Middle East. It was the greatest self-inflicted wound of the Iraq war. No other development or combination of events so destroyed the reputation of America as a positive and consistent defender of universal human rights. The electronic photos were gleefully transmitted to Arab audiences in nonstop coverage for the next several weeks.

It is hard to convey just how sick we all felt. In many senses, American public diplomacy has been playing catch-up ever since. But these battles are never over, and while Abu Ghraib was unquestionably the low point in our efforts to reach hearts and minds, even that horrible event had a silver lining. The existence of an enterprising, investigative media sector with proliferating outlets is a recent phenomenon in the Arab world. The Arab media's extensive and critical coverage of American conduct may actually have heralded a new openness and honesty about the political failings of states in the region. For the same Arab media that showed the devastating images of prison abuse for weeks on end had little choice but to cover America's response to its own mistake.

And what a response it was. What the Arab media got to cover next was the shock and horror expressed by the American people in reaction. And it had to cover the instant efforts of the American political system to come to terms with the breakdown. There were immediate calls for investigations and for official rebukes. So many investigative commissions were formed in the weeks following the scandal that most people lost track of them. There were promises of harsh penalties for the culprits and apologies to the victims. And there was no small amount of self-flagellation all across America. The American people made clear that they were disgusted with their own government.

In a world of omnipresent media, the Abu Ghraib event displayed to Arab viewers the differences between how open societies like America deal with their own failings and how the mostly closed systems of the Middle East handle theirs. On numerous occasions, I heard Iraqis comment to the effect that "at least you Americans have a real system of justice to deal with abuse." To those Iraqis, we are imperfect, but even our imperfections illustrate how high our commitment to rule of law is.

In the Middle East, where police abuses and prison torture are fairly routine, at least a few Arab citizens had to be asking, "Would our country handle a public scandal with half as much seriousness?" The answer, to the dismay of most Arabs, had to be a resounding "no." In fact, the mantra of the Arab press, which is still restricted, should be: "Allow us to provide the same coverage of our own government's failings as we gave to America's."

Journalists around the world share the same compulsion to cover events freely and to pursue the facts tirelessly. The global media is a restless and expansive force, keen to pry open what is closed. Journalists find their professional satisfaction in eliminating barriers to the truth, come what may.

In many closed societies, most media outlets are still operated by the state and strictly controlled, but this is not a condition that can remain for long in an era of proliferating media and multiplying electronic technologies. For example, the incident in Burma involving a protest by Buddhist monks in 2007 did not remain an obscure event in the internal affairs of a minor country. Instead, citizens became war correspondents and got the story out by cell phone and the Internet, leaping over the Burmese junta's information barriers.

Offering just a little openness, as is currently the common practice for closed societies in the Middle East, is not sustainable. Governments in the region realize that they can't really control the media unless they are prepared to become hideously totalitarian states, willing to torture and imprison those who dare to own cell phones or use the Internet to criticize their oppressors, much as Saddam did. America got a black eye from Abu Ghraib, but there were no cover-ups, no censorship of the media, and no official lies or sugarcoating. Instead, there were prison sentences for perpetrators.

In the new world of electronic connections and digital cameras, there is no hiding—not for Americans and not for tyrants and totalitarians of any ilk. Public diplomacy will be no match for the daily circulation of electronic images and information. If Vietnam was the first war fought in our living rooms via television, Iraq was the first conflict in which the digital camera was used to capture the raw realities of war.

For good or bad, the truth of life in America is broadcast to large audiences on a daily basis through a variety of technical means. In the aftermath of Hurricane Katrina, the entire world witnessed the shocking images of lawlessness, of poor American blacks dying from neglect in New Orleans. According to the journalist Jim Hoagland, the initial shock abroad came not from the sights of such human misery, which are commonplace in the Third World, but from the fact that they were occurring in the United States, which has always been quick to help others but also to lecture other governments on their shortcomings. He asks, "Will post-Katrina America be humbler, more cooperative, and more understanding of other nations' problems and failures?"[9]

The internationally connected media is creating a new global consciousness and candor around the common struggles of mankind and nations. Russia's President Vladimir Putin captured this sentiment as he reflected philosophically on the devastation of Hurricane Katrina: "I look at this and cannot believe my eyes. It tells us however strong and powerful we think we are, we are nothing in the eyes of nature and of God Almighty. . . . We are all vulnerable and must cooperate to help each other." Putin was undoubtedly speaking for much of the world. In this rare instance of American vulnerability, dozens of nations immediately offered to help, an offer that our government, in one of its clumsiest moves, initially declined. This decision was quickly reversed.

The global power of the media exerts a leveling effect on nations and institutions, however powerful they may be, by placing official shortcomings suddenly and painfully on display before an audience that potentially consists of billions. This transparency puts pressure on governments everywhere to admit their shortcomings and make improvements in governance.

Perhaps the most promising development in the Middle East is the revolution in public access to information through new media and satellite technology. Under Saddam Hussein, people could be imprisoned or tortured for being found with a cell phone or Internet service, and although televisions were allowed, programming was tightly restricted. One of the first things we observed within weeks of arriving in Iraq was that everyone wanted a satellite dish. The rush to purchase and install this symbol of sophistication and prosperity helped to generate brisk business in downtown Baghdad.

When asked to give the number one reason for being hopeful about the Middle East, my answer is: the satellite dish. Anyone who has flown at low altitudes over Middle Eastern towns and cities cannot help but observe how popular it has become.

The Arab media has a long way to go, according to a report by the United States Institute for Peace. It typically operates "in collusion with a reigning regional power to maintain the appearance of domestic social concord and the illusion of solidarity among Arab states' points of views," which means that censorship is still a fact of life, that many media outlets remain instruments of governments, and that the United States and Israel are portrayed as victimizers. Nevertheless, according to the report, "cracks are beginning to show in the tight state monopoly over media because of an inability to control access to 24/7 global electronic media, including the Internet."[10]

The report concludes that the Arab media is in the midst of "a highly dynamic transition." Low-cost access to satellite technology in recent years has resulted in "an explosion of Arab satellite television channels and aggressive competition among them for market share, which has translated into more Arabs having access to real-time information." More and more limits are being stretched or broken. For example, in the absence of real "citizen-based politics" in the Middle East, media programming often mimics the kind of "authentic public debate" one finds in representative government elsewhere. For now, news and entertainment shows can only imitate participatory democracy, but they will likely hasten the arrival of the real thing. Unless there is a dictatorship that completely forbids access, people will keep seeking out news and information, which ultimately is likely to challenge the monopoly on power that is common in Arab states.

AMERICAN POPULAR CULTURE

The fact that Arab households are more and more accessible to Western programming presents unprecedented opportunities as well as new challenges for America's reputation abroad. The issue of Western cultural programming is probably the least understood, the least discussed, and yet possibly the most consequential factor in America's image problems abroad. Media reports on Muslim attitudes toward

America typically focus on disagreements with Washington policies, not Hollywood products. Yet the popular culture largely shapes how the American way of life is seen by much of the world, and it generates disdain for America throughout the Islamic world.

There is much about American popular culture that is healthy and is regarded as appealing by many outside of the United States, especially the young, even in Arab and Muslim countries. From our own perspective, even when programming crosses over the line of what is usually considered healthy, it is tolerated as part of our expansive view of freedom. This outlook is generally not accepted in the Muslim world, and it affects Muslim perceptions of America's legitimacy as a source of democratic and moral values.

We think of our own society as sophisticated, intelligent, and highly advanced. Many Muslims have a different impression. While they admire our democratic values and the success of our economy, they don't think of our social or cultural values as worthy of emulation. In fact, it is quite the contrary. For many traditional Arabs and Muslims, the downside they see in allowing greater openness in Arab societies is precisely that it means providing their own young with access to the moral values of the West. Many Muslims view America as selfish, materialistic, promiscuous, and too willing to trade off families and communities for a socially destructive individualism.

Cultural products are among America's leading exports, and yet there is little discussion of their impact on America's image abroad. What worries much of the world is not merely the dominance of American popular culture but its content and effects. In the course of three short decades, American culture has moved from *Leave It to Beaver* and *Gone with the Wind* to *Baywatch* and MTV. While the former once defined the center of gravity in American values and beliefs, the latter are increasingly viewed as representative. As Internet access and satellite programming become more and more available in traditional Muslim societies, it is often the most debased programming, not older family films or classics, that makes its way into homes.

An unpleasant fact is that many Muslims fear and are prepared to resist the growing pervasiveness of American culture in their countries. For instance, one of America's leading development policy objectives is to advance rights for women. Empowering women economically can bring major breakthroughs in Third World communities. Yet in many Muslim locations, one can find stiff resistance to the lifestyle modernization that is often presumed to come along with economic empowerment.

Responding to Western pressures after 9/11, Saudi Arabia loosened the strict censorship that had been applied to the media and liberalized some standards for women, such as in driving automobiles or fraternizing with men. But at major rallies in Saudi Arabia recently, traditional Muslim women expressed their opposition to creeping Western lifestyles. One spokeswoman said, "Saudi women are the luckiest in the world and Saudi Arabia is the closest thing to an ideal and pure Islamic nation. We don't want imported Western values to destroy that."[11] Western aid workers are likely to conclude that these women are brainwashed. Yet sizeable portions of the Saudi female population are in the frontlines of resisting liberalization, presumably for their own well-considered reasons. "This is a choice," said Samia Adham, a female professor of statistics. "We choose to be ruled by Islam. We will make changes, but within our own religion and in our own way."[12]

The few polls that have bothered to investigate attitudes among Muslims toward American culture confirm the existence of a problem. On the one hand, America's generous assistance following the tsunami disaster in the Indian Ocean resulted in markedly higher general approval of the United States in Indonesia—a 2 to 1 favorable view instead of 2 to 1 unfavorable, as previously. Impeding further progress in this direction, however, was the Indonesian public's concern about "Western influence" in the area of culture. In a rare case of the State Department addressing the cultural dimension of anti-Americanism, its own newsletter reported that "by a margin of 62% to 28%, Indonesian Muslims say they have an unfavorable view of American culture, with their aversion focusing on American lifestyle ('immoral,' 'free sex') and clothing ('immodest,' 'too sexy')."[13]

Muslims have typically been slow to speak up about American cultural excesses for fear of generating a backlash; however, a growing number see it as too critical an issue to ignore any longer. Mustafa Akyol, for example, a prominent Muslim moderate who is engaged in multicultural dialogue, says that while Muslim radical rage at America is "irrational and ill founded, many mainstream Muslims are put off by the moral decline that seems to have pervaded American culture during the second half of the twentieth century. They worry that it will be exported to their children and societies." [14]

In an essay called "Show Us the Other America," Akyol acknowledges that American moral values are "in better shape than a glance at U.S. television or other indicators might have one believe." But, he says, the dominant worldview that comes through to non-Westerners mostly by way of American popular culture is a philosophical materialism that encourages "pleasure seeking, selfishness, and hedonism," the consequences of which many devout Muslims around the world find "horrifying." [15]

Meic Pearse picks up this same theme in his book *Why the Rest Hates the West*. Pearse reports that many around the globe see Western societies abandoning their heritage of virtue for a worldview that "denigrates religion, depreciates family, discards honor, and is preoccupied with amusements and sexual permissiveness." [16] According to Pearse, it is not merely the overt vices of American popular culture that trouble many Muslims, but also a deeper social atomization that it produces within Muslim communities—"personal irresponsibility; dehumanizing impersonality; and other wounds to traditional families, communities, and conceptions of the person." [17]

HOLLYWOOD HEGEMONY

American film, television, and music now account for over 80 percent of the world's cultural programming. Many indigenous forms of dance, music, and art that are distinctive to regional and local cultures are being pushed aside by an aggressive American marketing machine.

Most producers, screenwriters, and entertainment celebrities could not imagine themselves participating in economic or military imperialism, yet in cultural terms they are agents of a new form of global colonialism that increasingly runs roughshod over indigenous cultures and sensibilities. The unsettling aspects of economic globalization are that it displays little allegiance to sovereign nations and scant concern for the interests of communities, while it effectively colonizes small economies.

When criticism is aimed at American economic power abroad, the entertainment sector of America can normally be counted on to concur. And yet Hollywood's growing hegemony over the world's cultural programming is also an aspect of American power. Its effect is hardly distinguishable from that of economic globalization; and in fact it must be understood as a major economic phenomenon. But unlike those products that move around the globe through trade agreements and treaties, cultural products cross the world electronically in seconds, oblivious to geographic boundaries and cultural differences.

Traditional diplomacy focuses mainly on such things as bilateral trade and state-to-state relations—the kind of activities over which states have at least some control. By contrast, although cultural exports have major implications for U.S. policymakers, they operate almost entirely outside of traditional checks and balances. In fact, the working assumption within the corporate culture of entertainment and media giants is that their own products and practices are beyond scrutiny and debate. Producers of culture dismissively assume that if someone has a problem with their product, it is the consumer who has the responsibility to change.

American popular culture thrives in an unregulated and unaccountable environment made possible by the First Amendment. Its creators and promoters are largely oblivious to any responsibility for advancing cultural health and a more balanced view of America. Indeed, the leading lights of the entertainment world generally regard their libertarian views as synonymous with freedom and as something to be universally encouraged.

When discussion in Washington turns to the problem of Muslim attitudes toward America, as it often does, the conversation almost always focuses on the failings of the U.S. government to promote a more favorable picture. But the larger picture of America lies beyond official influence. The contribution of popular culture to anti-American attitudes is rarely discussed in official circles. One reason is that raising complaints about the purveyors of American popular culture is typically seen as the first step to censorship, and thus the topic is considered taboo.

Many American personnel working in Muslim countries have a greater interest in changing Muslim customs and practices that are considered out of step with Western practices. Why be concerned about your own music and film culture alienating Muslims when your primary interest is in transforming Muslim communities and cultures? Many Muslims note the irony that Americans are eager to change other people's cultures, even at the risk of provoking anger, but unwilling to engage in a broad conversation about the failings of their own culture.

The solution is not to weaken the protections of the First Amendment, but to call for re-examination of attitudes among the producers of American culture, along with greater awareness of the sensibilities of other cultures, beliefs, and traditions. There is need for more dialogue between cultures and nations, with an eye toward forming reality-based perceptions on both sides.

ARAB POPULAR CULTURE

If the worst of American popular culture is often counterproductive to the goal of generating sympathy for the United States in the Arab world, perhaps an alternative approach would be to take an interest in Arab popular culture as the path to liberalization. Arab entertainment products are likely to be a more authentic voice for Arab and Muslim aspirations. And while Arab pop culture stretches the highly restrictive social norms that are still commonplace in much of the Muslim world, it nevertheless is tame by contemporary Western standards and respectful toward Islam.

Charles Paul Freund, a senior editor at Reason Foundation, describes the powerful influence of a contemporary Arab music that is circulating widely in the Middle East. "Much of Arab culture remains a place of restricted, traditional and narrowly defined identities, often subsumed in group identities," says Freund, yet many more recent musical genres are showing openness to more flexible gender roles. Some "confront the nature of Arab identity directly," an identity that in the most traditional communities is shaped wholly by the group and not the individual.[18]

New Arab musical genres are thriving and are encouraging a vitally important shift in Arab identity. The most important aspect of Arab music videos, Freund writes, is that "they offer their audience an imagined world in which Arabs can shape and assert their identities in any way they please." Arab pop music expresses a kind of individuality, but without the "isolation and futility" that are associated with the individualism of the West and are lamented in much of Arab literature.[19]

In addition, says Freund, Arab pop culture "subverts state power, challenges restrictive social and moral norms, portrays socially marginalized groups in sympathetic terms, seeks solutions to societal problems, portrays women in roles of power and ultimately increases social tolerance." While some of this will be discomfiting to those steeped in traditional culture, it will also undermine the authoritarian systems that have often succeeded in controlling and manipulating "traditional folk culture and high culture, either by harnessing them to their own purposes or destroying the types of high culture they have not liked." No authoritarian system, observes Freund, "has ever been able to deal effectively with pop culture."[20]

If mainstream Arab pop culture is an effective conduit of certain "liberal" Western values in the Muslim context—promoting greater openness yet generally respectful of traditional mores—what might happen if Americans took an interest in supporting Arab pop culture instead of pushing their own so aggressively?

Public Diplomacy: Where Do We Go from Here?

Most of the programs promoting America's values and interests abroad were created during the Cold War, for the objective of winning the ideological battle with Soviet-style communism. Through much of the 1990s, it was widely assumed that America no longer needed capacity for ideological warfare. As a result, many public diplomacy programs were trimmed, eliminated, or simply neglected.

Efforts to revitalize a coherent strategy of public diplomacy will have to deal with the fragmented nature of America's public diplomacy programs. The State Department is responsible for public diplomacy policy and oversees public information programs at diplomatic posts. The Pentagon operates information warfare programs. USAID has a variety of programs that directly affect attitudes toward America and operates training programs for foreign media. The National Endowment for Democracy carries out a variety of programs that entail disseminating information about American democracy. The Broadcasting Board of Governors is responsible for overseeing the broadcast of balanced news and cultural programs through the Voice of America and its surrogate outlets. According to Stephen Johnson, a senior policy analyst at the Heritage Foundation, these entities operate "in separate universes, much like America's intelligence agencies before September 11."[21]

The United States will not make headway in reversing negative opinion of America without bringing cohesion to its fragmented public diplomacy programs. Official policy reforms, however, are a necessary but insufficient step in the direction of a sound and comprehensive public diplomacy strategy. All the governmental pipelines of information might operate together in coherent fashion, but that would not address the problem of American credibility. The U.S. government is simply not the most trusted source of information in the eyes of vast numbers.

Developing a new core strategy for confronting anti-Americanism abroad will require less dependence upon government information programs, media strategies, and official messages. In short, the next generation of public diplomacy programming should not be official-centric. A new, more encompassing strategy will require thinking outside the box of official public diplomacy.

The new focus must start with an appreciation of the enormous asset that America has in its own citizens and their civic and educational institutions. Any initiative that facilitates partnerships and dialogue between American citizens and their counterparts in Islamic countries will yield significant dividends. Ordinary citizens are America's best ambassadors for the simple reason that they don't have agendas beyond the pursuit of friendship and trust.

The next phase of programming will also need to focus on cultivating indigenous civil society. That process should begin with a major assessment of the rapidly evolving role of nonstate sectors and intermediary organizations in shaping attitudes and policies in the Middle East, and should include a review of how Western aid can strengthen indigenous civil society while curbing the worst antidemocratic influences that can take root. The strategy needs to emphasize building broader ties to foreign publics via mediating organizations and expanding the direct ties of American citizens to their counterparts abroad, whether through travel and exchanges or though electronic links.

No particular approach is going to yield an immediate payback, but any program that promotes volunteerism and unofficial ties across all sectors of society should be preferred. The range of potential people-to-people and institution-to-institution ties is as unlimited as America's private sector itself.

Business, in particular, is a largely untapped resource in this regard. During my time directing private assistance for Iraq, several IT companies stepped forward to recommend projects with the emerging Iraqi business sector that held the promise of lasting people-to-people ties. One American IT company created a state-of-the-art electronic conference center and made it available to anyone who wanted to do international business long-distance. Another technology company sponsored a promising Iraqi IT entrepreneur and invited him to serve as an apprentice at their corporate headquarters. Upon his return to Iraq, he not only worked to train and equip other Iraqis in more advanced technology and business management, but also assisted the U.S. firm in making business inroads.

Similarly, the American Society of Civil Engineers assembled an entire team of volunteers to promote training opportunities for Iraqi engineers. The team created a "tool kit" of educational products along with training modules that could be forwarded to training sites electronically or carried into the country by U.S. contractors. Here is a private association operating on its own initiative and partnering with the U.S. government to provide capacity building for Iraqis, at no cost to the government.

Numerous firms and institutions stepped forward to donate computers, medical equipment and supplies, textbooks, and lab supplies. Several law schools volunteered to "adopt" an Iraqi counterpart and provide long-distance help and friendship around common interests. Where military shipping was not available, FedEx stepped in, offering to donate shipping services valued in the tens of millions of dollars.

Civic organizations volunteered to engage in people-to-people relationships and offered assistance. For example, Sister Cities International created partnerships with several Iraqi cities. Many civilian and military staff serving in Iraq who had a background in the Boy Scouts initiated efforts to develop scouting programs for kids patterned after the American model. Rotary Clubs sponsored a partnership with the hospital in Basra to provide prosthetics care.

New nonprofits sprang up to promote good will and trust among the Iraqi people. Operation Iraqi Children, founded by the actor Gary Sinise, organized donations of toys for Iraqi children. Spirit of America, whose purpose was to bring valued gifts to Iraqi children via American troops in the hope of promoting trust, was born partly out of frustration that government systems for getting donations into Iraq were bogged down in excessive red tape. Jim Hake, the group's founder, was an entrepreneur who was convinced that American citizens had a lot at stake in Iraq and thus needed to do their part; and that where government programs were incapable of getting the job done, the private sector had to step in. Hake wanted to prove that private systems, or "new economy" networks and connections, could deliver donations faster and better, even in the dangerous environment of Iraq.

The number of Iraqis who have had direct contact with Americans still remains small. But most of those who could travel to the United States and encounter real Americans have gone home overwhelmed with good memories.

One delegation of Iraqis brought to the United States consisted of five businessmen who had their hands amputated under Saddam. They were sponsored by a Texas foundation and prosthetics clinic that provided them with new artificial hands. I was able to join them for a special lunch at the State Department to honor them on their last day here after traveling to various destinations in the heartland. With tears in their eyes, they talked about how generous and warm they found the American people—how they were a people committed to family and faith, much like in their mostly Muslim homeland. From my experience, that one act of generosity did as much good as hundreds of official acts and meetings combined.

I took away from numerous experiences such as this one the simple conclusion that Americans are by far the best salespeople for their own society. When citizens of foreign countries encounter the unvarnished truth about the American people, they are almost always changed forever. They return home with a determination to convince their peers that Americans are, in fact, good people.

People-to-people exchanges have positive influences far out of proportion to the size of the project or the amount of money spent. Any effort to increase the flow of Arab citizens to America will involve problems with visas, responsibility for which is now in the hands not of the State Department but of the Department of Homeland Security, which takes an uncompromisingly hard line on visas, especially for young male Arabs.

While the visa issue is being addressed, there are numerous opportunities for long-distance connections involving business, trade associations, civic organizations, schools and universities. Opportunities for digital connections are limited only by the availability of the technology. Especially promising are opportunities to build ties among professional associations, where citizens organize around common interests and expertise without official ties or agendas. Anything that contributes to reducing the vast digital divide inevitably encourages both the development of a knowledge-based society in the Middle East and the advancement of education.

Helping to cultivate a new generation of leaders who are committed to reform is not possible without expanding the range of educational opportunities within Arab countries. There is no short-term fix or silver-bullet remedy for the problems of Islamic education, and efforts to help are usually fraught with the danger that we appear too eager to "reform them." Once again, the key is to align U.S. programs with Muslim organizations and universities that have an interest in reforming their own societies. Anything that promotes a deeper understanding between our societies would be beneficial, especially ties between institutions of higher learning.

The influence can actually flow both ways. For example, the suggestion has been made that instead of trying to dictate Arab curricula, we would get off to a better start with Arab publics by "asking Arab civil society to help Western schools to combat ignorance." This action "would be a powerful symbolic response." [22]

Other possibilities include providing more scholarships for students from the Middle East to attend universities in the United States or universities in the region with Western curricula such as American University Cairo or Beirut. Another would be to expand U.S.-sponsored universities in the region to include cities like Kabul, Baghdad, or perhaps Kurdistan. American philanthropists have been considering providing financial support for major new academic programs for women, for example in Bangladesh, where access to a university education is very limited.

Yet another option would be an initiative to send Muslim American scientists, professors, journalists, and business managers on short-term volunteer assignments in the Muslim world to provide training and technical assistance. This work is already being attempted by American NGOs that are promoting more educational opportunities in the Muslim world. For example, the Academy for Educational Development is working with ministers of higher education in the region on teacher training, English-language competency, and the improvement of institutional design on all levels. Any short-term exchange program that matches Westernized Muslims with their friends and relatives in the Middle East will likely produce enduring ties and expand opportunities for advancing democratic values.

Simply promoting literacy for its own sake in the Arab world would also be a step forward. The challenge of winning hearts and minds among populations with high illiteracy rates is doubly complex in the case of the Arab world. Not only are 70 million Arabs unable to read or write, but also a much larger number of the region's 280 million people do not fully speak or understand the standardized Arabic that is used in broadcast news, the academy, and official discourse.

In the end, more than government programs and funding initiatives will be required. Americans from all walks of life have a stake in this outcome, and they are their country's best advocates. Working through business, trade, and civil society organizations, Americans need to partner with reform movements, promote economic and social development, encourage moderate Arab intellectuals, and ask their own Muslim-American neighbors how they can help.

CHAPTER TEN

Civil Society and Nation Building: Prospects for Democratization

The fact is that the chief threats to us and to world order come today from weak, collapsed, or failed states. Weak or absent government institutions in developing countries form the thread linking terrorism, refugees, AIDS, and global poverty.

FRANCIS FUKUYAMA[1]

Voluntary associations are "the little schools of citizenship."

ALEXIS DE TOCQUEVILLE

NO SOCIAL OR political force on earth compares to the power of an increasingly connected global democratic civil society. Today, civil society is providing a voice to the powerless and the poor, and propelling advances in human rights and rule of law. It is at work throughout much of the developing world, cultivating citizenship and building social institutions from the ground up.

The key to bringing justice to the world's poor and oppressed is building institutions for democratization as well as for sustainable development. As morally imperative as it is to come to the immediate aid of the sick and impoverished, humanitarianism alone will not build nations. Much of the activity of private as well as public aid workers is fueled by pity. Too few aid workers think seriously about how important it is for the poor that they not need assistance permanently.

The true work of compassion and justice is building viable communities, economies, and nations. This cannot be accomplished without sound governance, which requires building or strengthening a variety of functioning institutions such as a free press, an independent judiciary, and the legal framework for private enterprise.

In this chapter we will consider how the growing strength of civil society around the world is giving an indispensable "bottom-up" boost to democratic institutions. It is irresistibly shifting power away from authoritarians and toward citizens and grass-roots associations. In recent years, civil society movements have toppled an authoritarian president in Kyrgyzstan, led millions of nonviolent demonstrators against Syria's military presence in Lebanon, and supplied a vigorous citizens' defense of the new democracy in Ukraine when it was suddenly imperiled.

We will also candidly confront the many stubborn obstacles to the advance of democracy and consider why long-term strategies must rely less on politicians and bureaucrats and more on grass-roots movements. The development of democratic nations is simply not possible without the underpinning of a robust civil society. As the development economist William Easterly put it, "democracy works, but imposing democracy from the outside does not."[2]

Civil society operates as the seedbed of democratic citizenship. It provides a space where citizens freely gather to promote their common purposes. Aided by the rise of communications technology, civil society may be the most significant force driving increased openness among regimes that have long resisted change. Fareed Zakaria, a columnist who has covered Arab-world development, has said that "to change a regime, short of waging war, you have to shift the balance of power between the state and society. Society needs to be empowered. It is civil society—private business, media, civic associations, nongovernmental organizations—that can create an atmosphere which forces changes in countries."[3]

If recent history is any guide, the long-term prospects for democracy are relatively promising. According to Freedom House, the number of free states—those that ensure a broad array of political rights and civil liberties—has expanded in the past three decades from 43 to 88, a rate of 1.5 per year.[4] There have been variations in the rate of progress, but the long-term trend is generally positive. Freedom House estimates that 75 percent of the world's countries are currently either free or "partly free." It should also be noted that the unfree countries are generally concentrated in specific regions. For example, only 28 percent of Middle Eastern countries are either free or mostly free, and this percentage represents a decline over the past twenty-five years. The Arab world basically lacks the institutions of democracy, including real political parties, a free press, and civil society. Nevertheless, there is no significant constituency in the world crying out for more state controls and repression, with the possible exception of Islamic extremists.

But it is necessary to understand the full meaning of "long-term." The key to long-term success in promoting freedom and democracy may lie in accepting the fact that it will take decades and probably centuries to achieve, as was the case with America's experiment in democracy.

AMERICA'S DRIVE FOR DEMOCRACY

The United States has established as one of its foremost foreign policy objectives the promotion of democracy abroad. The premise behind this policy is threefold. One, there is the assumption of a universal longing among all people to be free, combined with the moral conviction that freedom is the right and destiny of men and women everywhere. Two, there is the assumption that all individuals and societies have the capacity to be free. And three, there is the pragmatic claim that pressuring undemocratic governments to embrace wider political freedoms will serve America's national interests over the long term. The expected result is a better world in which more people are peacefully improving their own lives.

Few will argue with the basic idea of bringing democratic freedoms to more of the earth's inhabitants. But each of those premises is open to challenge and is often the subject of debate by those who hold a less optimistic view of the forces that are at work today in the human race. Promoting the expansion of democracy abroad has not always been a primary goal of the U.S. government. Until fairly recently, in fact, U.S. foreign policy was dominated by the "realist" school, known for its skepticism about the prospects for American democratic ideals to be quickly or easily transplanted to regions that have historically been hostile to democracy.

Realists will point out that not all cultures and religions are equal when it comes to providing the philosophical and cultural underpinnings of freedom, and that in many cases the transition to democracy may bring about undesirable results. Practitioners from the realist school can often be heard calling attention to the benefits of the more conventional approach to international relations—those of peace, stability, and the efficiency and predictability of operating in settled bilateral partnerships with known leaders, however imperfect they might be.

These arguments still carry considerable sway, especially with respect to the Middle East, a historically volatile region with little democratic history to draw upon. America's heavy reliance on Middle Eastern oil adds a further difficulty and illustrates how complicated a policy of democratization can be, especially when pushing too aggressively can interfere with economic or national security needs. Thomas Friedman of the *New York Times* states that there's an illusion behind the idea that America can "break the Middle East's addiction to authoritarianism without breaking America's addiction to oil." In the Arab world, he says, "oil and authoritarianism are inextricably linked."[5]

The project of establishing democracies around the world seems so logical, so inherently right. Democracy is our core American value. How could it be anything less than the central focus of our foreign policy?

The realist school responds by arguing that America has not historically been committed to global revolutionary purposes, and that

What is often there and waiting to surface are ancient hatreds and prejudices, nourished through the "intense partisanship" of tribe, clan, or religious sect. Where the organic cultivation of democratic disposition has not occurred, "a multi-party system merely hardens and institutionalizes established ethnic and regional divisions."[11]

Among many Muslims there is a desire to embrace a politically muscular religion and a new cultural assertiveness, which may result in more reactionary social policies mounting up in defiance of the West. Richard Haas asks, what if free Iranians, in the spirit of cultural and religious pride, decide they want to acquire nuclear weapons and use them against Israel? What if the result is a horrible destabilization of the region? These are among the questions raised by skeptics.

Exponents of the realist school such as Haas believe that the most recent experience in promoting democracy in the Middle East confirms their doubts. By democratic means, Hizbullah has gained strength in Lebanon. By means of the ballot box, Hamas scored an electoral victory in Gaza and the West Bank, throwing the Middle East peace process into doubt. By means of an election judged to be relatively fair, Iran is now ruled by an Islamic fundamentalist mystic who came to power promising to develop nuclear power as a path to restored national pride, who denies the Holocaust, and who has reiterated his hope of eliminating Israel. In Egypt, where the government yielded to U.S. pressure to provide more electoral choices, the oldest Islamic fundamentalist organization in the world, the Muslim Brotherhood, surprised the watching world by achieving major gains.

As the advocates of democratic civil society must admit, steps toward greater openness almost always produce mixed results. Communications technology and access to the ballot can be used to advance repressive and even violent ideas, as well as hopeful breakthroughs.

Alexandria, Egypt, was long one of the most tolerant and easygoing cosmopolitan cities in the Middle East, where Muslim and Christian families often joined together to celebrate each other's festivals. But when Western pressure following 9/11 led to greater freedom of expression, it resulted in attacks on Coptic Christians and their places of worship. Christians have been stabbed and churches have been repeatedly attacked. Muslim rioting broke out when authorities permitted a theater to present a play featuring a man who converted from Christianity to Islam, then switched back. According to a local democracy expert, "there is an acceleration of conflict, and that is worrisome." Sectarian hostility is reported to be palpably on the rise.[12]

A leading candidate in the presidential elections of Peru in the spring of 2006 was Ollanta Humala, whose family is steeped in "ethno-nationalism," a thinly veiled racist ideology that would attempt to purify and grant political supremacy to the "copper race," meaning descendants of the Inca. Running in a country where racial tensions lie just below the surface, Humala declared in an interview, "We are racists certainly." He added, "Everyone is a racist, because nationalism is something that is in the blood, just like it is with the Japanese in Japan and the Germans in Germany."[13]

Civil society itself can be a means for advancing antidemocratic beliefs. In India, a sizeable rural movement with revolutionary intent has grown with the help of the very technology that in other parts of India is raising democratic hopes. *Washington Post* reporter John Lancaster tells the story of "Comrad M," as he wishes to be identified, who speaks fluent English, is a master of the language of e-mail and the Internet, and is waging a Maoist war on the Indian state.[14]

In perhaps the most troubling setback for nation building, East Timor was hit with a surprising reversal in the spring of 2006 when it faced bloody riots and near civil war conditions, apparently produced by internal conflicts that had been simmering but were ignored by the political class. After a very troubled path to independence in 1999, East Timor was globally heralded as a success story for its internal development, for its advanced civil society, and for its political stability. Two weeks before the bloody breakdown in 2006, the World Bank president Paul Wolfowitz hailed the Timorese people for "the bustling markets, the rebuilt schools, the functioning government." Clearly, there remained deep fissures that were not visible to the naked eye of Western governments and were blithely dismissed by the Timorese government until it was too late.[15]

East Timor may have been the victim of unrealistic expectations and premature celebration. Western powers believed that peace and stability had been secured, and a substantial peacekeeping presence offered by the Australians was withdrawn. When fighting broke out, many police fled, and the military proved woefully inadequate. Over one hundred thousand people were forced to flee their homes. The East Timor case may be seen as a warning for American forces in Iraq and elsewhere.

Shedding more light on short-term prospects for democratization in the Middle East is the U.S. experience in Iraq. While the liberation of Iraq from the brutal reign of the region's most notorious dictator and military aggressor was widely appreciated by Iraqis, the situation now seems to suggest that political advantage under the new order will be gained by conservative religious parties. The new "democratic" Iraq will likely forbid the kind of grotesque abuse and routine torture that was common under Saddam, but will also hesitate to embrace the liberal political values of the West. The question is not whether Islam will rule the new nation, but *how*. The West's hopes for a measure of pluralism hinged on internal developments having to do with Islamic policies over which it has little influence.

Fareed Zakaria notes that many of the parties and political movements of the Middle East espouse views that are "deeply illiberal, involving the reversal of women's rights, second-class citizenship for minorities and confrontation with the West and Israel."[16] Democratization in the Middle East will not necessarily bring our cultures and regional interests into greater harmony. It may not lead to adoption of Western ideals of freedom, tolerance, or political liberalism—at least not in the short term.

When democracy is suddenly introduced, the first forces to enter the newly created space are those that managed to survive under oppression, when civil society was strangled; in many cases, that means religious groups and parties. Iraq had a thriving civil society sector before Saddam rose to power. Private associations included the Arab equivalent of the Boy Scouts, societies of scholars and poets, and women's groups. All these associations were ruthlessly destroyed by the dictator for the simple reason that they were the most effective source of independence and challenge to his authority, even though they were not inherently political. Had civil society endured, it would have been available to play a role in the immediate postwar period, forming the basis for new parties and for social integration and cooperation. Instead, it was religious factions and parties that moved into the vacuum.

Throughout the Middle East, mosque-based networks and organizations are the only groups that have survived authoritarian rule for the simple reason that even the worst dictators have not gotten away with suppressing the practice of Islam. In many cases, autocrats have cynically manipulated Islam in order to resist unfriendly secular parties and movements. It is unsurprising, then, that Islamic groups would be the first to gain advantage in a more open system.

The greatest difficulty in making the transitioning from Arab dictatorships to functioning democracy has to do with the traditional forces of society in that region. Thomas Friedman describes an "iron rule" of Arab-Muslim political life: "You cannot go from Saddam to Jefferson without going through Khomeini." He maintains that a period of mosque-led politics is unavoidable because "once you sweep away the dictator or king at the top of any Middle East state, you go into free fall until you hit the mosque—as the U.S. discovered in Iraq." [17] There are basically two powerful centers of political and social gravity in the Muslim world—the ruling elites and the mosques; and there is nothing between them. Dictatorial regimes all across the region have kept themselves in power by "never allowing anything to grow under their feet." That includes a "truly independent judiciary, media, progressive secular parties, or civil society groups—from women's organizations to trade associations." Friedman concludes that if we are not careful we will end up in a few years with Muslim clerics in power "from Morocco to the border of India." [18]

Supporters of democratization will counter by saying that this description merely reflects the natural stages of development, and in any event, if democracy is not the answer to every problem in the Middle East, neither is the status quo. Violence and conflict have been rising to a boil in the region even under existing regimes. Moreover, the only way to find out whether or not democracy is achievable is to try it. New parties, whether Hamas in the West Bank or the Muslim Brotherhood in Egypt, will need to learn to govern. The burden now falls on them to deliver results, which will require pragmatism and developing programs that produce results. These groups may or may not moderate themselves, but as Zakaria puts it, they will surely lose some of their mystical allure when they "move from being martyrs to mayors." [19] They will now have to face public demands for competent government, improved services, and economic development, or they too will presumably face the voters' wrath.

All this assumes, however, that the same natural evolution toward pragmatic rule exists everywhere democracy is planted and allowed to grow. It assumes that the interest of ordinary citizens in reliable government services can be counted on to trump the appeal of religious agendas and reactionary attitudes. Experts on the region acknowledge that the jury will be out on these questions for quite some time. The debate is not about the inherent superiority of democracy, or even whether U.S. policy should or should not attempt to advance democracy. The point in giving full attention to these doubts is to ensure that the policies and strategies that are adopted have the best chance of achieving good results in the long term.

Can democracy be installed by an outside power, as is being attempted in Iraq? How do states with little or no history in practicing democracy transform themselves into democracies from within? Is the longing for democratic freedoms truly universal, or is it possible that repressive elements in some regions will use democratic means to secure freedom for themselves while denying it to others, such as religious minorities or women? How can governments that desire to introduce more democratic freedoms move toward a more viable democracy?

Civil Society and Nation Building

The requirements for establishing a functioning democracy are twofold: one, building self-sustaining political institutions, grounded securely in the rule of law, that allow political and economic freedoms to flourish; and two, accepting the serious challenge of cultivating democratic citizens. Dispositions are as essential as procedures. In other words, democracy is made for democrats.

For any program to succeed in the long run, it must begin with the recognition that the path to democracy is filled with stubborn obstacles; that progress may be disrupted by frequent setbacks; and that in countries with histories of repression, conflict, and civil war, there are no guarantees of arriving at what most in the West would consider a functioning democracy in the foreseeable future. Building the foundations for democracy requires a long-term investment and avoidance of the temptation to reach for quick fixes. The best strategies must be accompanied by patience and a willingness to pay the necessary price, which may be steep.

Sustained progress in expanding political freedoms will need global movements of citizens—ideologically diverse, but linked in their determination to promote openness, pluralism, and basic freedoms. It will require grass-roots efforts to pry open closed states, apply the spotlight to human rights abuses, and lay the foundation for new institutions. It will require dealing with ethnic and religious conflict and with the economic stagnation that so frequently impedes democratic progress.

AMERICA THE RELUCTANT NATION BUILDER

Opinion differs on whether nation building—especially the kind involving military liberation—is a hallmark of America's mission in the world. Certainly there was a pattern of intervention long before 9/11. "Whether for reasons of human rights or of security," writes Francis Fukuyama, "the United States has done a lot of intervening over the past fifteen years, and has taken on roughly one new nation-building commitment every other year since the end of the cold war." [20]

Few would deny that the terrorist attacks of 9/11 fundamentally reshaped American attitudes about how far the United States should go to confront threats emanating from dictatorships or failed states. Following 9/11, the more cautious approach to intervention that had represented the status quo was abandoned in favor of a greater readiness to go on the attack against terrorist targets abroad. The new policy embraced a range of options including support for the use of force to remove dangerous dictators, combined with a greater willingness to engage in actual nation building. James Dobbins of the RAND Corporation says, "It now seems clear that nation building is the inescapable responsibility of the world's only superpower."[21]

Perhaps so, but it would be wrong to assume that the United States is anything but a reluctant nation builder. The attitude of the American public remains skeptical and conditional regarding costly interventions abroad, with liberals and conservatives generally setting different kinds of conditions. Liberals tentatively favor intervention in conflict-torn countries where grave humanitarian conditions call for outside assistance. Conservatives tend to look askance at purely humanitarian interventions but are generally willing to consider regime change in cases like Iraq where it appears there is a national security justification and where a new regime might be friendlier to the United States and its economic interests. But these patterns may shift with the winds of partisan politics.

Contrary to the impressions of many at home and abroad, America has shown willingness but not eagerness to engage in the controversial work of nation building. Just as notable as foreign interventions are the number of situations where American intervention might have been justified and was even encouraged by one domestic constituency or another, but America held back. "The United States has not embarked on such endeavors lightly," says Dobbins. "The costs and the risks associated with nation-building have remained high." For instance, America "withdrew from Somalia in 1993 at the first serious resistance. It opted out of international efforts to stem genocide in Rwanda in 1994. It resisted European efforts to entangle it in

Balkan peace enforcement through four years of bloody civil war. After intervening in Bosnia, it spent another three years pursuing a non-military solution to ethnic repression in Kosovo." [22]

The experience in Iraq may only reinforce a familiar pattern— intervention followed by many reconsiderations. It has demonstrated to persons of all political persuasions that exercises in regime change and nation building can be costly in terms of life and treasure, with outcomes that are at best uncertain.

The images of planting democracy that are most common in the American consciousness are the cases of Japan and Germany, which "set a standard for post-conflict nation-building that has not since been matched," remarks Dobbins. [23] Largely forgotten are the heavy investment and the time required to achieve those successes. The Marshall Plan began only in 1947, two years after the country was liberated, and Germany did not regain its sovereignty until 1955. Nation building, says Dobbins, is a "time and resource consuming effort." [24]

Germany and Japan had much going for them. Both were advanced states with modern administrative structures, albeit corrupted by antidemocratic ideologies during the period of fascist rule. Each had an ethnically homogeneous and relatively well-educated population. In each, a large effort was made by the United States and the international community to bring about "democratic transformation," which meant wiping away the machinery of militarism, the instruments of repression, and the remaining vestiges of state-worship.

Transformation meant not only replacing the superstructures of the previous government, but also putting into place the institutional underpinnings for a new state, including economic, social, and educational systems. Every effort had to be made to cultivate a democratic society with democratic citizens practicing democratic ideals. General MacArthur declared his determination to introduce American-style labor rights, to guarantee the right of free speech, and to implant liberal values in the education system. [25]

Japan and Germany are rare examples of what Paul Johnson has called "a revolution from above," and are not easily replicated. [26] The circumstances that allowed General MacArthur the time and resources needed to undertake a massive social and political rebuilding effort are simply not possible in many other settings.

As in Germany and Japan, the United States defeated a brutal dictator when it drove Saddam Hussein from power. But that may be where the similarities stop. The ethnically and religiously volatile Middle East was not likely to provide the same accommodating circumstances that existed in Japan and Germany.

What is remarkable about the public debate over Iraq is just how little it drew from a historical perspective on either side. European allies charged that America was simply following a romantic vision of what was possible, and that it was indifferent, if not willfully ignorant, to the stubborn realities that awaited. A realistic understanding of the difficulty, shaped by historical models, would probably have better prepared the public for the trials and setbacks ahead.

On the positive side, a more realistic understanding of the difficulty of postwar nation building would probably also have created a more objective system for evaluating the real progress that was accomplished by the Coalition Provisional Authority. Iraq was vastly harder to occupy and rebuild than Japan or Germany, and yet even in the midst of daily violence by a stubborn insurgency, substantive progress was made in building a new education system, improving health care, and repairing infrastructure. Sovereignty was transferred fourteen months after the military operation, and within the first eighteen months a constitution was forged and popular elections were held.

Yet the challenge was complex and demanding almost beyond description. Following the military liberation, the state that previously existed in Iraq just melted away. The police and military dissolved and disappeared, leaving the country in a state of lawlessness. The entire civil service abandoned their duties. Little of the governing infrastructure escaped the widespread looting and destruction. There was no legitimate political authority to speak of, and there were no legitimate political figures, such as Nelson Mandela in South Africa, available to rule.

Civil Society and Nation Building

The United States and its allies became fully responsible for a country the size of California with no legitimate political institutions, no functioning bureaucracy, no constitution, no rule of law, and few qualified Iraqis with sufficient public support to be placed in positions of leadership. There was no choice but to become an occupying and nation-building presence in an Islamic society in the heart of the Arab Middle East. It is hard to fully comprehend the difficulty of the odds. The only institution that proved to be resilient was the one that had previously held power, the Baath Party. Recent evidence shows that remnants of the party formed a significant component of the insurgency, supplying tactical brains and operational support for the armed rebellion.

The vast majority of American civilians who signed up for the postwar rebuilding effort in Iraq did so not because they were caught up in arguments about WMDs or because they harbored a desire to carry out vengeance for 9/11. They signed up because of their enthusiasm to help build a new nation in the heart of the Muslim Middle East. In private conversations, they frequently expressed the hope and expectation that Iraq would become a thriving Western-style democracy with a modern administrative state.

Many on the team had at least a vague familiarity with the successes of Germany and Japan, and this influenced their view of the task in Iraq. Few fully appreciated the extent of the differences in the circumstances. Reorganizing and renewing an industrialized economy, as in postwar Germany and Japan, is far easier than building a new one in a country where none previously existed.

The conditions following World War II that permitted outside powers to rule over and rebuild nations are not likely to exist in many of the conflict-prone regions of the world today. A Western, nominally Christian nation is almost certain to run into difficulty in building institutions that affect core values, beliefs, and practices in the Muslim Middle East. The challenge is further complicated by history, by negative perceptions of U.S. power objectives in the region, and most of all by distrust over issues of religion and culture.

Francis Fukuyama identifies two critical components to postwar reconstruction: one is "state building," the other "nation building." Though often confused, they are different functions.

The first function, state building, includes stabilizing the country after the conflict, offering humanitarian assistance and disaster relief, rebuilding the infrastructure, and jumpstarting the economy. State building, according to Fukuyama, is about "creating or strengthening such governmental institutions as armies, police forces, judiciaries, central banks, tax-collection agencies, health and education systems, and the like." This first phase, he adds, "is well understood, and although difficult, it lies within the capability of both the United States and the broader international community."[27]

The second phase, nation building, begins after stability has been achieved. As Fukuyama explains, it consists of "creating self-sustaining political and economic institutions that will ultimately permit competent democratic governance and economic growth." This second phase is far more challenging than the first, and it is more important in the long run. The key word, Fukuyama says, is "self-sustaining." Nation building is really about "creating or repairing all of the cultural, social and historical ties that bind people together as a nation." As critics have pointed out, this function is very difficult for outside powers to accomplish. Outside intervention will likely falter in time unless the occupying power is able to leave behind "stable, legitimate and relatively uncorrupt indigenous state institutions."[28]

Iraq illustrates the difficulty of carrying out either of these functions well, particularly the nation-building part. The United States has done a commendable job in building a new system of civil administration with improved standards of transparency and accountability. It has clearly improved services. It has put in place a variety of new laws favorable to a modern administrative state and a functioning private economy. In fact, any balanced system of grading would issue good to excellent grades for the job done in improving health, education, banking, currency, and a variety of other functions of public administration.

Most will acknowledge, however, that the job of nation building proved significantly harder than expected. American success in building a viable political society in Iraq—one in which diverse people join together around a shared sense of national history, identity, and destiny —remains quite uncertain. Anyone who served in Iraq will likely point out that "drilling down" into the subsoil of a historically fragmented nation to reverse deep patterns of ethnic and religious division was vastly harder than initially imagined.

In Germany and Japan, the social, political, and economic changes —the "political transformation"—that were engineered in the postwar reconstruction effort outlived the American occupation. In Iraq, many of the same expectations accompanied the liberation but soon followed a path of retreat in the face of the complicated social and political realities on the ground. Many people slowly came to the realization that it would take years or decades to build a middle class, to privatize state-run industries, and to cultivate a free-market entrepreneurial economy. And many worried that these changes might not come fast enough to sustain the fledgling democracy.

Nations are complex fabrics of history, of blood ties, of cultural or religious belief systems, and of shared or disputed aspirations. As is often remarked, Iraq is an "artificial" construct as a nation, consisting of three regions that were cobbled together by the British after the collapse of the Ottoman Empire. It struggled through various regimes before Saddam, and whether or not it evolves peacefully toward a functional nation-state in the traditional meaning of the term remains to be seen. Its history is filled with violence and suffering, punctuated by intermittent periods of peace. Iraq has little experience with what the historian William Polk calls "constructive civil order."[29]

Constructive civil order may emerge, but it will be difficult to create a cohesive federal system in which the internal parts—chiefly, the northern Kurds, central Sunnis, and southern Shiite regions— function together as a whole. From the beginning of the postwar period, the drift was toward the familiar and safe affiliations of tribe, religion, or region. The gravitational pull was toward fragmentation and sectionalism. Every effort to fashion a whole out of the parts, whether in forming the Governing Council, forging a constitution, or fashioning political parties, involved powerful pressures in the direction of communal affiliation, not nationhood.

The jury may be out for another decade on whether it is possible for America to transplant a Western-style constitution that diffuses and separates power, guarantees minority rights and religious freedom, and empowers all citizens equally. Many high-minded Iraqis professed an interest in the contents of the newly adopted constitution, but even the best were drawn inexorably by the course of daily political life back to deeply ingrained attitudes and historical patterns associated with religious, tribal, and ethnic factions. A long history of grievances militates against the rapid adoption of such essential democratic values as tolerance, pluralism, and compromise. Even the political parties, which one might have hoped would form the basis for social integration and pluralism, became ethnically or religiously homogeneous, only exacerbating social divisions and illustrating how democracy reflects as much as it shapes society. Unlike Germany and Japan, national identity in Iraq is a weaker force than ethnic, tribal, or religious identities.

BUILDING DURABLE INSTITUTIONS

Building democratic nations is messy, and it is difficult. Successful "revolutions from above" are likely to remain exceedingly rare. The key to long-term success in democratization and nation building starts with the realization that top-down strategies of political change face severe odds. If the daily operations of a democracy are little more than a superficial layer of official dealings and remote machinations that are otherwise irrelevant to the daily lives of the people, real democracy will not likely take hold.

Constitutions, pro-democracy parties, a free press, and sound governance reforms at the top are all essential, but political transformation will not occur unless there is a welling up of democratic hopes, intentions, and capacities from within society. For democracy to build momentum, the tide of culture, religion, and history must be moving in the direction of democratic values. Internal societal transformation must be allowed to progress, and that is the work of civil society.

Candor requires acknowledging that in most regions of the world where democracy is needed the most, it is stymied by a variety of obstacles that must be directly confronted if a new order is to be established. Some fledgling democracies are overwhelmed by internal dysfunction, humanitarian disasters, or refugee crises. Many are plagued by religious intolerance, pervasive illiteracy, economic stagnation, and weak institutions of state.

Some democratic societies must rise from the ashes of deep ethnic conflict or civil war, requiring the presence of U.S. or international peacekeeping troops. For nation building to work in these cases, some hard compromises are necessary, according to Marina Ottaway, "including military coercion and the recognition that democracy is not always a realistic goal." Nations, says Ottaway, were once forged by "blood and iron," but today we try to build them "through conflict resolution, multilateral aid, and free elections," approaches that have "not yielded many successes."[30]

Many governments have long histories of corruption and cronyism. In many of these cases, it isn't democracy that immediately takes root, but what Freedom House calls "pseudo democracy"—a system that has the "false trappings" of democratic process and a "façade" of electoral competition, but in reality is ruled by a crony-capitalist oligarchy through intimidation and corruption.[31] Democracy is little more than a paper construct unless it is built on democratic habits, aptitudes, and skills among large numbers of citizens. Democracy is only possible, in other words, if citizenship is cultivated.

CIVIC POWER: REFORMING REGIMES FROM WITHIN

Evidence from every region of the world suggests that wherever democracy is either being advanced or defended against erosion, it is owing to the power of citizen movements. "People power" is a major

233

source of pressure for decisive change in many nations that move from authoritarian rule to democracy. A Freedom House study found that "the force of civic resistance was a key factor in driving 50 of 67 transitions" from a dictatorial system, or 70 percent of countries experiencing such transitions.[32]

Fareed Zakaria argues that regime change in closed societies is not possible without the aid of civil society groups operating deep within. Where civil society groups have grown from within, regime change has occurred naturally, such as in Ukraine, Georgia, and Kyrgyzstan. In Iraq, where a regime had spent almost three decades destroying the underpinnings of civil society, the new state had to start at the most elementary stages. Zakaria concludes that U.S. policy must see regime change as a byproduct of civil society. "Look around the world today," he says, "and you will see regime change in places where Washington has no such policy and regime resilience in places where it does."[33]

To see how civil society drives democratization, one need only review the reactions of autocrats to the rise of a civic sector that sets out to enforce accountability. After years of allowing grass-roots activism, the Russian parliament in the fall of 2005 considered steps to bring all NGOs under strict state control. Russian policy is increasingly forcing all private organizations, from medical charities to human rights groups, to register with the state and have their activities monitored.

Holly Cartner, a spokeswoman for Human Rights Watch, described the Russian action as a "new chapter in the government's crackdown on civil society." She added, "Now that the Kremlin has neutralized other checks and balances, NGOs remain among the last independent voices that can criticize the government and demand accountability in Russia."[34] The drive to control NGOs came from ardent nationalist members of parliament, the most antidemocratic elements in Russia.

Aiding local civil society is easiest within those systems that are already open enough to permit outside support. Policymakers are

Civil Society and Nation Building

forced to confront the fact that in tightly controlled states, such as in many Muslim nations, outside intervention may actually work against the ultimate goal of liberalization. The best current example of this is Iran, where the State Department sent $85 million in fresh support to civil society groups for advancing freedom. Almost immediately, some of the human rights activists with external ties were imprisoned for their activity. Abdolfattah Soltani, an Iranian human rights lawyer who spent seven months in prison, said that this kind of support "has a negative effect, not a positive one." Soltani said that repressive states like Iran see external support as a pretext to clamp down further on human rights activists, claiming they have secret relations with foreign powers.[35]

Vahid Pourostad, editor of *National Trust*, a newspaper with ties to Iran's democratization movement, urges America to study the history of Iran more carefully before acting. Whenever the American public supports something, he says, the Iranian people do the opposite. "Generally speaking, it is impossible to impose something from outside. Whatever happens will happen from inside."[36]

The United Nations and other major institutions have come to recognize the central role of grass-roots civil society in advancing democracy. A UN report released in June 2004 argued that "effective engagement with civil society and other constituencies is no longer an option—it is a necessity in order for the United Nations to meet its objectives and remain relevant in the 21st century."[37]

NGOs increasingly serve as the eyes and ears of the international community in identifying human rights abuses. Groups devoted to monitoring abuses dispatch field officers around the globe and file detailed reports. Much of the monitoring is done by groups such as faith-based organizations that are simply there on the ground, delivering humanitarian assistance to refugees and other at-risk populations. In Darfur, for example, the most effective action to halt violence and restore peace and security, according to Joe Loconte, "has come from the institutions of civil society—namely, independent human rights organizations—not from any UN officers, agencies or commissions."[38]

Commenting on how the nation of Georgia transitioned to democracy via the "Rose Revolution," President Mikheil Saakashvili attributed this success to civil society. What made peaceful change possible, he said, wasn't military power, but a network of local institutions and partnerships. "There is the internet, TV, NGOs. Americans helped us most by channeling support to free Georgian news media. That was more powerful than 5,000 Marines." Saakashvili added, "you can't impose civil society from outside—you see that in Iraq." It involves a struggle that can take decades, but there is no alternative path.[39]

Freedom House concludes that once an opening for political change appears and a transition to democracy is under way, it is essential for donors to continue "to support pro-democracy civic groups as a means of ensuring that there is civic pressure on the new authorities to continue down the path of liberalization and reform." Freedom House has called for a "paradigm shift" among development agencies and other funding sources, to better understand the importance of "indigenous civic resistance directed at challenging authoritarian rule." The priority should be to "provide significant resources and knowledge to NGOs, civil society groups, and the fostering of broad-based indigenous coalitions."[40] These coalitions generate the environment where groups work together and deal with differences, where democracy is learned and new leaders are recruited and trained.

There are plenty of past successes to draw upon. For example, the history of democratic liberation movements in Eastern Europe is filled with examples of how American agencies fostered the growth of local NGOs in the 1990s. According to government documents, vigorous USAID support for local nongovernmental organizations was a "critical element of strengthening civil society in the region."[41] This included assistance in developing parties, conducting elections, and creating grass-roots civil society organizations.

Similarly, USAID provided generous support for civil society organizations in South Africa that opposed apartheid and then assisted in the transition to a new system, often in the face of serious resistance by the government. By the time the new government came to power, "there was a fairly strong civil society foundation upon which to build."[42]

GROWING INSTITUTIONS FOR ECONOMIC EMPOWERMENT

Perhaps the most compelling point that skeptics of democratization make is that for democracy to be sustained, it must be accompanied by the development of durable and transformative social and economic institutions internally. Democracy may be the evolutionary outgrowth more than the creator of those institutions. Addressing the sweeping reversals that seem to be occurring in Latin America, Jorge Castaneda writes that "democracy, although welcomed and supported by swaths of Latin American societies, did little to eradicate the region's secular plagues: corruption, a weak or non-existent rule of law, ineffective governance, and the concentration of power in the hands of a few."[43]

The campaign to promote global democracy often focuses on political liberalization. But reforming or removing a dictator is not enough. Building democracies is difficult in the absence of a thriving middle class and a sense that political empowerment will lead to economic advancement. In fact, citizen support for new democratic governments can quickly wane if newfound political freedoms do not yield economic improvement. Commenting on the obstacles to raising up economies from the ashes of failed regimes or conflict, James Dobbins states: "No post conflict program of reconstruction could turn Somalia, Haiti, or Afghanistan into thriving centers of prosperity."[44]

Although the precise relationship of democracy to economic progress is disputed within expert circles, it is clear that economic liberalization and the expansion of democratic freedoms go hand in hand. Whether economic growth produces political liberties, or democratization delivers the fruit of prosperity, there is evidently a positive relationship, and the two are mutually reinforcing. Democratization does not guarantee economic advances, nor does economic improvement by itself guarantee the rapid development of a deep, broad democratic culture grounded in political liberalism. Local circumstances yield different outcomes. But it is hard to imagine economic prosperity coexisting with political authoritarianism for long. Similarly, democracy surely raises popular expectations that standards of living will improve.

The relationship of democratization to prosperity can be observed in Asia, where economies are growing dynamically. A variety of Asian nations have become genuine democracies, including South Korea, Taiwan, the Philippines, Thailand, and more recently Indonesia. Throughout the region, says Francis Fukuyama, "democratic transformation has been underpinned by strong economic growth."

China is experiencing spectacular economic growth, and the hope and expectation of many China watchers is that the rise of capitalism will likely permit incremental gains in personal and religious freedoms. But there are real doubts as to whether the Chinese government intends to allow more progress toward openness and pluralism. In a September 2005 conference titled "Building a 'Harmonious Society' in China: Non-Governmental and Faith-Based Organizations As Agents of Social Change and Stability," the Center for Strategic and International Studies explored a variety of entities and activities that are thriving outside of the official state. The premise was that while China was becoming more comfortable with economic entrepreneurship, social entrepreneurship, and new concepts of "investing in China's reservoir of social capital," these trends would inevitably yield gains in the area of political liberalization.

The unfolding experiment in China illustrates how a limited embrace of freedom by state authorities may not be sustainable. China now has 111 million Internet users and 30 million bloggers. Authorities have declared commentary on politics, economics, and foreign affairs out of bounds, but propaganda czars do not have the resources to police the unruly arena of Web-based communication. The accessibility of the Internet is giving rise to a tech-savvy young urban population that is increasingly capable of outsmarting their unelected rulers and censors. There are simply too many easy ways around the controls. "Blogging represents a grassroots media," notes Mao Zianghui, one of China's leading bloggers. "We can use it to solve social problems."[45] Fang Xingdong, founder of a service provider that registers fifty thousand new bloggers each day, says, "There's no other use for the internet that will bring greater reform to Chinese society."[46]

True democratization ultimately requires the establishment of strong government institutions that stand firmly on the side of freedom and rule of law. Because the tendency in American political debate is to favor limited government, especially among conservatives, it is difficult for many to imagine any good coming from stronger governments. But that is often precisely what is needed to promote economic liberalization and prosperity in the developing world. Development is probably not possible without competent government institutions, grounded in the rule of law, with strict curbs on corruption, and modern laws covering banking, credit, and property.

The poor are in possession of large quantities of financial assets, but their wealth cannot be directed to more profitable use without adequate land and property titling or reasonable business registration laws. A major rush is on throughout the developing world to reduce the time, cost, and regulatory nightmare often involved in starting new enterprises. Obtaining licenses, registering property, and gaining access to credit can take months or years, greatly increasing the barriers to opportunity.

This is especially true in regions of the world where economic development has been systematically neglected, for example the Arab Middle East. It is often said that democratic states are not evolving in the Arab world because existing powers refuse to develop institutions, starting with those that expand the middle class, such as education and health care. The Arab Middle East has no choice but to confront the unsustainable situation in which Arab populations are growing at 4 percent annually while economies languish with a 1 percent annual growth rate, which has led to festering problems of unemployment.

From Syria to Morocco, according to *Newsweek*'s Stephen Glain, "financial institutions are too primitive and regimes too inept to meet their economies' basic need for capital." Banks, though flush with oil wealth, are reluctant to lend money, and stock markets are largely ignored. Trade is stagnant and foreign direct investment is less than half the global average. In comments to *Newsweek*, Jordan's Prince Hassan stated, "Arabs have been humiliated by their own governments." [47]

Things were not always this way. Arabs and Muslims were once known for producing and peacefully trading a wide array of fine products including textiles, jewels, and iron and glass works. "The free flow of goods and money informed the character of early Islam," says Glain, and "part of Muhammed's appeal was his reputation as an honest merchant." The pilgrimage to Mecca was big business, as reflected in the motto of the day: "May your pilgrimage be accepted, your sins be forgiven and your merchandise not remain unsold." [48]

Yet today, Islamic and Arab states are in crisis. The staggering oil wealth of many Arab states has actually stunted the development of a diversified economy and general prosperity. Oil wealth may be the single greatest cause of economic and political stagnation. Nearly all of the world's oil states are undemocratic; most are dictatorships. In too many Arab states, religious conservatism, paranoid obsessions about secret police, and narrow tribal loyalties all contribute, says Glain, to "dysfunctional dictatorship, rotten at the core." [49]

Any effort to reform corrupt and incompetent states must be accompanied by the creation of new institutions to harness capital for productive use, as well as modern laws aimed at reviving private enterprise, capital markets, and international trade.

Speaking on the nation-building project in Afghanistan, Ashraf Ghani and Clare Lockhart state that "credible institutions and public finance would contribute more to security than would the deployment of troops." It is not merely the availability of money that counts, they stress, but "such things as rule of law, transparency and predictability." It is exclusion from the right to make decisions in their own countries, not resentment of the West, that is feeding resentment among the poor—and that will drive reforms in Arab and Muslim states. "The need for functioning states," they conclude, "has become one of the critical issues of our times." [50]

Proof that economic as well as political liberalization is possible in predominantly Muslim societies is offered by the experience of Muslim Asia. In the Muslim societies that are open and thriving, moderation appears to have established itself, as in Turkey and Malaysia, for example. Pakistan, a Muslim nation in which Islamic political parties have tended toward moderation, is growing at 8 percent annually. Says Fareed Zakaria, "for all the noise, fundamentalism there is waning. If you are comfortable with the modern world, you are less likely to want to blow it up." [51] Observers are worried about the direction of Pakistan in light of events in late 2007, when a state of emergency was declared and supreme court judges were dismissed. It remains to be seen whether Pakistan is trending democratic or relapsing into authoritarianism.

CHAPTER ELEVEN

Conflict and Reconciliation in the Context of Nation Building

"Words fail you when you come to a place like this."[1] These were the only words that Paul Wolfowitz, president of the World Bank, was able to utter while visiting the genocide museum in Kigali, which features large stacks of human bones and skulls. The memorial was built to honor and remember the one million Rwandans who were slaughtered with ruthless efficiency by simple machetes in the course of ninety dark days in 1994.

In April of that year, Rwanda descended from a nation-state into a Hobbesian state of nature. The entire country, from the capital to the most remote village, imploded in a genocidal nightmare. No one was spared the horror. Every sector was affected, and every sector contributed. As President Paul Kagame has stated, "Rwanda experienced a total failure of leadership. Every institution failed: the government, business and even the church."[2]

Every institution failed, including—it must be stated—civil society. No honest treatment of the global rise of democratic civil society can bypass the sobering reality of ethnic and sectarian conflict and its corrosive power. Although civil society is the principle force advancing "bottom-up" democratic ideals all around the world, civil society alone is not sufficient. It is not a substitute for strong democratic institutions and rule of law. In many cases, it is too weak a force by itself to prevent conflict from breaking out. It too can become corrupt, as the experience of Rwanda and dozens of other countries suggests.

The lesson from dozens of crippling conflicts that dot the landscape of the developing world is that nation building can succeed only if internal divisions are resolved. Where a past conflict has crippled a country, forging ahead with a new social contract requires a just political settlement and social reconciliation.

The Dark Force of Conflict

If anything has the potential to derail the more optimistic trends noted in this book, and to reinforce the existing divisions between the "haves" and the "have-nots" of the world, it is conflict and civil war. Although democratic civil society is on the march across the globe, the unpleasant fact is that in dozens of locations, the forces of progress are impeded and in some cases overwhelmed by what may be the darkest dynamic on earth today—ethnic and sectarian conflict. Upwards of fifty nations today are at or near civil war conditions and are deeply dysfunctional.

Some observers believe that ethnic conflict has become the dominant global trend. Robert Kaplan, a correspondent for the *Atlantic Monthly*, takes a pessimistic view on the direction of history. A closer look at experiments in democracy, be believes, reveals that they are mostly "episodic," followed by rebel incursions, coups, and dysfunctional states. He predicts a "coming anarchy," with deteriorating economies in southeastern Europe, deepening ethnic conflicts in places like the Balkans, complete dysfunction in much of Africa, the continued erosion of nation-states, and growing ethnic violence fueled by resource scarcity.[3]

We dread conflict and have a difficult time contemplating it, says Kaplan, yet for many others it is understood as a way of life. While the West is preoccupied with how to manage middle-class entitlements, there is a large number of people on the planet "to whom the comfort and stability of a middle-class life is utterly unknown," and who "find war and a barracks existence a step up rather than a step down." Only when people attain a certain economic, educational, and cultural standard does the natural aggression that is a part of being human become "tranquilized."[4]

Writing in *Foreign Affairs*, John Rapley describes the arrival of a "New Middle Ages" in an essay by that title. Replacing nation-states, he says, are gangland cultures in which numerous "mini-states" emerge with little more than symbolic ties to the nation, each with its own localized economy, social structures, and even political systems; each operating in highly fragmented territories with many overlapping authorities. This is a world of shantytowns governed mostly by their own armed gangs, who deliver services on the basis of patronage.[5]

Some countries are retreating from the modern nation-state before even passing through modernity, says Rapley. "Large sections of Colombia have gone this way," he writes, "as have some of Mexico's borderlands and vast stretches of the Andes and the adjoining rain forest." Other countries, such as Afghanistan and Somalia, "are more or less governed by warlords." Private militias have carved up large swaths of the Congo, Papua New Guinea, and the Solomon Islands. The list "continues to grow," says Rapley. "The state's retreat is a global phenomenon."[6]

Military planners are anticipating a new "loose and shadowy" form of unconventional war that is replacing the types of wars that were waged for centuries by nation-states. In these struggles, writes the military historian Martin Van Creveld, "the radius of trust" is limited to the tribe, immediate family, or guerrilla comrades, which means that political settlements operating at the level of nation-state are far harder to come by. Borders mean little, while the "sedimentary layers of tribalistic identity and control mean more." Van Creveld predicts that "religious fanaticism" will play a larger role in armed conflict than during any time in the previous three hundred years.[7]

Much has been made of the "flattening" of the globe, thanks both to the end of the superpower rivalry between the United States and the Soviet Union, and to advances in communication technology.

Closed societies everywhere are being pried open, and individuals have unprecedented opportunities to make their voices heard. Accompanying this flattening process, however, is an equally consequential fragmentation, provoked by long-simmering sectarian prejudices and ancient animosities that were held in check for decades by superpower competition and repressive regimes.

Many impoverished and disenfranchised individuals in the Third World are embracing ethnic or religious identity in order to gain solidarity and power, while many politicians are willing to exploit group allegiances. The genocide in Rwanda was an example of a communal conflict involving darkly prejudicial ethnic attitudes that festered for decades, then spiraled out of control. In fact, those attitudes were cultivated and exploited by previous governments.

Although ethnic and religious strife is the emphasis of this chapter, conflict may also arise from mafia-like criminal gangs and their armed militia, feeding off weak or corrupt states. In some cases, conflict involves simmering border disputes that periodically draw in militaries or militia from neighboring states. Conflict may stem from competition over natural resources needed for survival. Whatever the cause, these conflicts destabilize entire regions and leave severely weakened institutions in their wake.

Another point of clarification: It must be noted that ethnic consciousness or pride is not bad in itself. In fact, the strong and familiar bonds of ethnicity are one component of community and a source of social strength. Low-income people in particular often form strong kinship ties to help meet their collective needs. Social networks cannot be understood without an appreciation of the role played by ethnic and religious bonds. Perhaps most importantly, the vast majority of ethnic enclaves live at peace with their neighbors and are tolerant toward other ethnicities.

Even so, the fact remains that the majority of violent conflicts in the world today are ethnic or sectarian in nature.

Of all the conditions that stymie social and economic progress, the most consequential is civil conflict. According to the UN, "22 of the 34 countries that are the farthest away from achieving the Millennium Development Goals are affected by current or recent conflicts." Poor countries often find themselves stuck in a cycle of deepening poverty and intensifying violence, which feed voraciously off each other. And as the UN report explained, "countries emerging from violent conflict are also prone to relapse." [8]

Where conflict is a fact of life, governments and aid agencies spend most of their resources and time caring for displaced people, providing humanitarian assistance to the swelling numbers who have been cut off from livelihoods, and trying to reconcile warring factions. Monies that could otherwise be used to build viable states and encourage social and economic development are diverted into the military sector. According to UN data, the world now channels upwards of $1 trillion annually into military expenditures. In the worst environments, even NGOs are often forced to exit. Away from the watchful eye of outside civil society groups, human rights abuses may escalate.

The vast majority of conflicts occur within nations, not between them. During the period of 1990–2002, there were 58 major conflicts in 46 locations around the world. Only three were interstate; all the rest involved subnational groups within countries. [9] Whereas conflicts with a neighboring country may strengthen solidarity within a nation, conflicts involving subnational ethnic and sectarian groups can rip away at trust and leave enduring scars. Conflicts may be deep-seated and date back decades or even centuries. During the Cold War, many regional conflicts were assumed to fit into the patterns of allegiance shaped by the Soviet-U.S. confrontation. Today they have their own internal dynamics, without either encouragement or restraint from superpowers or their regional proxies.

The worst conflicts are often linked to "failed states," a term that refers to a governing system so dysfunctional that it can't muster the political or security strength to curb lawlessness and violence. In failed states, political and police powers are often limited to a small radius around the capital and are used for protecting an embattled ruling elite, with large portions of the country left largely ungovernable. This can be the situation in newly established sovereign states, such as Afghanistan, where the central authority simply doesn't have the means to govern over its entire region.

It is impossible to build states that are viable or legitimate in the eyes of their citizens without gaining and employing the capacity to protect individual rights. That means having adequate legal and judicial systems and professionalized police and military, in order to exercise a monopoly on violence in the nation. This is the capacity that is frequently lacking in high-conflict areas, where achieving a political settlement among factions is difficult and the process of building legitimate and competent institutions is slow. In the wake of ethnic or sectarian conflict, institutions and economies are in shambles. Governments are left with depleted resources after years of heavy investment in security and police functions, and the political power of those in charge is tenuous. Frequently, much of the best talent that would otherwise be available to run government and business has fled the country.

The result is "weak states," which may have some legitimacy and even the best of intentions but are too emasculated to function well. In a weak state, the government loses control of its functions to other actors. According to the Brazilian economist Olympio Barbanti, "administrative chaos in under-financed governmental bodies often causes the transference of responsibilities from the central state to NGOs, local governments, and the private sector. The result is that such organizations assume duties that may go well beyond their capabilities, which causes further conflict."[10] In other words, many functions of government in weak or failed states are effectively privatized into the hands of whatever forces are available to carry them out—including forces that may exacerbate division.

The power of communal conflict is often hard for Westerners to comprehend. Steeped in the values of tolerance and pluralism, Westerners tend to project their ideals onto the world. We may assume that the answer to conflict is rapid democratization. We take for granted the presence of a certain degree of trust and good will. Our greatest error is in assuming a level of literacy that doesn't exist, or even some schooling in the principles of Western liberal democracy. In many countries where democracy is being presented as the answer to a host of problems, sizeable majorities are illiterate.

We may assume that internal divisions are about political issues that are essentially manageable—for example, conflicting philosophical ideas such as big government versus small, or the interests of the rich versus the needs of the poor. On such issues, reasonable people might find solutions in compromise.

But ethnic or sectarian conflict is rarely about sound governance, or grievances over access to health care or education. Conflicts in the developing world often center on group identity and collective power. In the case of a besieged ethnic minority—such as the Rwandan Tutsis, the Bosnian Muslims, or the Albanian Kosovars—the issue that generated violence was group defense and survival.

The West has had its own experience with disputes among ethnic and religious constituencies, but these are mostly nonviolent. The sectarian hatred that leads to violence or civil war is foreign to most liberal minds. When a conflict is about the survival of a particular ethnic group, it usually produces the demonization of a competing group, based upon ethnic or religious characteristics.

The depth and intensity of these conflicts is at the center of the controversial debate over democratization involving the "realists," represented by people like Robert Kaplan, and what some call the "romantics," who are bullish about prospects for continued progress toward the universal values of democracy.

Repressive regimes violate Western liberal sensibilities, but if one were compelled to identify some virtue in their existence it is that they are often able and willing to suppress ugly ethnic conflicts. Repressive regimes accept a variety of illiberal practices, but in so doing they sometimes prevent equally illiberal conditions from emerging—general violence, civil war, or genocide. These are tradeoffs that must be taken into account when democratization strategies are designed.

When bad regimes are replaced or forced to reform rapidly, outcomes can be highly uncertain. It is clear that highly repressive states rarely follow a smooth path to becoming open, tolerant societies. Democratization that is pressed forward too rapidly or recklessly can yield unintended consequences. Suppressed ethnocentric constituencies are suddenly free to act upon their base beliefs and attitudes. The pathway is cleared to settle old scores.

Free elections can produce illiberal results. Says development economist Bill Easterly, "a big problem with democracy and development, particularly with uneducated voters, is that politicians could appeal to voters' gut instincts of hatred, fear, nationalism or racism to win elections." Without core protections, "majority ethnic groups can exploit minority ones." In many ethnically divided countries, politicians exploit ethnic animosities to build coalitions that seek to redistribute income from "them" to "us." This problem is especially prevalent in Africa, says Easterly.[11]

Pro-democracy efforts are forced to figure out how to enable individuals to relinquish the safe and familiar categories of group identity and protection, and to pursue the higher road of democratic nationhood. Trading in narrow group identity for the more universal identity of citizen often proves too difficult for either local government authorities or outside NGOs to manage. In some cases, entirely new states must be created to accommodate dominant ethnic groups.

The tortuous path that may lead from tyranny to democratic pluralism was exemplified in the effort to construct a multiethnic democracy in Yugoslavia following decades of rule by a communist state. The moderate multiethnic forces had a difficult time overcoming the ethnic parties that rose to power when elections first occurred in the mid-1990s, securing both the presidency and most of the seats in the parliament.[12] The Muslims, Croats, and Serbs developed their own radical nationalist parties and struggled for dominance. Pro-democracy forces were simply no match for the deeper forces of group loyalty.

How does a nation bring about democratic consolidation after a period of intense ethnic conflict, such as in Bosnia-Herzegovina? Is it even possible to overcome ethnocentric enmity? What is clear is that older forces of nationalism and ethnic belligerence don't just disappear. One can only hope that they will fade away as political arrangements are put in place to encourage compromise and moderation, and civil society groups work at promoting cooperation and integration.

In the 1990s, the international community attempted to link groups throughout the former Yugoslav state to global civil society, drawing them into the norms and practices of democracy. How effective these steps were in helping ethnic constituencies overcome alienation and embrace the norms of citizenship remains to be seen.

For democracy to take root, all factions must believe they have a place at the table and a stake in the nation's future. Institutions must be built and operating procedures accepted by a cross-section of national constituencies, resulting in a political order that is viewed by most as at least nominally legitimate. Progress toward that goal can be greatly aided by elites who work to promote trust and establish the rule of law. In many cases, however, political elites prove ineffective in curbing ethnically inspired conflict because they too succumb to the temptation of relying on narrow appeals as a way to gain and hold power.

Perhaps most importantly, for democracy to take root, civil society must be free to flourish and to take on the role of encouraging democratic norms and practices. As the experience in the former Yugoslav state illustrates, civil society may be present, but limited in influence to a small number of enlightened elites with little reach beyond the NGOs or the universities that typically support them.

Ultimately, the normative values of democracy must be internalized by the people and put into practice in their daily lives. Otherwise, democracy becomes little more than a shallow set of procedures. In all too many cases, democracy movements gloss over the realities of ancient animosities, relying too optimistically on a thin veneer of contrived cooperation. Grass-roots empowerment can even become a vehicle for ideologies that are intolerant and hostile to the ideals of human worth and equality.

★   ★
★

IRAQ

In Iraq, ethnic and sectarian divisions were the major roadblock to building a new political order where large majorities would be able to trade in narrow loyalties for a new moral vision of citizenship. As the conflict dragged on, it became more and more clear that the insurgency was not essentially about poverty, lack of services, or nationalism in the face of foreign occupation, although certainly those played a role. Neither was it fueled primarily by an imported Islamism, although this element was especially brutal and effective in pitting Iraqis against each other. The central issue was a sectarian minority suddenly losing the power it had exercised for decades. In short, the insurgency was fundamentally about a struggle for group power.

The Coalition Provisional Authority in Iraq was widely criticized for not appreciating soon enough the magnitude of the country's ethnic fault lines and not addressing the divisions quickly enough. If there was a shortcoming, perhaps it was a failure to move immediately after the military operation to construct a national framework for reconciliation that would have provided an opportunity for ordinary Iraqis to experience a catharsis.

There is a body of trained specialists who are skilled in conflict mediation and reconciliation, usually associated with NGOs or international agencies that could have assisted in arranging a nationwide reconciliation summit. As reconciliation experts will point out, people who have been persecuted or tortured sometimes find it impossible to move on unless they come to terms psychologically with what they were subjected to. This opportunity was not presented to Iraqis in a forum that might have allowed national healing and reconciliation.

A national conference on reconciliation would have established the magnitude of Saddam Hussein's atrocities, openly confronted the sectarian wounds that had been opened, and invited Iraqis to forgive each other and move forward. In the midst of seemingly more urgent priorities such as providing security, restoring services, and getting an interim government in place, the priority of reconciliation lost out.

But even if the means existed to coordinate an elaborate and difficult exercise such as this in Iraq, it is hard to imagine a new national compact emerging out of it with the power to cancel out centuries of sectarianism and tribalism. The likelihood is that ethnic tension was bound to boil over one way or another, and that neither the Coalition nor the international community could have managed the process with any credibility. And there simply were no Iraqi institutions or indigenous leaders with the necessary moral authority or political legitimacy to convene such a gathering. There were no Iraqi leaders, either indigenous or among the exiled community, who carried a moral stature remotely comparable, for example, to South Africa's Nelson Mandela. What Iraq did possess was a history of pain and division, without the social or political institutions to manage it.

The practice of relying on tribe instead of national institutions was deeply embedded in the culture and had a long history. In countries like Iraq where tribalism is a dominant characteristic, many issues of daily life—including law, morality, family, professions, land and wealth—have been sorted out for centuries through communal governance and longstanding customs. The tribe provides the solace, the mediation, and the protection that individuals need to survive. Those patterns are reinforced under the kind of dictatorship built by Saddam Hussein, as people are forced to rely more and more on tribal and familial bonds.

Not surprisingly, from the earliest days following the liberation, the gravitational pull was in the direction of communal identity and solidarity. Many Iraqis were cautious about volunteering to help forge a new nation because they feared retaliation should their former abusers return to power, or because they lacked confidence in the unknown and untried. After decades of having all things decided by a single dictator, few Iraqis had any experience with taking initiative.

Family, tribe, and religious sect are the deepest and strongest bonds in human society, and are not easily cast off in exchange for the abstract promise of some alternative system of justice or security.

Communal identity and loyalty trumped Iraqi nationalism in determining the allegiances of the Iraqi people.

All of us who served in the Coalition Provisional Authority had our experiences of trying to get Iraqis to think like Iraqis and not as members of a splinter group with its separate identity and independent sense of sovereignty. The tug of communal loyalties proved too powerful even for those who were invited by the Provisional Authority to serve in the new government as civilian workers, police, or soldiers. In time, we could detect a growing desire among the factions to keep score on how power was being allocated among groups, especially at the cabinet level. As responsibility for government was transferred to the Iraqis, discussions among the Iraqis turned almost immediately to the question of who would get positions, hiring authority, and money. Would this or that position or perk go to a Kurd, a Sunni, or a Shia?

In what seemed like the most damaging development of all, when new political parties formed to participate in democratic elections, they promptly organized around ethnic and religious homogeneity. Rather than transcend or defuse sectarianism, the entire apparatus of the new democratic state—including civil society and political parties—came to mirror the tribal and ethnic breakdowns of the nation.

As this experience illustrates, participatory democracy is likely to reflect the underlying social and cultural realities. Having constitutions and procedures in place is not enough. True democracy that endures over time must embrace pluralism, religious tolerance, minority rights, and other liberties. These principles must either come from the pre-existing cultural or social subsoil, or be planted and cultivated where they are absent. Democracy must grow from the roots of society, even though constitutional arrangements are put in place from the top.

In Iraq, the early stages of democracy were overwhelmed by the issue of communal divisions. Assessing the situation at the three-year mark, Kanan Makiya, a powerful Iraqi exile who had helped make the case for liberation, commented: "The failure lies in the inability of Iraqi leaders to rise above their own groups and confessional allegiances." Makiya noted the lack of a visionary moral leader who was able to think and act "beyond the self-interest of their group." Instead of moral leadership, he saw the "elevation of victimhood into a quality," especially among the Shiite leadership. The Shiites, he said, placed "Shiiteness over Iraqiness." [13]

Makiya was describing a familiar pattern involving the deep wounds of a long-suppressed ethnic group. The Shiites, although a sizeable majority of the population in Iraq, had been kept out of power under Saddam Hussein, and were frequently persecuted and even slaughtered. It is not surprising that upon liberation they would immediately want to secure their rights and take their place as the majority, and above all prevent a return to power by the Sunnis who had supplied the power base for Saddam.

Similarly, one can understand why the Sunnis, the privileged minority that had long dominated Iraq, would worry deeply about their status under the Shiite majority. A variety of measures such as better security and improved services could have had a palliative effect for the Sunnis, but the real issue was their new sense of powerlessness in the face of a majority that might decide to govern without their input.

The Kurds had their own history of persecution as an ethnic minority under Saddam, and they had managed to gain partial autonomy and protection from the regime in Baghdad in the early 1990s. Their objective, not unlike the Sunnis, was to guarantee that no majority at the national level would again threaten the Kurdish people.

The Kurds and Sunnis played off each other as they jockeyed and negotiated their way toward securing the protections they felt they needed to survive as a group. For the Kurds, the purpose was to achieve rights and protections for themselves not as Kurdish Iraqis but as ethnic Kurds interested in maximizing their autonomy within the new nation. The fights from the past that shaped their fears in the present were all about ethnicity.

When democracy is forced to accommodate constant skirmishing among groups defined by ethnicity or religion, the process comes to be seen by most participants as a zero-sum game: one group's gain is another's loss. Such a view makes it difficult to attain a political compromise in which most people are able to transcend ethnicity.

There were a variety of constituencies in Iraq that tried to advance a more pluralistic vision. They were heavily concentrated in Baghdad and generally included those who had married outside their ethnic group, or were well educated, moderate in their Islamic faith, or familiar with democratic practices in secular nations. But again and again, those constituencies and their enlightened leaders tended to be outmaneuvered as parties and politicians catered to the grass roots for support.

This deeply entrenched group identification is very difficult for Westerners to fully comprehend. Our tendency in Iraq was to fall back on what was familiar in our own experience, which usually meant offering a vision of economic opportunity, better services, and democracy. But economic aid and reconstruction assistance "cannot fix the problem," as Stephen Biddle of the Council on Foreign Relations remarks. "Would Sunnis really get over their fear of Shiite domination if only the sewers were fixed and the electricity kept working?" Economic growth would likely ease tensions at the margins, but in the near term, "survival trumps prosperity, and most Iraqis depend on communal solidarity for their survival." [14]

Small steps in the direction of democracy may exacerbate ethnic divisions. In an ethnic conflict, says Biddle, "rapid democratization can further polarize already antagonistic sectarian groups." This is especially true in countries with little prior history of compromise, where one group mobilizes its constituency and rises to power by "demonizing" other groups, with which it must then deal. [15]

The symbol of Iraqi liberation became the ink-stained finger, which indeed spoke to the enormous courage of Iraqi citizens who defied the insurgency to cast a ballot. But as we are learning, more important than the ink-stained finger are attitudes, beliefs, and habits of life, which may be oriented either toward the democratic ideals of pluralism and tolerance or toward exclusionary group power.

In Bosnia, as the social and political environment became increasingly poisoned by nationalist ideology in the early 1990s, the multi-ethnic element of civil society was first silenced, and then it cracked under pressure. Elites and political parties solidified around ethnic identities, and civil society was gradually replaced by ethnic community.

Civil society groups can certainly be ethnically homogeneous, but to truly be a part of civil society they must seek peace and justice for all persons and groups in society. Ethnic or religious differences should not get in the way of the democratic ideal. For democracy to evolve, there must be a minimum of consent over procedures and principles. Replacing ethnic divisions requires building new institutions that foster trust and generate economic opportunity, the very activities often curtailed by violence.

The experiences of past decades pose numerous questions for policymakers. Where do the qualities of liberal society come from and how can pro-democracy leaders and movements bring them into being? How do ethnically demarcated societies become ethnically diffused? Where there is a burden of nationwide conflict, how do you change the political and cultural DNA of an entire country in hopes of creating a future of democratic pluralism?

MODELS FOR OVERCOMING CONFLICT: THE RWANDAN EXAMPLE

A steady stream of Westerners now make their way to Rwanda, driven in many cases by curiosity over the grisly events of 1994. For a Westerner visiting one of the country's genocide memorials, the first shock happens when his soul is forced to absorb the moral horror of the primitive killing that went on there over the course of three months. The second shock happens when the visitor's mind engages in the grim calculation of the ruthless proficiency that was required to accomplish a massacre of that scale.

One of the many remarkable aspects of the violence was the sheer speed and brutality of it. The genocide was launched on April 6,

1994, and by the end of the month, perhaps half of the nation's Tutsi population was already dead. The killing then continued at a slower pace, but by the time three months had passed, 800,000 Tutsis and 100,000 moderate Hutus, also deemed enemies, had been eliminated. The killers in Rwanda slaughtered with an efficiency that exceeded the Nazi concentration camps, according to Jack Fischel, a professor of history at Millersville University who has studied the two cases in comparison. The Hutus killed at "three times the rate at which 6 million European Jews were killed by Nazis in the 1930s and 1940s." Rwanda, says Fischel, was the site of "the most efficient mass killings since Hiroshima and Nagasaki."[16]

What force within human nature is powerful enough to generate so ferocious a hatred and so tireless a determination to wipe out an entire people? Yes, evil exists, but how could it have amassed its force with such fury, advanced with so little resistance, and consumed an entire country—all while the world willfully turned a blind eye?

Paul Rusesabagina, who was present during the genocide but has become a controversial figure for politically charged comments he has made, has nevertheless identified conditions that must be in place for genocide to occur. Requirement number one is that the world look away. Along with international indifference, he says, there must be a "cover of war." In other words, onlookers are encouraged to conclude that this is a war involving military combatants, not civilians. The other prerequisites have to do with conditioning the people. One is that ordinary citizens be "deputized," that is, conditioned to commit or accommodate atrocities. Perhaps the most important requirement is that "ethnic grievances must be manipulated and exaggerated" as a means of conditioning the killers.[17]

These prerequisites were all in place in Rwanda and the result was approximately one million innocent people being mercilessly slaughtered in a killing juggernaut.

★ ★
★

THE ANATOMY OF GENOCIDE

Genocides are not completely spontaneous and unpredictable. They don't just happen, taking everyone by surprise. The 1994 genocide in Rwanda, as hideously irrational as it was, had origins in a real history that can be rationally explained. It is also a history that could have been altered at various times, and had it been, an ethnic holocaust would have been prevented.

According to Bill Church, who heads a leading think tank in the Great Lakes region of Africa, "the 1994 Rwanda genocide was not just a hundred bad days in their lives that came out of nowhere and could not have been predicted or stopped."[18] It was preceded by numerous forewarnings for the entire world to hear. There had been smaller massacres before, along with political instability and assassinations. A variety of diplomats and military observers familiar with the country spoke of ethnic volatility in the early 1990s. In August of 1993, the UN High Commission on Refugees in Geneva warned of a "threat of ethnic killings in Rwanda." In March of 1994, the Belgian foreign minister saw an impending disaster—a prediction that went mostly unheeded.[19]

The 1994 genocide "was the Hutu government's final solution which was connected to a 40 year history of genocide ideology and also constant and targeted killing of Tutsi/Hutu population starting in 1959," says Church.[20] An ideology of ethnic hatred was perpetuated by government actions, and was built into the schools and the private sector. It was "a racist pseudo-philosophy spouted by the government that manipulated the majority's feeling of inferiority," as Professor Fischel puts it.[21]

This ethnic division had roots in colonial misrule. The traditional rulers of Rwandan society prior to the twentieth century were Tutsi kings. During World War I, the Belgians occupied Rwanda, and later they received a mandate to rule the country under the Treaty of Versailles. For much of Rwanda's history, the people groups "shared the same culture and religion, spoke the same language, intermarried, and lived side by side on the same hillsides," according to Uma Shankar Jha and Surya Yadav, who have studied the genocide.[22] Between the Tutsis and the Hutus there were some differences of trade and class, but it was the Belgian colonists who introduced the idea that they were separate races, citing minor physical differences that were previously inconsequential. The Belgians suggested that the Tutsis, who on average were thinner and taller and had lighter skin, must have had some European ancestry and thus were superior. The Hutus, darker and shorter on average, should therefore serve the Tutsis.

The Belgians fomented an ideology of racial hatred in order to divide and rule, says Church. Pitting Rwandans against each other served "to divert attention during the years of African Independence fervor in the 1950s and 1960s." For purposes of social control, the Belgians introduced the practice of having each individual classified on a government identification card as either a Hutu or a Tutsi—a practice more poisonous than any other. Even political parties organized along ethnic lines. It was this manipulation of racial attitudes that accounted for the eventual unfolding of ethnic violence.

In speeches, Rwanda's President Paul Kagame regularly condemns the colonial practices that "sprouted antagonism between Hutu and Tutsi." During the period of Belgian rule, he states, "colonial masters and religious preachers capitalized on 'divide and rule' policy," developing the idea that "Rwandan people are divided into distinctive ethnic groups, insisting that one group is naturally more intelligent than others and therefore has to rule over the rest."

The Hutus, the country's ethnic majority, eventually threw off colonial rule by an uprising in 1959, but the ethnic divisions planted by the Belgians had taken root and grown. The result was state exploitation of the minority Tutsis. The Hutus insisted that they were the emancipators of the Rwandan people and they blamed much of the country's trouble on the Tutsis.

Serious strife emerged during the Hutu reign as early as 1963 and resulted in the deaths of twenty thousand Tutsis. Several outbreaks of persecution followed through the early 1970s, driving a quarter million Rwandans, most of them Tutsis, into neighboring Uganda, which became a staging ground for an eventual Tutsi challenge to Hutu rule.

When limited democratization was introduced during the early 1990s, it became clear that small steps toward democracy do not guarantee political liberalization where the seeds of pluralism and tolerance have not been cultivated. On the contrary, the Hutu regime exploited democratic politics to rally the majority against their purported racial enemy.[23] The 1994 genocide was the final episode in a long-running drama in which, according to Professor Fischel, "the Hutu led government imagined that by exterminating Tutsis they could create a better world."[24]

On April 6, 1994, the Hutu president's plane was shot down by forces suspected to be associated with hard-line Hutu elements, operating inside and outside of the government, who had resisted efforts to broker a transnational government. But the hard-line Hutus instantly and predictably blamed the assassination on the Tutsis; and some would argue it was planned precisely that way.

Within hours, government radio stations called upon the Hutus to attack the homes of their Tutsi neighbors, spurring a "frenzied campaign of loot, rape, murder and arson."[25] Fleeing Tutsis took asylum in any space that was accessible—hospitals, hotels, churches, schools, and sports stadiums—but were soon overwhelmed by Hutu mobs and slaughtered en masse.

From Neighbors to Killers

The Rwandan genocide is widely regarded as one of the darkest chapters in human history. With minimal provocation, ordinary citizens and workers turned into butchers who killed on the basis of ethnic hatred. Indeed, genocide on the scale that occurred in Rwanda is not possible without the participation of ordinary citizens. According to eyewitness reports, teachers killed their pupils, customers killed shop owners, and neighbors killed neighbors. Husbands were reported to have killed their wives in order to save them from a more terrible death.[26]

Jean Hatzfeld, a French reporter with a background in human rights, notes that in Nazi Germany, "when the decision to commit genocide was actually made, the army, police, government services, and various sectors of civil society—educational institutions, railroads, chambers of commerce, churches—had already long been prepared to carry it out." The last phase in the destruction of the Jews "began without a hitch," he says, and "things in Rwanda went equally smoothly."[27]

Hatzfeld was able to arrange lengthy interviews with dozens of the killers who have since been convicted and jailed. He found men who described a day of killing as an ordinary day at work, but "less wearisome than farming." These men had "rampaged across the fields, singing as they went, hacking to death 50,000 out of 59,000 of their neighbors." One killer described the activity in mundane terms: "A man is like an animal: you give him a whack on the head or the neck, and down he goes."[28]

It all began almost effortlessly, according to a convicted perpetrator named Pancrace. He said a messenger from the organizing officials first went house to house summoning everyone to a meeting. There, a municipal judge announced matter-of-factly that "the reason for the meeting was the killing of every Tutsi without exception. It was simply said, and it was simple to understand." Pancrace said there were only a few questions raised about the details of the operation. One of them came from "some guys who asked if there were any priorities," to which the judge replied: "The only worthwhile plan is to start straight ahead into the bush, and right now, without hanging back anymore behind questions."[29]

Pancrace described a typical day: "During the killing season we rose earlier than usual, to eat lots of meat, and we went up to the soccer field at around nine or ten o'clock. The leaders would grumble about latecomers, and we would go off on the attack. Rule number one was to kill. There was no rule number two. It was an organization without complications." Alphonse similarly described a straightforward operation: "We would wake up, wash, eat, relieve ourselves, call to our neighbors, and go off in small scouting parties" to kill. There were no changes in the daily routine, only nonstop hacking to death.[30]

Pio drew comparisons between his lifelong occupation of farming and the "job" of killing. "We can't say we missed the fields," he remarked. "Killing was a demanding but more gratifying activity."[31]

The only requirement for the job was to show up with a sharp machete, and no serious instructions were given "except to keep it up." Adalbert noted, "A number of farmers were not brisk at killing, but they turned out to be conscientious." By this he meant they were willing to learn, "doing it over and over." He explained that "repetition smoothes out the clumsiness," as it does "for any kind of handiwork."[32]

Some of the "fumblers" had to be dealt with harshly and be compelled to "finish off a wounded person." According to Fulgence, "The culprit had to keep tackling the job to the end," and the worst thing was "being forced to do this in front of your own colleagues." Being incompetent at this task and failing to improve was considered shameful. "If you proved too green with the machete, you could find yourself deprived of rewards," said Jean-Baptiste. "If you got laughed at one day, you did not take long to shape up. If you went home empty-handed, you might even be scolded by your wife or your children."[33]

Joseph-Desire described how the peer support system would help the "bunglers." "If you are born timid," he remarked, "this is difficult to change, with the marshes running with blood. So those who felt relaxed helped out the ones who felt uncomfortable. This was not serious so long as it kept going."[34]

Little boys were encouraged to imitate their fathers, just as they learned the skills of sowing and harvesting in the fields. "That is how many began to prowl after the dogs, to sniff out the Tutsis and expose them," said Ignace. "That is how a few children began to kill in the surrounding bush." Clemintine explained further that boys were first shown how to imitate machete blows as if they were harvesting grain.

Next they got to practice their skill on dead people, then on living people they had captured during the day, and "the boys usually tried it out on children, because of their similar size."[35]

Elie explained that "the Rwandan is accustomed to the machete from childhood. Grab a machete—that is what we do every morning. We cut sorghum, we prune banana trees, we hack out vines, we kill chickens."[36]

In his interviews with the killers, Hatzfeld sought out "the secrets in their souls." But few moral insights emerged from the conversations. Instead, there were mostly passionless descriptions of a killing machine and how it worked.

One exception was Pio, who described the feeling of being physically and mentally taken over by "a stranger in me." Pio said: "We no longer saw a human being when we turned up a Tutsi in the swamps. I mean a person like us, sharing similar thoughts and feelings. The hunt was savage, the hunters were savage—savagery took over the mind."[37] Pio admitted that he did the killing, but he said it was as though "I let another individual take on my own living appearance, and the habits of my heart, without a single pang in my soul."[38]

Alphonse offered a similar observation as he reflected on the slaughter: "Man can get used to killing, if he kills on and on. He can even become a beast without noticing it. In a way, I forgot I was killing live people."[39]

Hatzfeld found evidence in his interviews to support the thesis that genocide had long been in the moral bloodstream of Rwandans and was never confronted. One perpetrator, Elie, stated: "I think the idea of genocide germinated in 1959, when we killed lots of Tutsis without being punished, and we never repressed it after that."[40]

When the Hutu leaders swept to power after declaring independence from the Belgians in 1962, the Hutu administration, according to Hatzfeld, "depicted all Tutsi as scheming, treacherous speculators and parasites in an overpopulated country." Crimes against Tutsis usually went unpunished. Hatred of Tutsis surfaced again and again in the following decades, making its way into laws, political speeches, and even humor. Popular radio stations aired comedy sketches and songs openly calling for the destruction of the Tutsis. The comedy skits were said to be so clever that even Tutsis found them funny. One Tutsi observer recounted: "They were clamoring for the massacre of all the cockroaches, but in amusing ways. For us, the Tutsis, those witty words were hilarious." [41]

The most sobering reminder of the power of ethnic hatred to penetrate to the deepest levels of a nation's moral fiber came in the form of shocking reports of churches and monasteries being used to entrap Tutsis. African Rights Watch has filed detailed reports on the conduct of two Catholic nuns who were responsible for the deaths of between five and six thousand Tutsis. A militia leader recalled that the nuns "got the Tutsis out of their hiding places and handed them over to us." According to this account, "those two nuns collaborated with us in everything we did. They shared our hatred for the Tutsis. I did not do anything without first discussing it with Kizito and Gertrude." In another case, African Rights Watch reports that five thousand Tutsis were held at the health center of a monastery. When the center was surrounded by Hutu soldiers and civilians, the religious workers who had been sent to protect the monastery joined the attackers. Men, women, and children were hacked, stoned, and burned to death. [42]

It is not that the Catholic hierarchy was indifferent to this behavior. In fact, Pope John Paul II was the first to use the term "genocide" in reference to the killing fields of Rwanda, on April 27, 1994. What happened in remote locations on the ground involving nuns and even a priest, however aberrant, is only further evidence that the germs of ethnic suspicion and hate can infiltrate every sector of society under the right conditions.

A NATION IN COLLAPSE

This detailed treatment of Rwanda's descent into genocide is offered in part to illustrate the destructive power of ethnic conflict as well as the magnitude of the difficulty involved in raising up a new nation where there is a history of ethnic strife. But Rwanda also offers the story of a nation that is attempting to rise above its past by relying on a "bottom-up" strategy of social transformation.

Some would conclude that the country had no future, least of all as a democratic nation. Rwanda sits in one of the most war-torn regions of Africa. The 1994 genocide left an already fragile political order in ruins.

Rwanda was essentially a collapsed and deserted state. Three and a half million people had fled, and the survivors who stayed were wandering warily from place to place, stunned, overwhelmed with fear, and hopeless about the future. Just about everyone was displaced in one way or another. Everything had been politicized and poisoned, according to one observer, and the populace was left in a general state of paranoia.

Rwanda's national institutions had disintegrated, and there were no revenues to fund a new government. No schools operated; banks had been robbed and looted; and there were no functioning services. For months, law and order was nonexistent and a cloud of insecurity hung over the country. Many former soldiers and militia attempted to regroup, hoping to carry on the genocidal campaign with support from outside the country. Many perpetrators would remain at large; many had fled the country and would remain menacingly at arm's length just across the border. New authority had to be instituted, and personnel and resources assembled to take up the urgent work of establishing security and capturing and trying hundreds of thousands of perpetrators.

Demographic factors further stacked the odds against a rapid recovery. Half the surviving population was under age eighteen, and 67 percent was under thirty-five. Of the surviving children, 30 percent had lost one or both parents. As is common in weak or collapsed states, Rwanda suffered badly from a lack of technical proficiency. The killing had spared no occupational category, least of all those with education or training, such as teachers and government workers. The civil service had been decimated, and educated elites with Western advanced degrees fled the country, many determined never to return.

A new Government of National Unity was formed, consisting of five political parties and led by the Rwandese People's Front. Paul Kagame's initial responsibility under the new government was to secure life and property for all Rwandans, so as to begin knitting together a new nation based upon the rule of law, individual rights, and pluralism. After becoming president, he set out to refute the skeptics who believe that new nations cannot be born from the ashes of old ones.

President Kagame is on a mission to prevent the Rwandan people from returning to their nation's genocidal past. He knows that he must completely exorcise the demon of ethnic hatred, but this task is far beyond the capabilities of any government; it is the work of society, and not merely the state. Kagame believes the country must undergo a deep and broad transformation. His aim is to build new governing institutions with firm foundations, and to cultivate a moral vision for citizens living together in a peaceful, just, and pluralistic society. Most of all, he believes it is not possible to build a new nation in the wake of massive ethnic violence without a large majority of the citizens firmly rejecting the past and embracing a new ethic of citizenship.

One might think that Kagame's strategy would be simply to get the Hutus and the Tutsis to sit down and recognize each other and realize their need to live together in peace. That's what neighboring Burundi settled on as a strategy. In Iraq, senior government positions are being allocated to Sunnis, Shiites, and Kurds in proportion to the country's ethnic breakdown. But Kagame sees this model as unworkable over the long term. Why preserve ethnic categories at all when one considers their superficial origins and unjustified nature, as well as the manner in which they have been exploited? Kagame's purpose is to create a nation, not of Hutus and Tutsis, but of Rwandans.

★ ★
★

Bottom-Up Reconciliation

President Kagame believes in the need for new government and constitutional policies to prevent ethnicity from raising its head again. The government is undoing policies that institutionalized sectarianism and discrimination, and instead encouraging a culture of respect for human rights and rule of law. Kagame has presided over the establishment of a constitution that holds it illegal to identify a person by ethnic or religious group.

But it requires more than acts of government to put decades of ethnic ideology and struggle for power behind. The Kagame administration recognizes that an entire society must embrace the foundational belief in the worth and dignity of all human life. The centerpiece of nation building in Rwanda is deep, authentic reconciliation among the people themselves. Kagame believes that the reconciliation process cannot simply involve a small subset of the nation's government or NGO elites; it must involve the entire nation and be owned by the people to the greatest extent possible.

A basic tenet of Rwanda's National Unity and Reconciliation Commission is that before colonialism there was an effective unity among the Rwandan people. The commission stated that "Hutu, Tutsi and Twa were all Rwandans on an equal footing, that Rwanda was a common country for them all and no groups could prevail over others in terms of citizenship claims." Therefore, Rwandans are capable of being one people again.[43]

"National unity and reconciliation is the duty of each and every one; it constitutes the pillar of national life of all Rwandans," the commission declared.[44] "Everybody has to do something," said the executive secretary, Fatuma Ndangiza. Elites must buy into the process, but success ultimately depends upon ordinary Rwandans. The commission has stated a determination to avoid "acting and behaving as a professional institution of experts." Instead, it is making a broad effort across the country to allow Rwandans to be heard, to address issues, and to take ownership of the renewal process. The people themselves must come to terms with their own conscience, with their grief and anger, and arrive at a place of forgiveness. Rwandans "need to make a thorough self-assessment" and "discuss truly and openly about their cohabitation."

The Rwandan people were asked to verbalize their own views of what went wrong in their nation, a time-consuming and painful process. Suppressing the facts of what happened would drive the demon of ethnic hatred out of view, but not out of existence, according to officials involved.

Not everyone in a nation of nine million is going to participate in a reconciliation process or find it helpful. Some simply don't want to remember what happened, let alone revisit and dwell on it. Some survivors worry about whether the truth will really come out and whether justice will really be done. Those who might have been perpetrators or somehow complicit in the atrocities may feel that the process is only generating shame for them and perhaps encouraging the relatives of victims to respond with retribution rather than forgiveness. Many survivors suspect that perpetrators are only seeking the best outcome for themselves under the laws that provide for restoration. By current law, a perpetrator is entitled to certain benefits if he writes a letter of apology to a victim's relatives and meets with him.

One Rwandan I spoke with, who works for the U.S. government, had remained in the country and survived the genocide but his mother was hacked to death. In early 2006, he visited with the person who killed his mother, but wasn't convinced that the killer was truly repentant. He couldn't help but wonder why the apology was so long in coming and suspected that it was motivated less by sincere remorse than by the legal advantages it brought.

The community-based, bottom-up approach to reconciliation also yielded useful information on what kind of society Rwandans want, and what they believe their government's policies and standards should be. For example, citizens stressed that policy in the future should not be imposed from the top, and that leaders must do a better job of explaining their policies and proposals to the people. Many stressed the need to build the capacity of local governing institutions, with no more domination by "one-man" models of leadership. Others spoke of mounting a full-scale effort to protect the people from corrupt officials and to ensure "transparency and dignity" in all contracts and government programming. Above all, people wanted citizen participation and input in determining policies.

These results should give cheer to those who believe ordinary people can't be trusted to embrace democratic ideals. According to Fatuma Ndangiza, "the people themselves said 'governance matters.'"[45] The people called for an end to the use of ethnic quotas by schools and for strict policies of nondiscrimination to allocate jobs on the basis of merit.

Bottom-Up Justice

Finding healing as well as a sense of justice for genocide victims is difficult and complex work. Standards that large numbers of Rwandans consider equitable are needed to guide the distribution of funds for victims and for the care of widows and orphans. The country must deal fairly and effectively with the resettlement of dislocated people. During the late 1990s, three million refugees slowly returned and had to be repatriated. The lack of available land for returning refugees is a big issue, especially when land for the most part is not deeded or titled.

Greatly complicating the challenge of reconciliation and the establishment of social peace is the need to reassimilate many of the perpetrators back into society. Upwards of half a million people had participated in the slaughter in one way or another. It would be impossible to imprison all of them, and neither would it serve the future security interests of the county to allow many of them to remain across the border in neighboring nations. Many combatants have slowly returned, some turning themselves in under new rules that provide conditions for their re-entry into society.

Rwanda has also had a severe problem of prison overcrowding, which has prompted charges of inhumane treatment. Officials have had little choice but to release large numbers of low-level offenders who must be settled back into communities. In early 2006, as many as 55,000 prisoners—the population of a small American city—were released.

A severe shortfall of lawyers and other legal personnel has made it nearly impossible to manage the enormous genocide caseload. The government estimates that it would take a hundred years to resolve cases through the conventional court system. This reality, along with a desire to apply local customs in the resolution of genocide cases, led officials to rely on alternative institutions that are grounded in indigenous traditions of justice.

Genocide-related cases involving high-level organizers were tried by the International Criminal Tribunal for Rwanda (ICTR) and by the government in conventional courts. But the national government also authorized a substantial role for local "gacaca" courts, which are village-based courts that rely on organic law rooted in local custom. There are 169,442 gacaca judges, serving in 12,103 courts. They are elected by the community based upon standards of personal integrity and trustworthiness.[46]

Under the gacaca system, defendants have the right to present witnesses and evidence on their own behalf in public trials. There is also a right of appeal to higher courts. But beyond this, the process of establishing justice does not presume to follow the exact standards of international law. In fact, the goal of the courts is not to mete out precise justice for perpetrators, but rather to promote reconciliation and restitution in ways that contribute to community building and social peace. Attempts are made to arrive at the best understanding of what happened and then apply a plan for restitution and a return to community that all parties agree to. Settlements usually involve a requirement of community service. For example, a defendant may agree to help construct a house for the relative of a victim or work for a local dairy cooperative for a specified amount of time.

Not surprisingly, given the volume of cases and the informal nature of the system, the process has been marked by more than a few imperfections. Some gacaca judges have been accused of bias, of bearing grudges against defendants, and in some cases, of being genocide perpetrators themselves. As international observers have pointed out, defendants have been confronted with unsubstantiated accusations and guilt by association. There were bound to be cases of alleged perpetrators being wrongly detained.[47]

Because the overriding objective of this process is peace and reconciliation, faith-based leaders have been encouraged to support the gacaca system and to ask their followers to respect its jurisdiction. One religious figure observing the process emphasized the importance of former perpetrators offering "their hands"—the same hands that killed —to serve and restore. "Churches are a place of healing," said Fatuma Ndangiza, executive secretary of the National Unity and Reconciliation Commission, and they specialize in "matters of the heart." Rwanda, she believes, cannot move forward without healing. She reports dramatic growth recently in new churches that are organized around a clear departure from the past.[48]

The role of religious organizations in advancing peace and reconciliation cannot be overstated. According to one religious leader, "truth sets some one free and liberates his or her mind." Rwandans must be helped to believe that they are not natural criminals, and that genuine reconciliation can mark a fresh beginning. Faith-based organizations and congregational leaders have joined together under an umbrella group to guide the process forward.[49]

As President Kagame acknowledged, all sectors contributed to the violent breakdown in Rwanda, including religious figures in several cases. But he believes that the overwhelming majority of congregations not only share his passion for renewal, but are also well positioned to preside over the healing of the nation's wounds. Faith leaders have come together to take account of past failures and to face the challenge of reconciliation and social inclusion in the future.

Civil society leaders know that the obstacles to achieving reconciliation and economic development are great. They also know how critical their role will be in preventing reversals. Civil society, according to the national commission, "arises out of need." The need today is for civil society to organize against the sins of the past and prevent them from returning.

Exemplifying that role is Bishop John Rucyahana from the Anglican Church in Rwanda, who lost many friends and relatives in the genocide and is now helping to coordinate the nationwide network of pastors and churches to promote reconciliation. In an interview, Bishop John explained how communities are born or reborn in the midst of oppression and pain. When the people suffer under bad regimes, they gather around new associations for protection and renewal. What matters most is what shape these voluntary associations take. Sustainable social progress must be "bottom-up," he stressed. "Communities must find their destiny in building the nation." [50]

THE ROLE OF GOVERNANCE

National rebirth in the wake of genocide cannot be imagined without a strong commitment to creating new institutions, new laws, and new leadership. President Kagame believes that the only way to avoid a repeat of past failings is to confront them directly. If the problem in the past was "anti-people" leadership, the answer now is to train a new generation of "strong leadership for a growing democracy" and equip the people to be citizens.

Many of Kagame's speeches dwell on the need to understand global standards of good governance and the need for citizens to expect it. Constitutional protections for individual human rights are important, but so is a new consciousness among the citizens. "First of all," Kagame says, "leaders at different levels ought to adopt a good culture of transparency, accountability and always be people's interests minded." [51] He has received wide acclaim for dealing effectively with the country's problem of corruption.

Conflict and Reconciliation in the Context of Nation Building

Kagame regularly reminds the people how previous corrupt regimes used ethnic discrimination to keep themselves in power and to prevent democratic culture and constitutional government from developing. He maintains that if Rwandans are helped to understand how they were exploited by outsiders and made to hate each other in the past, they will not again fall for the self-loathing idea that Africans are somehow bound by a law of nature to behave savagely toward each other. Kagame stresses the need for "resisting any sort of ideology and actions that are likely to divide the Rwandan people."[52] He speaks of creating a "culture of cooperation" and a healthy "culture of patriotism" that focuses on pride in nation rather than ethnic grouping.

In a private interview at his home, Kagame talked about building new institutions and new leadership, and about changing the culture from the bottom up. "Democracy," he said, "is about choice; about making informed and ethical choices." He repeated those words with emphasis: "*informed* and *ethical* choices." Conflicts in dozens of nations have revealed that citizens may be informed, yet also very wrong.

The Rwandan experiment in nation building would not be possible without a rebirth of ethics. A major focus of the National Unity and Reconciliation Commission is civic education, including workshops on how to foster citizenship and an attitude of service.

Kagame believes that although international friendship and assistance are needed, the reconstruction of a painfully torn nation must be carried out by Rwandans. He is skeptical in particular toward many outside NGOs. In many cases, he thinks they lack sufficient understanding of the history and culture of the country, and thus bring unrealistic expectations. To all outsiders, he offers a stern caution: A variety of activities carried out in a humanitarian spirit are simply not adequate. What counts is the "quality" of those actions—meaning whether they materially advance the work of building a nation with a new ethic of citizenship.

★   ★
★

Economics and the Struggle for
National Rebirth

The prospects for Rwanda's government may be tied to its ability to deliver real economic improvements to its people. Poverty may not have been a core causal factor in past conflicts, but persistent poverty is clearly recognized as an obstacle to putting the atrocities of the past securely behind.

Poverty can either create division or be identified as a common enemy around which a previously divided people come together. At least one Rwandan official, the minister of youth and sport, is attempting to capture the minds of the young by telling them they "must convert hatred of the past to hatred of poverty." For now at least, the goal of reducing poverty is serving to draw people together.

Rwandan officials recognize that social and economic development is paramount, and that the clock is ticking. The country needs economic growth in order to deliver social justice. "We can't talk about reconciliation in the absence of growth, education, and governance," said Fatuma Ndangiza.[53] Many of the underlying tensions in a country with a history of conflict have to do with the interlocking problems of underdevelopment: lack of sufficient food or clean water, basic services, and most importantly, jobs. Today, 60 percent of Rwandans are unemployed or underemployed.

Located in the interior of Africa, Rwanda is landlocked, with no easy access to ports. There are no waterways, no functioning railroads, and few adequate roads. The infrastructure is in a bad state of underdevelopment and neglect. Electricity is erratic even in the capital city and depends on expensive diesel-powered generators that are supplied by daily caravans of fuel trucks traveling long distances and crossing dangerous borders. Few in the countryside have electricity at all. It is very difficult to build a manufacturing economy or to bring technology into the country without capacity to generate power.

Subsistence agriculture remains the only form of livelihood for the overwhelming majority of Rwandans. For most, it is their entire way of life. Just about every acre of tillable land has been developed for cultivation, and in many cases, subdivided in order to accommodate new families. Land scarcity combined with rapid population growth remains one of the major challenges confronting Rwanda. The lack of an equitable land policy can quickly lead to tensions and threaten the national peace. Most observers believe that the shortage of arable land in Rwanda has been one factor in ethnic hostility.

Since 2003, the government has embarked on a land reform program that aims to establish clear private ownership of agricultural plots and to stop the subdivision of farms. For purposes of long-range development, the government has little choice but to try to increase the productivity of land under cultivation, and also to encourage migration into towns and cities, where a diversified labor market is more likely to emerge.

Rwanda is in need of much help to advance economically. It badly needs to boost exports and foreign exchange, and to do this requires infrastructure and foreign investment. Like many developing countries, Rwanda has attracted a variety of social entrepreneurs who want to try out new ideas on the frontiers of nation building. One firm organized by an American in his twenties is attempting to develop small solar-powered generating units in order to serve institutions such as businesses, schools, and libraries that currently lack adequate electricity. Another has drawn up plans for an elaborate system of fiber optic wiring, hoping to make high-speed Internet service available to companies that open operations in Rwanda.

Paul Kagame himself has proven effective at drawing the attention of the world to his experiment. In particular, he has succeeded at generating support from the U.S. business and faith communities. Kagame has personally won the trust and inspired the engagement of America's most prominent faith leader, Rick Warren, who pastors a 25,000-member church and is the author of *The Purpose-Driven Life*, which has sold 25 million copies worldwide. Warren is building a unique partnership with Rwandan congregations in the hope of advancing peace and reconciliation and strengthening their capacity to provide badly needed services.

President Kagame has attracted high-level interest in the American business community. Dozens of entrepreneurs and CEOs are championing Rwandan economic development and using their influence to leverage American business support. Two Chicago investment partners, Joe Richie and Dan Cooper, are getting commitments from companies to help export Rwandan coffee to American retail stores, to develop telephone services and open a call center in Kigali, and to improve agriculture and natural resource development.

CHAPTER TWELVE

Habits of the Heart: The Case for a Global Civic Culture

DEMOCRACY IS EASY to be for. But it is far harder to achieve than is commonly assumed. Democracy was made for democrats, and its ultimate success depends upon more than conducting periodic elections. Democracy cannot exist without institutions that cultivate citizens who are capable of exercising both the rights and the responsibilities of freedom. Moreover, those institutions upon which democracy rests must themselves be grounded in humane and democratic values. What the world really needs is a civic culture and a democratic ethos, not merely more elections.

The thesis that has been presented in this book is that America's chief export today is its heritage of democratic civil society. Americans, through their philanthropic giving and participation in nongovernmental organizations, are contributing to Third World development in ways and at levels that now eclipse traditional foreign aid. More important, American norms of philanthropy and civil society are spreading rapidly across the globe in both the developed world of Europe and Asia and in the underdeveloped world of Africa and Latin America. A proliferating array of nonprofits and volunteer-based organizations are finding effective "bottom-up" solutions to the pressing social and economic problems of the Third World.

At the same time, indigenous civil society is taking root wherever information technology and government openness allow it to grow, and it is linking electronically with its counterparts around the world. For the first time in history, a dynamic and globally connected civil society is emerging, independent of government. This is the single greatest force for global progress in democratization, human rights, and rule of law. Civil society belongs to citizens working together voluntarily toward common purposes and often in opposition to change-resistant governments. It sets the stage for citizens everywhere to participate in charting the direction of their societies.

In spite of all the obstacles discussed in this book, democratic civil society is evolving as an unstoppable force. Thanks to the universal advance of communications technology and the increased global consciousness of citizens everywhere, very few of the world's repressive political systems will manage to resist pressure for greater openness. In time, dictators will likely find it impossible to maintain totalitarian rule as it has been known over the past century.

This is why civil society is so important. It is the bridge to democracy and the wellspring of the civic virtues that sustain its growth.

THE WEST'S VISION OF CIVIL SOCIETY AS THE SEEDBED OF DEMOCRACY

The term "civil society" has a rich history as an integral part of Western political life and public philosophy, although some confusion remains over what it is and does.

Nearly everyone acknowledges that civil society, at a minimum, encompasses the entire web of voluntary associations that dot our social landscape: neighborhood groups, civic associations, charitable enterprises, places of worship, families, fraternal orders, and local voluntary networks "of a thousand kinds," as Alexis de Tocqueville put it. But just as importantly, civil society is linked to a moral order that undergirds democracy. It is inextricably linked to democratic political values.

According to Adam Seligman, "The very idea of civil society

touches on and embraces the major themes of the Western political tradition."[1] Among the major sources for the idea are classical philosophy, the Scottish Enlightenment, early American Protestantism, and Catholic social thought.

There was a burst of interest in civil society during the revolutionary period in the seventeenth and eighteenth centuries. John Locke's writing on the subject was especially prescient in light of today's global struggles with terrorism, genocide, and civil conflict. To Locke, civil society represented a passageway for men to leave a barbarian "state of nature" and enter into a commonwealth of free citizens. It was a means to reconcile liberty with order.

Perhaps no one left a more influential or enduring legacy on the American understanding of civil society than Alexis de Tocqueville, the Frenchman who traveled to America in the 1840s and studied its institutions. Tocqueville understood the organic roots as well as the requirements of democracy. He saw the institutions of civil society as important not merely because they perform innumerable functions in countless locations every day, but because they generate individual character and democratic habits. Through these institutions and networks, citizens develop the capacity to be helpful, trustful, and respectful toward others.

A variety of prominent twentieth-century figures sought to renew interest in civil society, including Robert Nisbet, Daniel Bell, Robert Bellah, Robert Putnam, William Galston, Peter Berger, and Richard Neuhaus. To varying degrees, these people addressed the problem of declining participation by citizens in the civic affairs and responsibilities of Western democracies.

Whatever the differences, civil society thought has always been concerned with the individual citizen in relationship to a democratic society and state. "What was common to all attempts to articulate a notion of civil society," says Seligman, "was the problematic relation between the private and the public, the individual and the social, public ethics and individual interests, individual passions and public concerns."[2]

Civil society is a public sphere, though not governmental. It is a space in which freely organized and self-regulating civic associations form and take direction from their voluntary members in pursuit of shared purposes and meanings. It is mostly a social mechanism, not political or economic. Civil society alone cannot supply the answers to deep economic problems or inequities. It is hardly an adequate antidote to disease and life-threatening poverty. Neither is it a substitute for sound government. While it offers individuals a defense against unwarranted intrusions by the state, it also requires the state's protection and at least modest support. Though not a substitute for political parties, civil society offers an arena for advocacy and debate over public concerns. It is, as one observer stated, a "non-legislative, extra-judicial, public space in which social difference, social problems, public policy, government action and matters of community and cultural identity are developed and debated."[3]

Civil society is certainly an instrument for checking and dispersing power. Conceptions of civil society have been enriched by a core principle of Catholic social thought, namely the concept of "subsidiarity," which holds that powers and responsibilities in a well-ordered state must be balanced and distributed, and that local communities in particular must be protected. According to Catholic teaching, "it is an injustice, a grave evil and a disturbance of right order for a larger and higher organization to arrogate to itself functions which can be performed efficiently by smaller and lower bodies."[4] Subsidiarity is grounded in a vision of man as intelligent, free, and social by nature and a vision of society in which free persons organize to advance common goals within an ethical framework. Closely linked to subsidiarity is the notion of the common good, which has strong support in Catholic moral teachings.

Civil society is a generator of vital social capital. In the real world of people's daily lives, civic associations are often formed to solve a community problem, to promote an idea, or to meet a social need. But civil society isn't merely about solving problems. The business of civil society is to create citizens.

Voluntary associations were "little schools of citizenship," according to Alexis de Tocqueville, who noted the creative tension that existed between self-interest and the public interest. He acknowledged the reality of self-interest as a factor in democracy, and one that provided much commercial energy and vitality, but he said that Americans tended to explain their actions by the "principle of self-interest rightly understood." By this he meant an enlightened regard for themselves that prompted them "to assist one another" and be willing to "sacrifice a portion of their time and property to the welfare of the state."[5]

Tocqueville saw the reciprocal ties of civil society as the "necessary" foundation upon which "the progress of all the rest depends" in democratic society. While large, paternalistic, and controlling states act like a parent, keeping its subjects in "perpetual childhood" and robbing them of their dignity, it is associational life that ennobles people and elevates them above narrow self-interest. Through civic participation, "feelings and opinions are recruited, the heart is enlarged, and the human mind is developed only by the reciprocal influence of men upon one another." These effects, he maintained, are not natural, even among democratic countries. They must be "artificially created, and this can only be accomplished by associations."

Civil society reinforces the very things democracy depends upon: social solidarity and a sense of mutual obligation. It takes isolated individuals and weaves them into the larger social fabric, linking them to purposes beyond narrow private or parochial interests. It was for this reason that Tocqueville saw voluntary associations as the basis of national greatness.

At the same time, voluntary associations play a critical role as mediating institutions, as a buffer between the individual and the large impersonal structures of the state and the economic market. Its basic dynamic does not involve seeking profit or power. Although civil society may be closely linked to small-scale, local commercial enterprise, it is not an economic sphere where self-interested persons compete for advantage. Although civil society does include many advocacy groups promoting improvements in human conditions, it is not generally understood as part of the political sphere where individuals and factions join forces to gain power. Rather, civil society is a social sector where individuals enter into horizontal relationships of trust and collaboration.

As Jean Bethke Elshtain puts it, the "sturdy but resilient institutions of democratic civil society" are the surest foundation for democracy and a check on the centralizing and totalizing tendencies of the modern state. Civil society is a bulwark against statist ideology and the grandiose dreams of national community that are often pursued by ideologues and demagogues, in democratic as well as totalitarian states. The thicker the layer of civil society, the greater the restraint on centralized or authoritarian government.

The weaker this layer of civic association, the stronger is the vertical relationship of the individual and the state—a relationship characterized by power, authority, and dependence. When civil society atrophies, the individual is left more and more powerless and isolated in a society where all roads lead to lawyers, courts, and social agencies.

One of the essential elements of democratic culture, and a by-product of civil society, is trust. Francis Fukuyama has described how societies with strong bonds of social trust and collaboration possess powerful advantages over those characterized by individual isolation and social fragmentation. Trust is a form of social lubricant that smoothes human transactions, whether civic or commercial, and a glue that secures bonds of human association. Strong communities, says Fukuyama, are rooted in and maintained by the "moral bonds of social trust, an unspoken, unwritten bond between fellow citizens that facilitates transactions, empowers individual creativity, and justifies collective action."[6]

CIVIL SOCIETY IS LOCAL AND VOLUNTARY

The citizen in civil society is not first a political subject or the client of a large governmental system. The citizen is first an inhabitant of a neighborhood, town, city, or state, with all the rights and reciprocal obligations involved.

Tocqueville's colleague and contemporary Edmund Burke spoke of the need to tie individuals in free societies to subnational associations or "subdivisions" in order to engender a healthy patriotism and love for mankind generally. "To be attached to the subdivision, to love the little platoon we belong to in society, is the first link in a series by which we proceed toward a love of our country and of mankind," said Burke. The key product of these local associations is social sympathy, a regard for others and for the common good.

Civil society must reinforce the role of volunteers and civic organizers in the face of tendencies toward bureaucratization and the encroachment of trained and pedigreed "social service professionals." That encroachment often squelches citizenship and discourages volunteers from getting involved in meeting neighborhood needs. The irreplaceable role of the local "subdivisions" or "little platoons" is often overlooked. Policy analysts, political advocates, and humanitarian NGOs alike tend to perpetuate a bias in favor of the large over the small, the national or international over the local, and the professional over the amateur. That bias militates against the cultivation of democratic citizenship.

It is worth asking whether large nongovernmental humanitarian organizations and advocacy groups—which often secure much of their funding from government and whose accountability is uncertain —really fall under the definition of civil society. In its truest form, civil society consists of associations that are of, by, and for the people themselves. If giant, publicly funded nonprofits are to be included, this inclusion should be conditioned upon a demonstrated commitment to the growth of local, indigenous civil society.

Building durable democratic societies requires the careful and painstaking cultivation of citizens at the bottom of society. Without citizens, says Jean Bethke Elshtain, "there is no democratic culture."[7] Democratization can receive a lot of assistance and encouragement from the top, but it is fundamentally a "bottom-up" enterprise.

The same principle applies to reducing poverty. The very condition of poverty involves matters of individual and social capacity. Escaping poverty requires that an assortment of local conditions be addressed. As the American urban activist Robert L. Woodson often puts it, solutions cannot be "parachuted into a neighborhood." Both the problem and the solutions exist in a local setting and within a particular "ZIP code," as Woodson observes. The conditions of poverty are thus not very susceptible to sweeping, abstract remedies designed by professional policymakers operating at a great distance from the problem.

Many of the counterproductive approaches tried over the past several decades failed principally because of the hubristic assumption that antipoverty activists and bureaucrats hold the key to empowerment of the poor. Instead, the poor themselves should be encouraged to take ownership of defining the problem and implementing a solution. There is much that governments and nongovernmental institutions worldwide can do to assist, but solutions to hunger, disease, and joblessness cannot be forced on communities. The answer to poverty is prosperity, and prosperity cannot be imposed from outside.

Both poverty alleviation and democratization require careful, layer-by-layer building around the existing assets of a society. When pressure is applied to accomplish more than may be realistic in the local context, the perfect becomes the enemy of the good. Civil society needs time and space to grow, and it needs certain conditions, including relative safety, rule of law, and support rather than resistance from powerful and potentially competing elements, such as ethnicity and sectarian religion.

For democracy to take root and become sustainable, the timetable for elections is of secondary importance. More crucial is that state authorities be either persuaded or forced to allow openness and freedom as an intermediate step, giving room for civil society to grow. The long-term cultivation of democratic citizenship depends on guaranteeing the right of voluntary associations and nonprofit groups to form and operate, whether these are women's groups, human rights organizations, independent media, or associations of free citizens ranging from choral societies to clubs for poets or birdwatchers. It is within these associations that individuals build trust and learn to collaborate in ways that strengthen democratic society. Once civil society is consolidated in a country, the likelihood of continued progress toward participatory democracy is improved.

DEMOCRACY IS THE OUTGROWTH OF A CIVIC CULTURE

Institutions are important, but more important are the ideas and values that they nurture. Institutions created by man, whether economic, political, or civic, reflect the men or women who create them. They can be morally good, bad, or neutral. Election bureaus and human rights commissions certainly qualify as institutions. But so did the Baath Party under Saddam Hussein, as did the government agency that designed and managed the concentration camps in Germany under Hitler, who rose to power by democratic means through the institution of parliament.

By contrast, civil society tends to be grounded in normative values. Most civil society organizations are made up of volunteers who are attempting to solve a social problem or improve the community. Civil society unavoidably touches upon matters of philosophy, morality, and religion—those elements that form the deeper layers of a nation's civic culture. Civil society involves institutions and associations, but also far more. It embodies the intangible values and beliefs that democracy rests upon. A healthy civil society—that which promotes the humane values of a liberal political order—generates an array of attitudes, habits, and skills that form social capital, the essential glue of democratic society.

The failure of societies and cultures to maintain ethical norms either creates deep divisions or causes many to resort to the domain of politics, which can be ill suited to adjudicate conflicting moral viewpoints because it involves the coercive powers of the state. For example, when voluntary efforts to achieve ethnic harmony through civil society fail, the likely result is the politicization of ethnic differences in the realm of political power. It is the mediating institutions of civil society that are "the value-generating, value-maintaining agencies in society," argue Peter Berger and Richard Neuhaus. "Without them, values become another function of the mega-structures, most notably the state."[8]

Americans tend to forget their own heritage of relying on voluntary associations to nurture civic and moral habits. According to Ryan Streeter, a scholar of civil society, it has been our primary associations, "from families to grassroots nonprofits to congregations to active professional associations," that have cultivated "a moral climate that most Americans consider desirable." The voluntary sector, more than any other, "possesses the capability to train our moral sensibilities and develop in us an active respect for the dignity of others."[9]

The term "civic culture" is used here because it conveys the idea of cultivation. "Culture" refers to the normative in contrast to the purely procedural factors of society. Culture is an integrated pattern of human beliefs, attitudes, and behaviors. A culture that promotes citizenship is one in which the idea of social responsibility is tied to customs, beliefs, and norms.

"Civic" pertains to a variety of intangible, even spiritual, qualities and requirements associated with being a citizen. A civic culture generates an environment in which every influence—including religion, morality, and the daily norms of life—propels the individual toward democratic behavior. A person socialized in civic culture understands all the rights and responsibilities of being free and independent. A product of civic culture is a true "democrat," committed to purposes larger than the self, and willing to think and act according to democratic values.

The notion of civic culture is offered here as an antidote to the deficiencies that often accompany campaigns for democracy.

One error is to assume that the implementation of democratic systems of government is equivalent to the advance of liberal principles such as pluralism, tolerance, and rights for all, particularly for religious and ethnic minorities. It is easy to blithely assume that the longing for democracy is always and everywhere a stronger force than the pull of ancient animosities or religious zealotry.

Second, it is tempting when talking about democracy to refer exclusively to the formal structures of constitutions, parties, and elections. Perhaps the best symbol of democracy in Iraq is not the ink-stained finger from the elections, but the millions of handshakes between Sunnis and Shiites that have yet to occur. Participatory democracy rests on the good will of the people. Elsewhere in the Middle East, elections have been used to advance radical Islamism, which at its core is undemocratic and illiberal.

Third, talk of democracy almost always refers to the affairs of state or of political society, when what is really needed is a civil society steeped in democratic values, to order and guide the daily lives of citizens. What are those values? Generosity, mutual assistance, self-sacrifice, fairness, trust and good will, minority rights and majority rule—apart from which there is no democracy.

If civil society is to serve democratic purposes, it cannot be seen as morally neutral—as an empty vessel into which any idea, attitude, or ideology is poured.

There is such a thing as bad civil society. For example, one of the Rwandan genocide perpetrators cited in the previous chapter mentioned having a problem with "habits of the heart." Killing was encouraged by the culture, and it became a customary practice. Bad civil society reflects and perpetuates the underlying ideologies of ethnic hatred and intolerance, while healthy civil society strives toward cooperation, reconciliation, and democratic pluralism. If civil society does not call upon individuals to yield a portion of their narrow parochial identity in favor of a larger democratic vision, it becomes merely an extension of the undemocratic environment operating around it.

★   ★
★

DON EBERLY

HUMAN DIGNITY: THE CORE IRREDUCIBLE CREED OF DEMOCRACY

Democracy can be planted anywhere, without regard to ethnicity, race, or religion, but it can thrive only when practiced by a certain type of person—the democratic citizen. The cause of liberal democracy is inherently moral, and some would even argue that it is religious. To believe in democracy is to believe certain truths about the intrinsic and inalienable rights of the human person.

Many who champion democracy are reluctant to discuss the normative—which is to say the moral and ethical—aspect of democracy. But democracy cannot coexist with evil beliefs about human beings. To promote democracy is to cultivate the moral life, which means the painstaking reinforcement of ethical and humane habits. It is possible for states to be democratic in name only, if the ideas and practices of democracy penetrate no deeper than elections. Ultimately, democracy as a value system and way of life must be drilled down into daily routines of society. In the end, the ennobling principles of democracy must live in people's hearts.

Democracy can never be separated from the need to cultivate the normative values that form its moral base. While customs and priorities will differ from location to another, there are certain foundational principles that are nonnegotiable.

Democracy is rooted in a fundamental truth: that all men are created equal. This philosophical doctrine forms the axis on which any civilization worthy of the name must turn. It is the central idea of the democratic nation. A culture that professes an interest in democracy but posits the inferiority of any man or woman because of color, class, or creed is built on a morally untenable foundation and is doomed to fray and even fail.

Viewed especially in the context of ethnic and sectarian strife, the fundamental truth that all men and women are created equal is the necessary foundation for human progress. Only after we embrace this as absolute truth—whether by means of religion or by natural reason —can we debate other claims without resort to hatred or violence. Democracy seekers everywhere must accept it without deviation, because it is the truth upon which the principles of tolerance and individual rights are based.

Building open societies, alleviating poverty, fostering opportunity, and planting democratic institutions are all linked to the ethic of human worth and dignity, which must be guarded and transmitted by a global civic culture. Cultivating trust and collaboration by sponsoring interethnic dialogue and engaging individuals from differing backgrounds in civic and humanitarian endeavors is the work of private, nongovernmental associations. A diversified and tolerant political culture can rise up from this subsoil of democratic civil society.

CHAPTER THIRTEEN

A Roadmap for Bottom-Up Nation Building in the Twenty-first Century

THIS BOOK ARGUES that a new, more effective model for poverty reduction and democratic institution building is rapidly emerging and that it will almost certainly improve the long-term prospects for many poor countries. A reliance on rule-driven, top-down bureaucracy is giving way to bottom-up strategies for curing poverty, creating entrepreneurial opportunity, and advancing democracy.

The engine of this global unfolding is an unprecedented growth in American-style civil society. As Peter Drucker and others have predicted, the challenges that confront communities in the twenty-first century will best be met neither by businesses nor by governments, but by nonprofits, often working in partnership with the other major social and economic institutions of society. It has been suggested that nongovernmental organizations will be as important in the twenty-first century as the nation-state was in the twentieth century.

There are few places on earth where national and international NGOs are not at work fighting poverty and promoting enterprise and democratization. Similarly, there are few places in the world that are not experiencing significant bottom-up growth in indigenous, local, volunteer-based civil society. One result of this associational revolution is unprecedented opportunity to forge problem-solving partnerships anywhere in the world. Another result is that results-driven innovation will be vastly more important than institutional spending driven by good intentions or the political need to "just do something."

Critics of government aid argue that this urge to just do something has yielded conventional bureaucratic approaches that have failed, because they are too sweeping, too constrained by top-down "development planning" agencies, and too indifferent to the private sector's indispensable role in generating economic growth. Grandiose, even utopian thinking has gotten in the way of simple solutions that could be formulated and implemented in partnership with the poor, as the development scholar Bill Easterly points out. Effective strategies to prevent the spread of disease, reduce malnutrition, purify water, and improve agricultural production have not been adopted because of the flawed methods employed by bureaucratic planners.

Alternatively, Easterly suggests, we can give the "searchers" a chance. Searchers are people who find manageable, achievable things that work and who are rewarded for their success and not merely good intentions or costly interventions. They often have modest goals and work in harmony with a poor village's natural wisdom and insights into problem solving. There is now unprecedented opportunity to link up these searchers and innovators and make them central players in the development process.

What can policymakers, businesses, private philanthropists, individual citizens, and NGOs do to spur experimentation with new ideas? What can all actors in the developed world, public and private, do to partner more effectively with indigenous civil society in order to build upon the problem-solving capacity that exists in every locality?

Foreign aid and development bureaucracies are not going to disappear. In fact, they will likely spend more money in the coming years. But there is a refreshing honesty emerging within what some have disparagingly called "the development industry." There is a dawning recognition that in a "flattened" and decentralized global environment shaped by local innovation, the standardized bureaucratic approaches get in the way of progress.

If there is a win-win proposition to suggest to all development actors—governmental, business, and humanitarian organizations alike —it is captured in a single word that Bill Easterly uses to describe the difference between top-down and bottom-up approaches to confronting poverty. That word is "homespun."

Homespun implies that the idea originated in the neighborhood and was developed in partnership with village elders; that it took indigenous insights, assets, and cultural norms into account. It also implies that for implementation to succeed, it must be done in collaboration with those who own the problem and have to live with the solution. Focusing on community-based or homespun strategies is a good starting point for the next stage of discussions about solutions to poverty, wherever they might be taking place—universities, aid agencies, business, NGOs, or private philanthropies.

Here are some questions that might be asked: Has the idea been tested locally? Does the plan treat the poor as partners in their own development? Does the action contribute to building durable institutions and sustainable progress? Is implementation guided by the idea that the poor will ultimately achieve their full dignity by becoming independent and self-sustaining, not needing foreign assistance or expert help at all? Such an approach would be genuinely transformational.

A world in which governments and bureaucratic institutions do not dominate is a world in which everyone has something to contribute: every organization and every citizen. Development then becomes a natural extension of every organization's mission in the world.

What follows is a "roadmap" for building communities and nations worldwide through indigenous civil society, markets, and rule of law. It is an invitation for all key sectors and organizations to think strategically about how they might help improve social, economic, and political conditions in the world. And it is meant especially for those donors, nonprofit leaders, business leaders, and even government officials who genuinely want to make a difference.

★   ★
★

DEVELOPMENT AND HUMANITARIAN NGOs

Focus less on charity and more on livelihood enhancement. Be more committed to building economic capacity among the poor, especially in generating "homespun" prosperity. Imagine a situation in which solutions are so effective in one location that you can move on to another. Work at making yourself obsolete. The surest way to reduce the need for international aid and humanitarian assistance is to make it temporary.

There are various economic strategies that deserve more attention than they are getting. Of particular value are programs to pool the capital of the poor through village banks and credit unions, microenterprise, and efforts to help the poor make better use of their assets such as land and property through legal reform.

Respond to the call for greater accountability. Private voluntary organizations (PVOs) and advocacy-oriented groups, make yourselves more accountable. A chorus of criticism is rising over a variety of issues, including practices that encourage dependence, failure to promote the development of local civil society, duplication of programs, and indifference to local culture.

When you advocate as an NGO, in whose behalf are you advocating? Where do you get your funds? Whether liberal or conservative, work to ensure that your agenda and message are shaped with input from the poor themselves, and not merely from intellectuals, ideological activists, and other elites who presume to know what the poor want or need.

Partner with Islamic moderates and modernizers. For development organizations working in the Arab world, study the UN's Arab Human Development Report, which is the least read yet most comprehensive and most promising roadmap for reversing the profound stagnation in Arab nations. It could serve as a template for development everywhere, with its focus on the importance of building institutions to serve the people, such as health care and education; on the urgent need to grow diversified entrepreneurial economies; and on the imperative of integrating Arab countries into the global system of trade and commerce. Also, miss no opportunity to partner with and empower moderate and reform-oriented Islamic elements.

Promote effective local peace building. NGOs operating in conflict-torn regions should assist in cultivating indigenous civil society that is committed to reconciliation and peace, especially wherever ethnicity or religion is a factor in the conflict. Getting disparate groups to work together on construction and humanitarian projects may be the surest path to ethnic peace. Faith-based organizations are uniquely positioned to cultivate interfaith networks and associations that can encourage mutual respect and partnership in building a just and peaceful society.

Demand sound governance as the key to nation building. NGOs everywhere should more forcefully call for improved governance, recognizing that widespread corruption, the absence of rule of law, and failed governmental systems perpetuate poverty and suffering and impede sustainable development. Of particular interest should be promoting sound NGO laws that guarantee the right of voluntary organizations to form, associate, and express themselves.

Promote people-to-people diplomacy. No organizations on earth are in a better position to promote broad and lasting ties between people from diverse ethnic and religious backgrounds than the voluntary associations that are already engaged in the work of citizenship. The bonds of connection are stronger because they involve citizens addressing common concerns, as compared with government officials whose mission is conducting the affairs of state. Today there are unprecedented opportunities to establish people-to-people ties, thanks to the rise of technology as well as the ease and affordability of travel into all but the most dangerous parts of the world.

AMERICAN AND MULTINATIONAL BUSINESSES (MDBs)

Think of yourself as a development expert. Stop assuming that Third World development is the exclusive domain of development agencies and stop being so deferential to pedigreed development professionals. You know a lot that they don't know about building organizations, generating innovation, and creating jobs. The objective of all development activity should be fostering healthy private sectors, which is precisely your line of work. Development is what you do.

Corporate social responsibility. Think critically about what you are doing to promote so-called "social responsibility." Recently, social responsibility agendas have become less focused on empowering the poor and more dominated by ideological agendas—in many cases, ironically, with a clear bias against business. Globalization certainly has its downside, but the answer is not to pretend that it is going to disappear or that the obligation of business is to become something it is not. Think objectively about whether your social responsibility agenda is truly conducive to improving conditions in the Third World.

Be more strategic in your philanthropy. World poverty reduction is one cause among many, and there are various reasons why a company might give to one cause and not another. But all too often, when a business supports humanitarian and development organizations, it asks too few questions about results on the ground. Develop a clear philosophy of giving, and whenever you give to an organization involved in social and economic development, investigate its effectiveness. Contribute wisely and hold nonprofits accountable.

Think about expanding your market development strategies. Too few businesses think proactively about how to expand their production and customer base into unserved populations in the Third World. Think about how your business can help generate more "wealth at the bottom of the pyramid," and how it might even improve its own bottom line by forming alliances with producers and distributors in emerging markets.

Adopt domestic and international service as part of your corporate culture. Businesses that encourage their managers and workers to engage directly in tackling the social and economic problems around them always report a variety of benefits, including higher levels of idealism, improved community relations, and lasting new relationships. Business leaders and entrepreneurs should know better the communities they serve, whether at home or abroad. They should travel more, and when they do, include trips outside the familiar and comfortable settings where business is normally transacted.

Take the lead in international disaster relief. American business donated an unprecedented $570 billion to relief and reconstruction efforts following the 2005 tsunami disaster in the Indian Ocean. Most of the money was transferred to large NGOs such as the Red Cross, which got the credit for the work. When the American private sector delivers compassion on this scale to a trouble spot using entirely private resources, it is an extension of the goodness of the American people, and the recipients of that generosity should know where it came from. Business should expect more credit and assert greater leadership over this activity.

Companies that directly engaged in tsunami relief worked with speed and expertise that matched or exceeded the performance of governments. Business is no longer a minor partner serving up the funds for relief activity and otherwise deferring to humanitarian professionals. The resources and leadership of business will be urgently needed in global disaster assistance.

Business associations such as the U.S. Chamber of Commerce and the Business Roundtable need to sponsor more dialogue between the business sector and nonprofit humanitarian groups in the hope of improving communication and coordination. If improvements cannot be made, and if a greater appreciation of business's unique contribution is not forthcoming, a leading business association should help create an alternative mechanism controlled entirely by business to pool and spend money.

Learn more about true market realities at the bottom of the pyramid. The world's poor are in possession of $9 trillion in assets and represent a huge potential market for those businesses that can figure out how to make inroads in less familiar territory. But little detailed information is available about many Third World cities and towns, and what is known is not organized in one location. Often, businesses that might be in a position to invest simply lack the data regarding on-the-ground conditions and policies in such areas as commercial law, banking, and governance. To better serve both the poor and individual companies, business associations should create a clearinghouse that specializes in gathering and disseminating information about developing countries, their market conditions, and business opportunities.

United Nations, Multilateral Institutions, and Global Forums

Admit failings. Be bolder in owning up to and even calling attention to the failings of forty years of development assistance. Speak about the indifference toward markets, profits, and prosperity that often exists among large development agencies. Recognize the indispensable part that business will play, both as a partner in traditional development, and in creating new producers and consumers among the poor. This candor will only win you more friends and supporters.

Demand more direct connections with real poor people. Don't just assume that the NGOs gathering at global forums are in touch with poor people.

Many of them occupy nice offices in cities well removed from the grinding poverty of Third World villages. Reserve a percentage of your conference registrations for poor individuals from every continent, representing only themselves and their experiences. Include successful female microentrepreneurs, the farmer who is improving production, the local co-op organizer, and the microfranchiser who is figuring out how to market and distribute affordable consumer products to the poor.

GOVERNMENT DEVELOPMENT PROGRAMS

The name of the game is results. Aid agencies are struggling to adapt to the new paradigm of the twenty-first century. For the most part, they realize that they no longer hold a monopoly on resources or expertise, and that many private entities are more innovative and results-focused.

Most literature and advertisements describing what aid agencies do highlight generous deeds and worthwhile projects. Aid agencies should accentuate long-term results as part of their mission statements, which would acknowledge up front that the public interest is not served merely by good intentions or generous spending. Aid agencies should focus on modest and manageable goals, taking on projects that are known to be effective and "scalable."

Set limits and conditions. It is better to achieve results on a more limited set of initiatives than to deliver comprehensive programs with questionable outcomes. Practice a tougher form of compassion, laying down strict conditions for delivering aid and assistance. Be willing to withdraw money and manpower entirely where it is doing more harm than good.

Hold nations accountable. Shine the spotlight on ineffective practices that are hurting the poor and especially stop coddling the corrupt. Spend more resources and time on pressuring and assisting governments to rein in corruption, practice transparency, and establish basic rule of law, especially in property rights, banking, and commerce.

Be innovative and flexible: Stop advocating sweeping, global poverty-reduction strategies. Instead, think in terms of becoming laboratories of innovation, investing in the development of small but effective remedies that can be replicated anywhere.

Pay more attention to local cultures and place more confidence in human wisdom than in the "science" of development.

UNIVERSITIES AND RESEARCH INSTITUTES

Every college and university potentially has a global role. Institutions of higher learning play an underappreciated role in globalization and Third World development. Colleges, universities, and technical schools host international students, send students abroad, and are increasingly operating at the crossroads of an electronically connected global information society. These are readymade networks for connecting Third and First World, North and South, rich and poor, developed and underdeveloped, haves and have-nots—and making a difference where it counts.

Institutions of learning are poised to play a central part in the emergence of global civil society. Their knowledge products, science, and technical capacity can be made available anywhere the material can be electronically received and downloaded.

Donors to universities could consider funding endowed chairs or research centers dedicated exclusively to the research of concepts and practices that could transform the Third World, including better irrigation, pest control, and soil preservation; affordable cures for disease; the conversion of waste into building products; low-cost methods of electrification, and more.

POLICYMAKERS

Organize a private sector war on poverty. The debate over foreign aid budgets and whether or not America is contributing enough to development agencies is distracting and counterproductive. Whether

America provides slightly higher or lower appropriations for government-sponsored development means little when private outflows in the form of philanthropy, remittances, and private voluntary organizations are exploding.

Between now and midcentury, somewhere between $30 and $40 *trillion* will shift hands from one generation to another in America, the largest transfer of wealth in world history. Given the economic disparities and inequities that are much reported both domestically and internationally, and taking into account the lead role increasingly played by the private sector in poverty reduction, the strongest possible case should be made for capturing a portion of those resources through changes in tax law, and channeling them into nonprofits that directly and exclusively serve the poor.

Streamline foreign aid policy. With the proliferation of agencies involved in some form of international humanitarian or development activity has come more duplication, competition, and fragmentation. The strong tendency of bureaucracies to defend their turf and advocate for their own expertise has produced more "stove-piping" in international development, whereby agencies bring narrow specialties rather than broad, integrated approaches to development.

In some European countries, international development programming is led by a cabinet-level official. While that may or may not be the answer in the U.S. system, Congress and the executive branch should undertake a thorough joint review of how to streamline and consolidate the planning and execution of all foreign development activity sponsored by the government, and greater authority should be placed with the senior official, which at present is the USAID administrator, who also serves as an under secretary of state.

Eliminate development earmarks. Coordination and implementation of the U.S. government's development programming is difficult enough even without the explosion of legislative "earmarks," which basically direct funds to specific organizations and projects that have gained favor with lawmakers. This has the result of severely constricting the flexibility of USAID, the lead development agency. If the U.S. government is going to maintain an aid agency, it must grant the resources and the flexibility needed for success, especially in formulating country-specific plans.

GRANT-MAKING FOUNDATIONS

Fund small, effective, indigenous organizations. Professional grant-makers from the major funding organizations of the world often share the same bias in favor of giantism, professionalism, and clientelism. Grant-making foundations should contribute to innovation and local experimentation, expanding beyond big humanitarian and development organizations to work directly with indigenous organizations. Alternatively, they can consider partnering with intermediary organizations, such as Geneva Global, that treat philanthropy as strategic investments and specialize in delivering local results.

Create a watchdog for the watchdogs. For years, the great concern was a lack of accountability in government programs. Today, that same concern holds in relation to nongovernmental organizations, and especially the proliferating array of advocacy-based organizations. They are now a global electorate, driving social and political change, organizing boycotts and protests, monitoring human rights, advocating for women, exposing corruption, and engaging in a host of other watchdog activities. But who are they? Who do they really represent? And who provides their funding?

Little is known about the most powerful international NGOs that have emerged as major global players. A consortium of major funders should partner to create an NGO monitoring organization or council whose sole purpose is to develop common global approaches to tracking, analyzing, and reporting on the financial and fiduciary matters of nonprofit organizations.

★ ★ ★

PRIVATE INDIVIDUALS

Target your dollars. To the individual American: in your capacity as a taxpayer, consumer, worker, and financial donor, you are actually the key to achieving the changes described above and to increasing accountability. None of the institutions above would function for a day without you. Ask the nonprofits you support for information about the amount of money spent on administration or advocacy. Ask your employer to explain the company's philosophy on philanthropy and service.

Adopt a poor person, country, or poverty-fighting organization. With all the proliferating opportunities to connect with needs around you, there is no excuse for not resolving to take steps toward engagement. Just do it. Get involved. Join and support an organization. Volunteer locally. Travel internationally. Serve in a short-term humanitarian assignment through your church, a service organization, or the Peace Corps. Host a foreign visitor. Develop long-distance friendships through the Internet. Organize a community fundraising drive. Become an expert on a specific Third World country and follow its politics and policies. Challenge your church, charity, or business to support a particular project.

If most citizens engaged in any of these activities on a regular basis, the full potential of global civil society would be fulfilled.

ACKNOWLEDGMENTS

This book is dedicated to heroes I have met in developing-world villages who imparted to me the treasures of wisdom about how poor people think and live with dignity in underdeveloped communities. It is dedicated to the fast-growing global community of the caring, which includes people from all walks of life, rich and poor alike, who practice a heroic form of generosity by devoting their lives to creating a better world.

It is dedicated to the saints who are determined to confront the evil of violence with their own lives—people like Bishop John Rucyahana, whose family suffered unspeakable atrocities during the Rwanda genocide yet he is at work building orphanages and promoting ethnic reconciliation.

It is dedicated to a new generation of African leaders who are determined to prove that Africans can build modern and just states grounded in the rule of law—leaders like Paul Kagame, who is determined to replace the ideology of ethnic division with the ethic of neighborly love.

It is dedicated to the youthful democrats of the world, like Sokol Ferizi from Kosovo, who is resisting despair over poverty, poor schools, and few job opportunities, by organizing a cadre of youth leaders determined to bring about a better future.

It is dedicated to some amazing Iraqis who became my friends, people who willingly faced death or imprisonment to advance justice and freedom for their countrymen—men like Ahmed al-Sammari, who returned to Iraq following the liberation to build a new Olympic program for Iraqi youth and who was kidnapped and is still missing for having done so; and like Ammar Shawkat, who left the security of a good job to dodge bullets in Iraq, hoping to see Sunnis and Shiites follow the path of moderation and peace.

It is dedicated to the many peaceful Muslim scholars and grass-roots reformers I've had tea with in Middle Eastern cities who are out to prove that Islam is compatible with tolerance and democratic values.

It is dedicated to former colleagues at USAID and the State Department, too numerous to mention, who care deeply about confronting poverty, disease, and conflict in the world.

It is dedicated to a new generation of thinkers who are convincing a skeptical world that prosperity and progress are possible for the Third World poor—people like Hernando De Soto, who is possessed of the simple idea that the poor want what everyone else wants: property rights, sound governance, and working economic institutions, so that they too can be entrepreneurs.

It is dedicated to a new generation of idealistic American business entrepreneurs I have met in remote parts of the world who are determined to deliver breakthrough solutions to disease, hunger, and grinding poverty. It is dedicated to the "wildcatters" working on the frontiers of Third World development, experimenting with new technologies to improve sanitation and housing, build alternative energy systems, or enhance agricultural productivity.

It is dedicated to the NGOs who are working to spread micro-lending programs—to people like Scott Hillstrom who insist that sustainable and scalable health care services can be provided in the developing world by means of commercial microfranchise models as an alternative to wasteful command-and-control delivery systems.

The Rise of Gobal Civil Society is dedicated to the hundreds who volunteered their valuable time to respond to my probing questions and who deserve credit for the good we all hope comes from the book's dissemination. And it is dedicated to my family—Sheryl, Preston,

Caroline, and Margaret—who have extended grace and patience when my professional life has taken me away.

Finally, I would like to thank the individuals and organizations who were directly involved in making this project possible, including the Bradley Foundation and the John Templeton Foundation, which provided generous support, as well as Neil McCauley and the very able staff at Encounter Books.

NOTES

Chapter 1 —Compassion: America's Most Consequential Export

1 Stephen C. Smith, *Ending Global Poverty: A Guide to What Works* (New York: Palgrave Macmillan, 2005), p. 32.

2 Ibid., p. 32.

3 Nicholas D. Kristof, "Meet the Fakers," *New York Times*, September 13, 2005.

4 Bill Gates, "Saving the World Is Within Our Grasp," *Newsweek*, October 1, 2007, p. 76.

5 Bob Davis, "Zoellick Fights for Relevance of World Bank," *Wall Street Journal*, October 9, 2007, p. A10.

6 Seth Mydans, "Suppression Up Close, Courtesy of the Internet," *International Herald Tribune*, October 4, 2007.

7 Michael Edwards, *Civil Society* (Cambridge, Massachusetts: Polity Press, 2004), p. 21.

8 Ibid., p. 3.

9 Sebastian Mallaby, "Aid Goes Online: The Development World Awaits Its Bloomberg," *Washington Post*, September 3, 2007, p. A1.

10 John Kay, "Khrushchev, Crosland and the Road to Mediocrity," *Financial Times*, February 28, 2006, p. 17.

11 Thomas L. Friedman, "'Patient' Capital for an Africa That Can't Wait," *New York Times*, April 20, 2007.

12 C. K. Prahalad, *The Fortune at the Bottom of the Pyramid* (Upper Saddle River, New Jersey: Wharton School Publishing, 2005).

13 Ibid., p. xii.

14 Ibid., p. xii.

15 Thomas Friedman, *The World Is Flat: A Brief History of the 21st Century* (New York: Farrar, Straus & Giroux, 2005).

16 Ibid., p. 387.

17 Ibid.

18 Ibid., p. 389.

19 Alexis de Tocqueville, *Democracy in America*, trans. Henry Reeve (New York:Vintage, 1954), Bk. II, ch. 5.

20 See Michael Edwards, *Civil Society* (Cambridge, Massachusetts: Polity Press, 2004), p. 23; Helmut Anheier, Marlies Glasius and Mary Kaldar, "Introducing Global Civil Society," in *Global Civil Society 2001*, LSE Centre for Civil Society and Centre for the Study of Global Governance (New York: Oxford University Press, 2001), pp. 3–22; and see "Nongovernmental organization" in *Wikipedia*.

21 *The Index of Global Philanthropy 2006*, The Hudson Institute, p. 26.

22 Stuart E. Eizenstat, "Nongovernmental Organizations as the Fifth Estate," *Whitehead Journal of Diplomacy and International Relations*, vol. 5, no. 2 (Summer–Fall 2004), p. 15.

23 Peter F. Drucker, "Civilizing the City," in *The Community of the Future*, The Drucker Foundation Future Series, ed. Frances Hesselbein et al. (San Francisco: Jossey-Bass, 1997), p. 1.

24 Ibid., p. 5.

25 Ibid., p. 6.

26 Ibid.

27 Everett Carl Ladd, "A Nation of Joiners," *Philanthropy Roundtable*, November 1999.

28 Stephanie Strom, "Many Charities Founded after Hurricane Are Faltering," *New York Times*, March 13, 2006, p. A12.

29 See the website of the Social Enterprise Initiative, Harvard Business School, p. 2; also see "Employment in the Nonprofit Sector," Independent Sector, www.independentsector.org/PDFs/npemployment.pdf.

30 "To Have, Not to Hold: The Rise of the New Philanthropist," *Economist*, February 25, 2006, p. 6.

31 "Doing Well and Doing Good," *Economist*, July 31, 2004, p. 57.

32 "To Have, Not to Hold," p. 7.

33 Everett Carl Ladd, "A Nation of Joiners."

34 Ibid.

35 "Doing Well and Doing Good," p. 58.

36 The *Index of Philanthropy 2006*, p. 28.

37 Arthur C. Brooks, *Policy Review Online*, March 19, 2006, p. 3.

38 "Doing Well and Doing Good," p. 58.

39 Ibid., p. 59.

40 Rana Foroohar, "Where the Money Goes," *Newsweek*, October 31, 2005, p. E18.

41 Ibid., p. E20.

42 Sharon LaFraniere, "Cellphones Catapult Rural Africa to 21st Century," *New York Times*, August 26, 2005.

43 Ibid.

44 Gary Johns, "The NGO Challenge: Whose Democracy Is It Anyway?" paper delivered at conference on "Nongovernmental Organizations: The Growing Power of an Unelected Few," American Enterprise Institute, June 11, 2003, p. 2.

45 Quoted by William A. Schambra, "Restoring Public Confidence in the Nonprofit Sector," presented to the Association of Fundraising Professionals, September 7, 2005.

46 Rana Foroohar, "Where the Money Goes," p. E20.

47 Ibid., p. E20.

48 See John Barkdull and Lisa A. Dicke, "Globalization, Civil Society and Democracy?: An Organizational Assessment," *Whitehead Journal of Diplomacy and International Relations*, vol. 5, no. 2 (Summer/Fall 2004), pp. 40–41.

49 Stuart E. Eizenstat, "Nongovernmental Organizations as the Fifth Estate," p. 21.

50 Ibid., p. 25.

51 Alfredo Sfeir-Younis, "The Role of Civil Society in Foreign Policy: A New Conceptual Framework," *Whitehead Journal of Diplomacy and International Relations*, vol. 5, no. 2 (Summer/Fall 2004), p. 29.

52 Ibid., p. 30.

Chapter 2—The Core Elements of Community and Nation Building

1 Alexis de Tocqueville, *Democracy in America*, trans. Henry Reeve (New York: Vintage, 1954), p. 129.

2 Robert D. Putnam, "Bowling Alone: America's Declining Social Capital," *Journal of Democracy*, vol. 6, no. 1 (January 1995), pp. 65–78.

3 Robert Ruthnow, *Saving America: Faith-Based Services and the Future of Civil Society* (Princeton, New Jersey: Princeton University Press, 2004).

4 David Ellison, "Church Brings Change Home," *Houston Chronicle*, April 30, 2006.

5 Tim Montgomerie, "Finally . . . a Breakthrough Idea for the Tories," *The Times* (UK), July 15, 2005.

6 Peter L. Berger and Richard John Neuhaus, *To Empower People: The Role of Mediating Structures in Public Policy* (Washington, D.C.: American Enterprise Institute, 1977).

7 Don Eberly, *America's Promise: Civil Society and the Renewal of American Culture* (New York: Rowman & Littlefield, 1998), p. 90.

8 Claire Hughes, "Survey Gives Faith-Based Groups High Marks in Hurricane

Aid," The Roundtable on Religion and Social Welfare Policy, December 2005.

Chapter 3—The Great Foreign Aid Debate: Stingy or Generous?

1 Quoted in *The Index of Global Philanthropy 2006*, The Hudson Institute, p. 8.
2 Bill Saporito, "The Jeff Sachs Contradiction: Celebrity Economist," *Time*, March 14, 2005.
3 From book review by William Easterly, "A Modest Proposal," *Washington Post*, March 13, 2005.
4 Ibid.
5 William Easterly, "The Utopian Nightmare," *Foreign Policy*, September/October 2005.
6 William Easterly, *The White Man's Burden: Why the West's Efforts to Aid the Rest Have Done So Much Ill and So Little Good* (New York: The Penguin Press, 2006).
7 Easterly, "A Modest Proposal," p. 3.
8 William Easterly, *The White Man's Burden*, p. 23.
9 Ibid., p. 26.
10 *Foreign Aid in the National Interest: Promoting Freedom, Security and Opportunity*, U.S. Agency for International Development (Washington, D.C., 2002), p. 3.
11 Cited from Ben Heineman Jr. and Fritz Heimann, "The Long War against Corruption," *Foreign Affairs*, May/June 2006, p. 78.
12 Jeffrey D. Sachs, "The End of Poverty," *Time*, March 14, 2005, p. 49.
13 From United Nations Development Programme database.
14 Shaohua Chen and Martin Ravaillon, "How Have the World's Poorest Fared since the 1980s?" *World Bank Research Observer*, vol. 19, no. 2 (2004).
15 "Recent Trends in Foreign Aid," *OECD in Washington*, no. 38, October/November 2002, p. 1.
16 "Who's Stingy," Editorial, *Wall Street Journal*, July 6, 2005, p. A14.
17 Carol C. Adelman and Jeremiah Norris, "America's Total Economic Engagement with the Developing World: Rethinking the Uses and Nature of Foreign Aid," The Hudson Institute, June 28, 2005.
18 "U.S. Aid: Generous or Stingy," transcript from debate hosted by the Center for Global Development and The Hudson Institute, January 13, 2005.
19 *The Index of Global Philanthropy 2006*, The Hudson Institute, p. 15.
20 "Sending Money Home," Inter-American Development Bank, 2006.
21 Ginger Thompson, "Mexico's Migrants Profit from Dollars Sent Home," *New York Times*, February 23, 2005, p. A8.
22 Ibid.

Notes

23 Robert Frank, "Checks in the Mail: For a Philippine Town, Monthly Allowances Pave a Road to Riches," *Wall Street Journal*, May 22, 2001.

24 "Remittances Increasingly Part of Globalized Economy," *New Republic Online*, December 17, 2005.

25 William Easterly, "A Modest Proposal," *Washington Post*, March 13, 2005.

26 Reuters, "EU Ministers See Study of Voluntary Tax That Would Aid Africa," *Wall Street Journal*, June 8, 2005, p. D11.

27 "The Blair Debt Project," Editorial, *Wall Street Journal*, June 7, p. 14.

28 "Africa in the Balance," Editorial, *New York Times*, July 6, 2005.

29 Quoted in "The End of Poverty," *Time*, March 14, 2005, p. 50.

30 Walter Williams, "Aid to Africa," *Washington Times*, July 20, 2005.

31 Thomas Dichter, "Time to Stop Fooling Ourselves about Foreign Aid: A Practitioner's View," Cato Institute Foreign Policy Briefing no. 86 (September 12, 2005), p. 2.

32 Ibid., p. 4.

33 Ibid., p. 7.

34 Ibid., p. 7.

35 Paul Collier, "Making Aid Smart: Institutional Incentives Facing Donor Organizations and Their Implications for Aid Effectiveness," USAID Forum Series, February 25, 2002.

36 Speech by Andrew Natsios, John F. Kennedy School of Government, Harvard University, October 16, 2002.

37 "Business against Corruption: A Framework for Action," UN Global Compact, International Business Leaders Forum, and Transparency International, 2005.

38 Sharon LaFraniere, "Africa Tackling Graft, with Billions in Aid in Play," *New York Times*, July 6, 2005.

39 Ibid.

40 Emily Wax, "We're a Thirsty Land of Empty Promises," *Washington Post*, February 20, 2006, p. A11.

41 Ibid.

42 Ibid.

43 Larry Rohter and Juan Forero, "Unending Graft Is Threatening Latin America," *New York Times*, July 30, 2005.

44 Ibid.

45 Associated Press, "Thousands of Brazilians Protest Corruption," *New York Times*, September 6, 2005.

46 Donald Greenlees, "In Jakarta, Cleaning House Is Slow and Painful," *International Herald Tribune*, May 9, 2005.

47 Tim Worstall, "Bill Easterly Is About to Spoil the Poverty Party," www.techcentralstation.com.

48 Jeffrey D. Sachs, "The End of Poverty," *Time*, March 14, 2005, p. 47.

49 Ben Heineman Jr. and Fritz Heimann, "The Long War against Corruption," *Foreign Affairs*, May/June 2006, p. 76.

50 William Easterly, "Can Foreign Aid Buy Growth?" *Journal of Economic Perspectives*, vol. 17, no. 3 (Summer 2003), p. 25.

51 "Millennium Challenge Account Update," White House Fact Sheet, June 3, 2002.

52 Quoted from "The United States and International Development: Fostering Hope through Growth," Bureau of Public Affairs, U.S. Department of State, May 31, 2005.

Chapter 4—From Aid Bureaucracy to Civil Society

1 Speech by Andrew Natsios to the John F. Kennedy School of Government, Harvard University, October 6, 2002.

2 Cited from presentation by Andrew Natsios at the Three Sector Conference, U.S. Chamber of Commerce, May 30, 2002.

3 William Easterly, "A Modest Proposal," *Washington Post*, March 13, 2005, p. 3.

4 Keith Henderson and Juliana Pilon, "Trust Civil Society," Commentary, *Elections Today*, vol. 10, nos. 3 & 4 (Summer/Fall 2002).

5 Stephen C. Smith, *Ending Global Poverty: A Guide to What Works* (New York: Palgrave Macmillan, 2005), p. 23.

6 Ibid., p. 43.

7 Kirk Magleby, "MicroFranchises as a Solution to Global Poverty," December 2005, at http://microfranchises.org/file.php?id=35, p. 6.

8 C. K. Prahalad, *The Fortune at the Bottom of the Pyramid: Eradicating Poverty through Profits* (Upper Saddle River, New Jersey: Wharton School Publishing, 2005).

9 Thomas Dichter, "Time to Stop Fooling Ourselves about Foreign Aid: A Practitioner's View," Cato Institute Foreign Policy Briefing no. 86 (September 12, 2005), p. 4.

10 Global Development Alliance, "Expanding the Impact of Foreign Assistance through Public-Private Alliances," USAID, at www.usaid.gov/gda.

11 U.S. Chamber of Commerce, 2005 Partnership Conference, "Corporate Citizenship and the Global Economy," p. 6.

12 Ibid., p. 7.

Chapter 5—Wealth, Poverty, and the Rise of Corporate Citizenship

1 Kirk Magleby, "MicroFranchises as a Solution to Global Poverty," November 2005, at http://microfranchises.org/file.php?id=35, p. 12.

2 Peter M. Robinson, "Business Can Help Build a Sustainable Future," USCIB, Policy Advocacy, Op-Eds and Speeches, September 14, 2005, at www.uscib.org/index.asp?documentID=3361

3 "Can Corporations Save the World?" *Forbes*, November 26, 2006.

4 Ibid.

5 Ellen Byron, "P&G's Global Target: Shelves of Tiny Stores," *Wall Street Journal*, July 16, 2007, p. 1.

6 Heather Timmons, "GE Chief Lays out Plans for Emerging Market Expansion," *International Herald Tribune*, May 31, 2007.

7 Kate Linebaugh, "Citigroup to Tap Low-End Market for Growth in Asia," *Washington Post*, August 29, 2007, p. D3.

8 Roben Farzad, "Extreme Investing: Inside Colombia," *Business Week*, May 28, 2007.

9 "Strengthening Public-Private Partnerships for Social and Economic Development," Report on Global Citizenship, Business Civic Leadership Center, September 2006, p. 3.

10 Ibid., p. 15.

11 John Sullivan, "The Business Case for Corporate Citizenship," Economic Reform Issue Paper no. 0410, Center for International Private Enterprise, December 27, 2004, p. 1.

12 Stuart L. Hart, *Capitalism at the Crossroads: The Unlimited Business Opportunities in Solving the World's Most Difficult Problems* (Upper Saddle River, New Jersey: Wharton School Publishing, 2005), p. 10.

13 "The Business of Giving," *Economist*, February 26, 2006, p. 5.

14 "Corporate Citizenship and the Global Economy," U.S. Chamber of Commerce, 2005 Partnership Conference, p. 4.

15 Michael Porter and Mark Kramer, "The Competitive Advantage of Corporate Philanthropy," *Harvard Business Review*, December 2002.

16 Ariana Eujung Cha, "Dot-Coms Are So '90s; In Silcon Valley, Doing Good Is the New Thing," *Washington Post*, August 9, 2005, p. A6.

17 "Corporate Citizenship and the Global Economy." p. 10.

18 John Sullivan, "The Business Case for Corporate Citizenship," p. 3.

19 Ibid.

20 Stuart Hart, *Capitalism at the Crossroads*, p. XI.

21 Ibid., p. xli.

22 Ibid., p. 21.

23 "Corporate Social Responsibility: An IOE Approach," International Organization of Employers Position Paper, March 2003, p. 2.

24 "The Role of Business within Society," International Organization of Employers Position Paper, May 2005, p. 8.

25 "Corporate Social Responsibility: An IOE Approach," p. 2.

26 Stuart Hart, *Capitalism at the Crossroads*, p. 189.

27 Hernando De Soto, *The Mystery of Capital: Why Capitalism Triumphs in the West and Fails Everywhere Else* (New York: Basic Books, 2000), p. 4.

28 Kurt Hoffman, "Lack of Investment Is the Tragedy in Africa," *Financial Times*, June 9, 2005.

29 Amit Varma, "India's Far from Free Markets," *Wall Street Journal*, June 16, 2005.

30 Ibid.

31 Ibid.

32 Barun Mitra, "India's Race to Reform," *Wall Street Journal*, July 29, 2005.

33 Ibid.

34 C. K. Prahalad, *The Fortune at the Bottom of the Pyramid: Eradicating Poverty through Profits* (Upper Saddle River, New Jersey: Wharton School Publishing, 2005), p. xii.

35 Ben W. Heineman Jr. and Fritz Heimann, "The Long War against Corruption," *Foreign Affairs*, May/June, 2006, pp. 83–84.

36 Kurt Hoffman, "Lack of Investment Is the Tragedy in Africa."

Chapter 6—Microenterprise: Tapping Native Capability

1 Hernando De Soto, *The Mystery of Capital: Why Capitalism Triumphs in the West and Fails Everywhere Else* (New York: Basic Book, 2000), p. 5.

2 C. K. Prahalad, *The Fortune at the Bottom of the Pyramid: Eradicating Poverty through Profits* (Upper Saddle River, New Jersey: Wharton School Publishing, 2005), p. xiii.

3 Ibid., pp. 10–14.

4 Pete Engardio, "How Strategy Guru C. K. Prahalad Is Changing the Way CEOs Think," *Business Week*, January 23, 2006.

5 Ibid.

6 Ibid.

7 Hernando De Soto, *The Mystery of Capital*, p. 10.

8 *World Development Report 2006*, The World Bank, www.worldbank.org.

9 "Economics Forever: Building Sustainability into Economic Policy," PANO Briefing no. 38, March 2007.

10 *Human Development Report 2006*, United Nations Development Programme, www.undp.org.

11 Ignacio Ramonet, "The Politics of Hunger," *Le Monde Diplomatique*, English ed., November 1998.

12 Stuart Hart, *Capitalism at the Crossroads: The Unlimited Business Opportunities in Solving the World's Most Difficult Problems* (Upper Saddle River, New Jersey: Wharton School Publishing, 2005), p. 1.

13 *Human Development Report 2006*.

14 Stuart Hart, *Capitalism at the Crossroads*, p. xli.

15 Ibid., p. 185.

16 John Lancaster, "Building Wealth by the Penny," *Washington Post*, March 14, 2006, p. A13.

17 Ibid.

18 Ibid.

19 Stephen C. Smith, *Ending Global Poverty: A Guide to What Works* (New York: Palgrave Macmillan, 2005), p. 13.

20 Ibid., p. 15.

21 Hernando De Soto, *The Mystery of Capital*, p. 20.

22 Ibid., p. 34.

23 Ibid., p. 6.

24 Stephen C. Smith, *Ending Global Poverty*, p. 37.

25 Hernando De Soto, *The Mystery of Capital*, p. 14.

26 Stephen C. Smith, *Ending Global Poverty*, p. 40.

27 Gautam Ivatury, "Retail Banking: Imagination Widens Reach," *The Banker*, March 1, 2006.

28 For more background read Stephen C. Smith, *Ending Global Poverty*, pp. 75–79.

29 Peter Greer, unpublished paper.

30 C. K. Prahalad, *The Fortune at the Bottom of the Pyramid*, p. 15.

31 Jeffrey Ashe, unpublished paper.

32 Ibid.

33 Gautam Ivatury, unpublished paper.

34 William Easterly, *The White Man's Burden: Why the West's Efforts to Aid the Rest Have Done So Much Ill and So Little Good* (New York: The Penguin Press, 2006), p. 14.

35 Interview of Koenraad Verhagen.

Chapter 7—The Great Tsunami of 2004

1 "Record Online Tsunami Relief Changes Ways of Giving," *Financial Express*, E-Globe, January 17, 2005.

2 Edward Iwata, "Tsunami Donors Creative in Giving," *USA Today*, January 17, 2005.

3 Brian Handwerk, "Tsunami Blogs Help Redefine News and Relief Efforts," *National Geographic News*, January 28, 2005.

4 "Record Online Tsunami Relief Changes Ways of Giving."

5 Ibid.

6 Ibid.

7 Sheeraz Haji, "Tsunami Relief Efforts Show Trends in Online Giving," *N-TEN Forecast*, August 30, 2005.

8 Opinion Analysis, Bureau of Intelligence and Research, U.S. Department of State, May 25, 2005.

9 "Tsunami Disaster Stirs Massive Aid Effort," *NewsHour with Jim Lehrer*, PBS, August 25, 2005.

10 Henry Shuster, "Tsunami Disaster Might Ease Terrorism," CNN, January 4, 2005.

Chapter 8—Conflict or Collaboration?

1 James Q. Wilson, "The Reform of Islam," *Wall Street Journal*, November 13, 2002.

2 Robert Satloff, "How to Win the Battle of Ideas in the War on Terror," *Policywatch* no. 919: Special Forum Report, Washington Institute for Near East Policy, November 19, 2004.

3 Ibid.

4 Richard Holbrooke, "Our Enemy's Face," *Washington Post*, September 9, 2005.

5 Robert Satloff, "How to Win the Battle of Ideas in the War on Terror."

6 Mark Leonard and Conrad Smewing, "Propaganda Will Not Sway the Arab Street," *Financial Times*, February 27, 2003.

7 Robert Satloff, "How to Win the Battle of Ideas in the War on Terror."

8 Ibid.

9 Ibid.

10 Samuel Huntington, *The Clash of Civilizations and the Remaking of World Order* (New York: Simon & Schuster, 1996).

11 Philip Jenkins, "Secularism and the Challenge of Faith," unpublished paper.

12 Paul Marshall, "Civil Society as a Global Template for Social Progress," presented at the Aspen Summit on Rethinking the Public Humanities, Aspen Meadows, October 20–22, 2004.

13 Philip Jenkins, "Secularism and the Challenge of Faith."

14 Philip Jenkins and Paul Marshall, "Sibling Rivalry among the Children of Abraham: Global Conflict and Cooperation between Islam and Christianity," Witherspoon Lecture, Family Research Council, July 18, 2003, p. 2.

15 Ibid., p. 3.

16 Ibid.

17 Mustafa Akyol, "Show Us More of the Other America: A Moderate Muslim's Prayer for American Faith and Family Values," *American Enterprise*, December 2004, p. 42.

18 Ibid., p. 43.

19 Ibid.

20 Ibid.

21 Victor Davis Hanson, "Democracy in the Middle East: It's the Hardheaded Solution," *Weekly Standard*, October 21, 2002.

22 Richard Norton, "The Challenge of Inclusion in the Middle East," *Current History*, January 1995, p. 1.

23 Ibid., p. 4.

24 Jillian Schwedler, *Toward Civil Society in the Middle East? A Primer* (Boulder, Colorado: Lynne Rienner Publishers, 1995), p. 10.

25 Richard Norton, "The Challenge of Inclusion in the Middle East," p. 2.

26 Ibid., p. 6.

27 Ibid., p. 6.

28 Ibid., p. 2.

29 "Akbar Ahmed to Lead Exploration of Islam in the Age of Globalization," Brookings Institution, November 14, 2005.

30 "Islam: A Primer—A Conversation with Roy Mottahedeh and Jay Tolson," Center Conversations no. 15, Ethics and Public Policy Center (September 8, 2002), p. 1.

31 Edward W. Said, *Covering Islam: How the Media and the Experts Determine How We See the Rest of the World*, rev. ed. (New York: Vintage Books, 1997), p. lv.

32 Timur Kuran, "Islam and Underdevelopment: An Old Puzzle Revisited," *Journal of Institutional and Theoretical Economics*, vol. 153 (1997), p. 49.

33 Cited in ibid., p. 58.

34 Ibid., p. 59.

35 "Islam: A Primer," pp. 3–4.

36 Imad-ad-Dean Ahmad, Minaret of Freedom Institute, "Building Muslim Civil Society from the Bottom Up," presented to the Meeting of American Muslim Social Scientists, Georgetown University, Washington, D.C., October 14, 2000, p. 2.

37 "Civil Society in Islamic Political Thought," Issue Paper, Institute of Islamic Political Thought, January 30, 2003.

38 Jillian Schwedler, *Toward Civil Society in the Middle East?*, p. 10.

39 Norani Othman, "Islam and Civil Society in Southeast Asia," The Ismail Centre, 2000.

40 Ernest Gellner, *Conditions of Liberty: Civil Society and Its Rivals* (London: Hamish Hamilton, 1994), p. 5.

41 "Civil Society in Islamic Political Thought," p. 5.

42 Ibid., p. 4.

43 Mohammad Khatami, "Pluralism and Civil Society," presented to the Eighth Session of the Islamic Summit Conference, Tehran, December 9, 1997.

44 Ibid., p. 3.

45 Ibid., p. 3.

46 S. Ismail, *al-Mujtama al-Madana Wad-Dawlah*, Arab Unity Studies Center (Beirut, 1992), p. 292.

47 Imad-ad-Dean Ahmad, "Building Muslim Civil Society from the Bottom Up," p. 1.

48 Ivan Doherty, "Democracy out of Balance: Civil Society Can't Replace Political Parties," *Policy Review*, April/May 2001.

49 Ibid.

Chapter 9—Understanding Anti-Americanism

1 Mark Leonard and Conrad Smewing, "Propaganda Will Not Sway the Arab Street," *Financial Times*, February 27, 2003.

2 "Arab Media: Tools of the Government; Tools for the People?" Virtual Diplomacy Series no. 19, United States Institute of Peace, August 2005.

3 Frank Newport, "Gallup Poll of the Islamic World," The Gallup Poll, February 26, 2002.

4 Associated Press, "Rumsfeld Gets Anti-Terror Lecture on Indonesia Visit," June 6, 2006.

5 "Arab Media: Tools of the Government; Tools for the People?"

6 Ibid.

7 Richard Holbrooke, "Our Enemy's Face," *Washington Post*, September 9, 2005, p. A25.

8 Glenn Kessler, "Campaign Methods Put to Test in Tour to Boost U.S. Image," *Washington Post*, September 30, p. A12.

9 Jim Hoagland, "Katrina's Global Lessons," *Washington Post*, September 7, 2005, p. A25.

10 "Arab Media: Tools of the Government; Tools for the People?"

11 Faiza Saleh Ambah, "Saudi Women Rise in Defense of the Veil," *Washington Post*, June 1, 2006, p. A12.

12 Ibid.

13 "Among Indonesian Muslims, Desire for Islamic Society Still Tempered by Traditional Values of Tolerance, Pluralism," Office of Research, U.S. Department of State, May 25, 2005.

14 Mustafa Akyol, "Show Us More of the Other America: A Moderate Muslim's Prayer for American Faith and Family Values," *American Enterprise*, December 2004, p. 42.

15 Ibid.

16 Ibid.

17 Ibid., p. 43.

18 Charles Freund, "Popular Culture in the Middle East: A Conduit for Liberal Values?" presented at the American Enterprise Institute, December 6, 2005, available at www.aei.org/news21673.

19 Ibid.

20 Ibid.

21 Stephen C. Johnson, "Improving U.S. Public Diplomacy Toward the Middle East," Heritage Lecture no. 838, The Heritage Foundation, Washington, D.C., February 10, 2004.

22 Ibid.

Chapter 10—Civil Society and Nation Building

1 Francis Fukuyama, *State-Building: Governance and World Order in the 21st Century* (New York: Cornell University Press, 2004), p. ix.

2 William Easterly, *The White Man's Burden* (New York: The Penguin Press, 2006), p. 116.

3 Fareed Zakaria, "How to Change Ugly Regimes," *Newsweek*, June 27, 2005, p. 31.

4 Adrian Karatnycky and Peter Ackerman, "How Freedom Is Won: From Civic Resistance to Durable Democracy," Freedom House, May 24, 2005, p. 5.

5 Thomas L. Friedman, "Addicted to Oil," Op-Ed, *New York Times*, February 1, 2006.

6 Fareed Zakaria, *The Future of Freedom: Illiberal Democracy at Home and Abroad* (New York: Norton, 2004), p. 17.

7 Ibid., p. 17.

8 Ibid., p. 31.

9 Richard Haas, "Freedom Is Not a Doctrine," *Washington Post*, January 24, 2005, p. A15.

10 Ibid.

11 Robert Kaplan, *The Coming Anarchy: Shattering the Dreams of the Post Cold War* (New York: Vintage, 2004), pp. 65–66.

12 Daniel Williams, "In Egypt, an Old Beacon of Tolerance Flickers," *Washington Post*, May 13, 2006, p. A10.

13 Monte Reel, "Race Is a Wild Card in Peru Runoff," *Washington Post*, June 3, 2006, p. A8.

14 John Lancaster, "India's Ragtag Band of Maoists Takes Root among Rural Poor," *Washington Post*, May 13, 2006, p. A1.

15 Joshua Kurlantzick, "The UN Success Story That Wasn't," *Washington Post*, June 4, 2006, p. B4.

16 Fareed Zakaria, "Islam and Power," *Newsweek*, February 13, 2006, p. 36.

17 Thomas L. Friedman, "Addicted to Oil."

18 Ibid.

19 Fareed Zakaria, "Islam and Power," p. 37.

20 Francis Fukuyama, "Nation-Building 101," *Atlantic*, January 2004.

21 James Dobbins, *America's Role in Nation-Building: From Germany to Iraq* (RAND Corporation, 2003), p. xv.

22 Ibid., p. xv.

23 Ibid., p. xiii.

24 Ibid., p. xix.

25 Allan Dowd, "The Exertions of Better Men: The Role of the U.S. Military in Planting, Protecting and Nurturing Free Government," *Whitehead Journal of Diplomacy and International Relations,* Winter/Spring 2005, p. 43.

26 Ibid.

27 Francis Fukuyama, "Nation-Building 101."

28 Ibid.

29 William R. Polk, *Understanding Iraq* (New York: HarperCollins, 2005), p. 3.

30 Marina Ottaway, "Nation Building," *Foreign Policy*, September 9, 2002.

31 Adrian Karatnycky, "Civil Power and Electoral Politics," Freedom House, 2005.

32 Ibid.

33 Fareed Zakaria, "How to Change Ugly Regimes," *Newsweek*, June 27, 2005, p. 31.

34 Peter Finn, "Grass-Roots Activism Faces Setback in Russia," *Washington Post*, November 24, 2005, p. A31.

35 Karl Vick and David Finkel, "U.S. Push for Democracy Could Backfire inside Iran," *Washington Post*, March 14, 2006, p. A1.

36 Ibid.

37 "We the Peoples: Civil Society, the United Nations and Global Governance," Panel of Eminent Persons on United Nations–Civil Society Relations, United Nations, June 11, 2004.

38 Joseph Loconte, "Reforming the Human Rights Agenda of the United Nations," Backgrounder no. 1877, The Heritage Foundation, September 13, 2005, p. 7.

39 David Ignatius, "Reality Check for the Neo-Wilsonians," *Washington Post*, January 26, 2005.

40 Adrian Karatnycky and Peter Ackerman, "How Freedom Is Won," pp. 10–11.

41 "Lessons in Implementation: The NGO Story," USAID, October, 1999, p. v.

42 Lynn Carter, "On the Crest of the Third Wave: Linking USAID Democracy Program Impact to Political Change," Office of Democracy and Governance, USAID, October 2001, p. 18.

43 Jorge G. Castaneda, "Latin America's Left Turn," *Foreign Affairs*, May/June 2006, p. 31.

44 James Dobbins, *America's Role in Nation-Building*, p. xix.

45 Sarah Schafer, "Blogger Nation," *Newsweek*, February 27, 2006, pp. 21–22.

46 Ibid.

47 Stephen Glain, "Slow Death," *Newsweek*, October 7, 2002, p. 22.

48 Ibid., p. 23.

49 Ibid., p. 22.

50 Ashraf Ghani and Clare Lockhart, "Rethinking Nation-Building," *Washington Post*, January 1, 2006, p. B7.

51 Fareed Zakaria, "How to Change Ugly Regimes."

Chapter 11—Conflict and Reconciliation in the Context of Nation Building

1 "Growing on the Ashes of Conflict," The World Bank: Conflict Prevention and Reconstruction, June 17, 2006.

2 Interview with President Paul Kagame.

3 Robert D. Kaplan, *The Coming Anarchy: Shattering the Dreams of the Post Cold War* (New York: Vintage Books, 2000).

4 Ibid., pp. 44–45.

5 John Rapley, "The New Middle Ages," *Foreign Affairs*, May/June 2006, pp. 95–103.

6 Ibid.

7 Cited by Robert D. Kaplan, *The Coming Anarchy*, p. 47.

8 "Conflict Prevention and Peace Building," United Nations Development Programme, www.undp.org/bcpr/conflict_prevention/index.htm.

9 Ibid.

10 Ibid.

11 William Easterly, *The White Man's Burden: Why the West's Efforts to Aid the Rest Have Done So Much Ill and So Little Good* (New York: The Penguin Press, 2006), pp. 127–28.

12 Steven Burg, "Bosnia Herzegovina: A Case of Failed Democratization," in *Democratic Changes and Authoritarian Reactions in Russia, Ukraine, Belarus, and Moldova*, Authoritarianism and Democratization in Postcommunist Societies no. 3, ed. Karen Dawisha and Bruce Parrott (Cambridge and New York: Cambridge University Press, 1997), p. 127.

13 Rajiv Chandrasekaran, "A Conversation with Kanan Makiya," *Washington Post*, March 19, 2006, p. B5.

14 Stephen Biddle, "Seeing Baghdad, Thinking Saigon," *Foreign Affairs*, March/April 2006, p. 8.

15 Ibid., p. 8.

16 Quoted in Dan Burke, "Holocaust, Rwandan Genocide Compared," *Lancaster* (Pennsylvania) *New Era*, April 3, 2006, p. B1.

17 Paul Rusesabagina, "Darfur," *Wall Street Journal*, April 5, 2006.

18 Interview with Bill Church.

Notes

19 Uma Shankar Jha and Surya Narayan Yadav, *Rwanda: Towards Reconciliation, Good Governance and Development* (New Delhi: Association of Indian Africanists, 2003).

20 Interview with Bill Church.

21 Cited in Dan Burke, "Holocaust, Rwandan Genocide Compared."

22 Uma Shankar Jha and Surya Narayan Yadav, *Rwanda: Towards Reconciliation, Good Governance and Development*, p. 36.

23 Ibid., p. 6.

24 Cited by Dan Burke, "Holocaust, Rwandan Genocide Compared."

25 Ibid.

26 Paul Rusesabagina, "Darfur."

27 Jean Hatzfeld, *Machete Season: The Killers in Rwanda Speak* (New York: Farrar, Straus & Giroux, 2003), p. 57.

28 Ibid., from inside cover.

29 Ibid., p. 11.

30 Ibid., p. 26.

31 Ibid., p. 65.

32 Ibid., p. 56.

33 Ibid., p. 38.

34 Ibid., p. 39.

35 Ibid., p. 40.

36 Ibid., p. 33.

37 Ibid., p. 34.

38 Ibid., p. 48.

39 Ibid., p. 49.

40 Ibid., p. 56.

41 Ibid., p. 55.

42 Wambui Kimani, "Nuns Accused of Genocide," *West Africa*, March, 2000, p. 20.

43 Report on the Evaluation of National Unity and Reconciliation, National Unity and Reconciliation Commission, Kigali, Rwanda, June 2002, p. 3.

44 Annual Activity Report, 2002, National Unity and Reconciliation Commission, Kigali, Rwanda, April 2004, p. 1.

45 Interview with Fatuma Ndangiza.

46 "Rwanda," Country Reports on Human Rights Practices, Bureau of Democracy, Human Rights, and Labor, U.S. Department of State, March 8, 2006.

47 Ibid.

48 Interview with Fatuma Ndangiza.

49 Summary Report of the National Summit on Unity and Reconciliation, National Unity and Reconciliation Commission, Kigali, Rwanda, May 2004, p. 14.

50 Interview with Bishop John Rucyahana.

51 Interview with Paul Kagame.

52 Paul Kagame, June 2002, p. 6.

53 Interview with Fatuma Ndangiza.

Chapter 12—Habits of the Heart

1 Adam Seligman, *The Idea of Civil Society* (New York: The Free Press, 1992), p. 3.

2 Ibid., p. 5.

3 Cited in Linda C. McClain and James E. Fleming, "Some Questions for Civil Society Revivalists," *Chicago-Kent Law Review*, vol. 75, n. 2 (2000), p. 301.

4 Kenneth L. Grasso, Gerard V. Bradley and Robert P. Hunt, *Catholicism, Liberalism and Communitarianism: The Catholic Intellectual Tradition and the Moral Foundations of Democracy* (Lanham, Maryland: Rowman & Littlefield, 1995), p. 24.

5 See Alexis de Tocqueville, *Democracy in America*, ed. Phillips Bradley (New York: Vintage, 1990), p. 68.

6 Francis Fukuyama, *Trust: The Social Virtues and the Creation of Prosperity* (New York: The Free Press), p. 10.

7 Jean Bethke Elshtain, "Not a Cure-All: Civil Society Creates Citizens, It Does Not Solve Problems," in *Community Works: The Revival of Civil Society in America*, ed. E. J. Dionne (Washington, D.C.: Brookings Institution Press, 1998), p. 28.

8 Peter L. Berger and Richard John Neuhaus, *To Empower People: The Role of Mediating Structures in Public Policy* (Washington, D.C.: American Enterprise Institute, 1979), p. 2.

9 Don Eberly and Ryan Streeter, *The Soul of Civil Society: Voluntary Associations and the Public Value of Moral Habits* (Lanham, Maryland: Lexington Books, 2002), p. x.

INDEX

DESIGN AND COMPOSITION BY CARL W. SCARBROUGH